MANITOU AND PROVIDENCE

MANITOU
and
PROVIDENCE

Indians, Europeans,
and the Making of New England,
1500-1643

Neal Salisbury

New York   Oxford
OXFORD UNIVERSITY PRESS
1982

Copyright © 1982 by Oxford University Press, Inc.

Library of Congress Cataloging in Publication Data

Salisbury, Neal.
Manitou and providence.

Includes index.
1. Indians of North America—New England—History.
2. Indians of North America—New England—First
contact with Occidental civilization. 3. New
England—History—Colonial period, ca. 1600-1775.
I. Title.
E78.N5S24   974'.02   81-11238
ISBN 0-19-503025-7   AACR2

Printing (last digit): 9 8 7 6 5 4 3 2 1

Printed in the United States of America

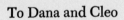

To Dana and Cleo

ACKNOWLEDGMENTS

No author is an island. Indeed, the sources of support on which I have drawn in writing this book are far too numerous to list individually; they include students, faculty colleagues, and the many others with whom I have discussed points of mutual interest through the mails, at conferences, or at libraries. Regrettably, I can mention only a few of the more substantial contributions.

Research fellowships at the Smithsonian Institution (1972–73) and the Newberry Library Center for the History of the American Indian (1977–78) provided the time, money, materials, and congenial settings for preparing this study (and much of the succeeding volume which will follow). In addition, I have benefited from the leaves of absence from teaching granted me by the Smith College Board of Trustees, with the support of my colleagues in the Department of History and of President Jill K. Conway. The Smith College Committee on Aid to Faculty Scholarship has kindly assisted me with a number of incidental expenses connected with the project. The staffs and collections of the Anthropology Library, Smithsonian Institution; Newberry Library; William Allan Neilson Library, Smith College; and Forbes Library, Northampton, Mass., have been especially helpful. In addition to the institutions credited for supplying the illustrations and permission to reproduce them, I would like to thank John Aubrey, Jane Becker, Kathleen Bragdon, Susan Dean, Wayne Hammond, and William Simmons for their assistance in locating certain items.

Brief passages in this book appeared previously in "The Conquest of the 'Savage': Puritans, Puritan Missionaries, and Indians, 1620-1680" (Ph.D. diss., University of California, Los Angeles, 1972; published University Microfilms, Ann Arbor, Mich., 1972); "Red Puritans: The 'Praying Indians' of Massachusetts Bay and John Eliot," *William and Mary Quarterly*, 3d ser., 31 (1974), 27–54; and "Squanto: Last of the Patuxets," in David G. Sweet and Gary B. Nash, eds. *Struggle and Survival in Colonial America* (Berkeley: University of California Press, 1981), pp. 228–46.

A number of individuals critically read portions of the manuscript in one or another incarnation and offered me the benefits of their insights: John Demos, Dena Dincauze, Lester Little, Calvin Martin, Kenneth Morrison, James Ronda, Dean Snow, William Sturtevant, Wilcomb Washburn, R. Jackson Wilson, and Mary Young. Francis Jennings has been most generous in his suggestions and support for a study that at once builds on and departs from his own. Three other outstanding scholars have not only contributed at many points along the way but gave me the benefit of a reading of the final manuscript—James Axtell, Gary Nash, and William Simmons. Without them, the book would not be what it is. Hilda McArthur proved a perceptive reader as well as a superb typist.

This book has been nurtured through a long evolutionary course over the last several years by the remarkable patience, understanding, and encouragement of Sheldon Meyer of Oxford University Press. Also at Oxford, Stephanie Golden proved to be a truly gifted editor. Like the scholars noted above, she contributed in many important ways to the book's final form.

The support and love of two others is far too basic to be conveyed here; for them, a separate space is reserved.

Northampton, Mass.   N.S.
June 1981

TECHNICAL NOTE ON THE TEXT

Dates in the colonial period appear, as in the sources, according to the Old Style Julian calendar, except those from January 1 to March 25, which are rendered according to the New Style Gregorian calendar.

Quotations follow the spelling, punctuation, and other usages of the edition cited except for the transliteration of "ye" and "yt" as "the" and "that," respectively.

CONTENTS

[T]here is a generall Custome amongst them, at the apprehension of any Excellency in Men, Women, Birds, Beasts, Fish, &c. to cry out *Manittóo,* that is, it is a God, . . . and therefore when they talke amongst themselves of the *English* ships, and great buildings, of the plowing of their Fields, and especially of Bookes and Letters, they will end thus: *Manittôwock* They are Gods: *Cummanittôo,* you are a God, &c.

> Roger Williams,
> *A Key into the Language of America*

[Y]ou may behold the good providence of God working with you in our preservation from so many dangerous plots and treacheries as have been intended against us, as also in . . . possessing the hearts of the salvages with astonishment and fear of us.

> Edward Winslow,
> *Good Newes from New England*

MANITOU AND PROVIDENCE

INTRODUCTION

HISTORIANS AND OTHERS have described the English conquest of Indian New England many times over, but with nearly always the same underlying assumption. Implicitly or explicitly, they have presupposed that the outcome was inevitable because of the incompatibility of Indian and English cultures and the inherent moral superiority of the latter. Such interpretations originated with some of the earliest English to write about the region, particularly those who commented on the plague epidemic which devastated the coastal natives from Cape Cod northward during the late 1610s. Thus such figures as the former Virginia leader John Smith and the anti-Puritan trader Thomas Morton, as well as many of the settlers who commented, regarded the epidemic as evidence that God intended the region for English colonization.[1] Among subsequent authors in the colonial period, this assumption was manifested most prominently in accounts that concentrated on the great Indian wars and presented the colonies' victories over the natives as those of God over Satan. Thus, in explaining the English victory over the Pequot in 1637—a victory that was achieved after English troops surrounded and burned a Pequot village and its several hundred inhabitants—the war's historians pointed to the blasphemy, witchcraft, and general sinfulness of the vanquished followers of Satan. More or less typical was Edward Johnson, who, in his *Wonder-Working Providence of Sion's Saviour in New England* (1654), described how the

3

Pequot had "blasphemed the Lord, saying Englishmans God was all one Flye, and that English man was all one Sqawe, and themselves all one Moor-hawks. Thus," he concluded, "by their horrible pride they fitted themselves for destruction."[2] When King Philip's War (1675-76) initially erupted, many New Englanders were less certain that God was on their side. Yet once the English gained the upper hand, it was clear that he had not abandoned them. Cotton Mather explained the remarkable turnabout in terms that were, by the time his *Magnalia Christi Americana* was published in 1702, familiar. "The *time limited* by Heaven for the success of the Indian *treacheries* was now almost expired," he wrote; "the blasphemy, and insolence, and prodigious barbarity of the salvages, was come to a sufficient *heighth* for the 'Lord God of Zabaoth' to interpose his own revenges."[3] Though the presentation of the conflict in these stock terms obviously served to rationalize the depersonalization of the Indians and the seizure of their lands, it was based on the belief system by which most colonists explained the world and the events and phenomena they encountered in it. While some early writers and later missionaries entertained hopes for the Indians' eventual assimilation to English culture, the volume of popular literature, especially that devoured by the colonists themselves rather than by readers in England, suggests that such hopes were never the sentiment of more than a distinct minority.[4]

For the Puritans' descendants in the nineteenth century, the explanation shifted to the inevitable triumph of "civilization" and "progress" over "savagery" and "barbarism." Whether welcomed or lamented, the conquest of the Indians and their land was considered central to the colonial experience in New England and fraught with dramatic and moral significance. Part of a national trend, this tendency had particular force among New England Yankees who longed for the romantic simplicity of their region's bygone frontier era. The work which perhaps best typified it was John Gorham Palfrey's multi-volume *History of New England* (1858-90). Though Palfrey's narrative was pervaded with tension that often made the outcome seem less than certain, his assumptions were nevertheless quite apparent. Commenting on the justice of the massacre of the Pequot, for example, he concluded that ". . . from the hour of that carnage, Connecticut was secure. . . . [Hence] it might be hoped that civilization was assured of a permanent abode in New England." Though Palfrey's undisguised contempt for the Indians was not shared by all readers of New England history during the nineteenth century, his explanation of the conquest varied little from those offered by his more liberal contemporaries. John William DeForest, for example, whose *History of the Indians of Connecticut* (1851) is a model of meticulous scholarship and who candidly detailed English atrocities, nevertheless concluded that, in the final analysis, the Indians' "own barbarism has destroyed them."[5]

The drama and primacy of the conquest found in earlier works have been largely absent from histories of New England produced in this century. Instead successive generations of scholars have focused on political, intellectual, and social history as conveying the essence of the region's colonial experience. The process whereby the settlers seized New England from its native inhabitants has been de-emphasized, when not completely ignored, even in the great monuments of twentieth-century historiography such as Charles M. Andrews's *The Colonial Period of American History* (1934-38) and Perry Miller's *The New England Mind* (1939-53), and continues to be so treated by the current generation of social historians despite the fact that the subject of (newly conquered) land is central to their studies.[6] The implication in all these works that Indian-English relations were unimportant suggests that the older assumptions of English superiority remain substantially unaltered. Indeed, those histories which appeared during the two

decades after World War II as part of the distinct but minor
category of "white-Indian relations" tended to perpetuate
earlier assumptions that cultural differences explained the
rapidity and relative ease of the English conquest. Thus Douglas Edward Leach began his history of King Philip's War by
noting that "here in the wilderness two mutually incompatible
ways of life confronted each other." This incompatibility was
defined most sharply by Alden T. Vaughan in the first edition
of his *New England Frontier* (1965). One society, wrote
Vaughan,

> was unified, visionary, disciplined, and dynamic. The other
> was divided, self-satisfied, undisciplined, and static. It would
> be unreasonable to expect that such societies could live side by
> side indefinitely with no penetration of the more fragmented
> and passive by the more consolidated and active. What re-
> sulted, then, was not—as many have held—a clash of dissimilar
> ways of life, but rather the expansion of one into the areas in
> which the other was lacking.[7]

With three and a half centuries of cultural stereotyping behind
him, Vaughan did not have to specify to his readers which society was which.

One irony of twentieth-century scholarship is that historians
such as Vaughan have reached their conclusions even while
acknowledging the limitations imposed by written evidence
that does not adequately reflect native perspectives.[8] It is only
very recently that some scholars have attempted to overcome
these limitations by applying insights and methods from cultural anthropology to their reading of colonial documents
dealing with Indians. Thus a few "ethnohistorians," as these
interdisciplinary practitioners are often called, have been able
to present native peoples in terms of their own histories and
cultures rather than those embodied in the stereotype of the
"savage."[9] In this study I have sought to incorporate the ethno-
historical approach to Indian history within a larger history of

Indian-European relations in early colonial New England. This approach has enabled me to focus on the historical experiences that shaped the composition, the culture, and the actions of each group, Indian as well as English, making each what it was at the time of its contact with the other. Accordingly, I have turned to the work of archaeologists, linguists, and ethnologists to investigate the long history of Algonquian-speaking hunters and farmers in New England, emphasizing both the continuities and the changes important for understanding their history during the colonial period. In addition, I have sought to reconstruct the little-known but critical period of relations between Indians and non-settler Europeans in northeastern North America that prepared the way for the beginning of actual settlement in New England. Finally, I have utilized recent work in the social and economic histories of the critical English localities, along with scholarship on the ideological ferment of the early seventeenth century, in order to understand and present the salient aspects of the settlers' English backgrounds. These perspectives directly inform the narrative of events concerning native-settler interaction.

As it emerges here, the conquest of New England rests on a set of interdependent explanations in which the stark contrasts between natives and settlers, while lacking the ahistorical, stereotypical quality of those presented in past histories, are no less dramatic. To begin with, the Europeans who explored and colonized the Western Hemisphere, including New England, were members of a population that had been exposed to and developed immunities to virtually every parasite that lethally infected humans on an epidemic scale north of the tropics. The peoples they encountered in the Americas, on the other hand, though remarkably healthy and well adapted to their native habitats, were completely sealed off from what William H. McNeill calls this "confluence of civilized disease pools" by the oceans, an Arctic cold screen, and the long tenure

of their ancestors. As a result, the diseases which Europeans,
had, in one way or another, "domesticated" found "virgin
soil" in an American Indian population that utterly lacked
defensive resources in the form of either immunities or even
analogous experiences with other diseases. The consequence
for the Indians was a massive depopulation—as high as 90
percent in many areas, including much of New England—
without which colonization could not have succeeded on the
scale it did.[10]

While epidemiological differences made the conquest of Indians by Europeans possible, they do not explain it, for the
newcomers did not truly conquer the Indians until they followed up the latter's demise by establishing their own hegemony. This occurred in New England when thousands of
settlers moved to occupy lands depopulated by two major epidemics. The availability of settlers in such numbers reflects the
phenomenal population growth that England had experienced
during the preceding century and a half.[11] Among the Indians,
on the other hand, a population that had been gradually but
steadily increasing for a number of centuries had just been
suddenly and catastrophically devastated.

Beyond the numbers and biological resources possessed by
each group were the factors that actually brought them together. The arrival of large numbers of settlers in New England could not have occurred without the complex of economic, political, technological, and other developments which
enabled and motivated certain Europeans to exploit and colonize the Western Hemisphere and its inhabitants. These
developments are familiar, but a review of them from a New
England perspective sheds light on the particular processes
there. Initial Indian contacts with Europeans in the late fifteenth and the sixteenth century were of two types: expeditions of explorers sailing for England, France, and Portugal
as these nation-states strove to match Spain's stunning achieve-
ments in Middle and South America; and fishing crews from

ports up and down Europe's Atlantic coast, representatives of increasingly powerful merchants who sought cheap, profitable sources of protein to market among their growing number of customers. Sometimes hostile, sometimes amicable, these contacts served to acquaint the two peoples, and their wares, with one another without inducing radical changes among either. Later in the sixteenth century, however, after the French had risen to dominate fishing in the North Atlantic, some of their merchants moved into a specialized fur trade with Algonquian hunters in what is now eastern Canada, rushing to corner a growing market hitherto dependent on more expensive Russian sources. The trade eventually had a decisive impact on the natives, for it drew them as both producers and consumers into a dangerous dependency on an unpredictable industry and pitted them in unequal, often destructive competition with one another. And though the trade by itself did not usually devastate Indian groups politically or culturally, it exposed them to European diseases and—particularly when it spread to those whose subsistence was primarily horticultural—to the attention of those in France, the Netherlands, and England who sought to advance their own and/or their countries' fortunes through the establishment of colonies.[12] Among the Indians, those in southern New England were especially vulnerable because of the combination of depopulation through epidemic disease and the region's demonstrated capacity for supporting intensive settlement and cultivation; among the European countries concerned, England was best prepared to take advantage of such a situation.

The key to this preparation lay in the burgeoning English population already noted, not simply in its numbers but in its changing character. England had moved far beyond any other European society in replacing the feudal relationships that had once prevailed with ones that were essentially capitalistic. Though, like France and the Netherlands, it boasted an innovating urban bourgeoisie, its capitalism was rooted in the countryside, dominating agricultural and nascent industrial production in the more heavily populated regions. The key to change in these regions was those members of the gentry and "middling sort" who (or whose ancestors) had bought or leased land from feudal lords and undertaken the raising of crops or livestock for commercial purposes. By the early seventeenth century, however, many smaller producers were threatened by the combination of economic and demographic growth. While some more marginal farmers and laborers turned to indentured servitude in the Chesapeake or the West Indies as solutions to their poverty and landlessness, others with sufficient financial resources and stable kin networks to remain independent found the recently depopulated lands of New England most alluring. Besides the attractiveness of its land, New England for many appeared as a religious haven. The family-oriented economic independence which characterized these farmers was elevated to a divine character trait in English Puritanism, and it constituted the basis of a radical critique of the political, moral, and ecclesiastical status quo in England.[13] The consequent persecution of Puritans helped to define their group identity, but they were at the same time radically individualistic. The prospect of a colony dominated by Puritans and Puritanism that would simultaneously fulfill their material goals was a truly utopian one for which thousands of English were willing to stake their lives and fortunes.

For the settlers, then, upheaval and conflict, plus a perception of themselves as righteous but deprived, were the experiences which informed their values and actions. The contrast with Indian culture in southern New England, shaped as it was by continuity, abundance, and stability, could not have been more striking. The fruit of the Indian experience was an ethos in which relationships in the social, natural, and supernatural worlds were defined in terms of reciprocity rather than domination and submission. Developed centuries earlier when hunting and gathering were the primary modes of subsistence, this ethos had survived and continued to prevail as agriculture brought larger populations and more sedentary settlement patterns to the southern portion of New England. To the natives here, the settlers appeared first as other human beings with whom they had to interact as best they could under the circumstances in order to maintain equilibrium in the world they shared. Only when they perceived the settlers as sources of permanent disequilibrium did some—at first in scattered and isolated instances, later in the Pequot War and in the pan-Indian movement led by the Narragansett—undertake efforts at direct resistance. For most colonists, on the other hand, the Indians represented the complete inversion of the world they sought for themselves as well as the concrete obstacle to their attaining it. This was enough to make the natives a potent symbolic enemy, as happened elsewhere in the Americas when Europeans sought to justify their invasions. But in New England the invasion also revealed the settlers' more atomistic and materialistic tendencies at the expense of what many of them, including their leaders, saw as a collective, divine calling. Accordingly, Puritan ideologues (outside of Rhode Island) sought to reconcile the reality of these tendencies with the myth of "New England"'s redemptive purpose by transforming each quest for land into a crusade against the "savage" Indians and by defining the social and cultural differences between the two peoples in terms of religious and moral absolutes. (This is not to deny the contentions of a number of recent historians that many settlers sought to re-create certain communal traditions in their New England villages and that most of them were subsistence- rather than market-oriented for much of the colonial period.[14] It is rather to suggest that the pursuit of particularistic economic and, in some cases, spiritual goals was the paramount motive in the "Great Migration" from England to New England and that the appearance of practices and ideas traditional in origin and/or communal in purpose represented the employment of familiar or conserva-

tive means to achieve these radical ends.) As a result, conflict
with the Indians affected the evolution of Puritan efforts to
formulate the meaning and purpose of "New England" far more
than Puritanism, per se, determined the colonists' actions.[15]

Thus the conquest was composed of two distinct phases,
phases rooted in concrete historical experiences rather than in
abstract "cultures." The Indians' encounters with traders and
explorers, and with their goods and diseases, constituted an
essential prerequisite to settlement by attracting the attention
of potential settlers and by rendering Indian societies vulnerable to conquest. But by themselves, these contacts did not
guarantee that outcome. That this was so becomes apparent
when we look elsewhere in North America and see that, when
land-hungry settlers did not immediately follow the explorers
and traders, Indians survived and interacted with Europeans
over long periods with varying degrees of advantage. The
sheer variety of these adaptive situations and their results suf-
fices to shatter any assumptions about the inherent cultural incompatibility of Europeans and native North Americans.[16] On
the other hand, where unequal contests for land quickly ensued,
the settlers were invariably successful. Thus as colonists occupied Indian lands around Plymouth and Massachusetts Bay
and on the lower Connecticut and Housatonic rivers in New
England, similar scenarios were being played out in New
Netherland and Virginia at the expense of other Algonquian-
speaking Indians. In all three areas, settlers effectively removed enough coastal natives by the mid-1640s to secure
beachheads which ensured them, their descendants, and those
Europeans who came later a permanence on the continent.[17]
In the final analysis, then, it was not simply the manifest differences between Indians and Europeans that explain the conquest but rather the unprecedented economic and social revolution that had begun to transform parts of western Europe,
particularly England, and was now spreading to North America.

one

FARMERS and HUNTERS

For so are we all Indians as the English are, and say
brother to one another; so must we be one as they
are, otherwise we shall all be gone shortly, for you
know our fathers had plenty of deer and skins, our
plains were full of deer, as also our woods, and of
turkies, and our coves full of fish and fowl. But these
English having gotten our land, they with scythes cut
down the grass, and with axes fell the trees; their cows
and horses eat the grass, and their hogs spoil our
clam banks, and we shall all be starved. —Miantonomi, Narragansett sachem, to the Montauk Indians
of eastern Long Island, summer 1642.[1]

MIANTONOMI'S IMPASSIONED, indeed desperate, plea
juxtaposed Indian memories of economic abundance, physical
health, and general social harmony with the looming loss of all
these at the hands of the relentlessly encroaching colonists.
That a leader of the most powerful Indian alliance in southern
New England would invoke such imagery suggests that it held
a good deal of meaning and power for Indians in 1642, that it
recalled a world they had once known but lost. Archaeological,
linguistic, and documentary evidence confirms the picture Miantonomi painted of that world and gives it historical context.
It was rooted in the cultures of the hunting bands which had
once flourished in southern New England and still did so in
northern New England and the Maritime Provinces where cli-

mate precluded the adoption of agriculture. Miantonomi spoke
to the Montauk, then, not merely of material loss but of the destruction of a deep-rooted, successful way of life. That way of
life is the starting point for our story.

Origins

The earliest millennia of human occupation in New England
were marked by a steadily changing physical environment to
which the inhabitants adapted on increasingly favorable terms.
As the Wisconsin continental ice sheet retreated, from about
15,000 B.C., the climate warmed, the sea level rose, and the flora
was transformed from tundra to spruce-lichen. This new environment attracted the great Pleistocene mammals—mastodons,
mammoths, and caribou—which, in turn, drew the "Paleo-
Indian" or "Big Game" hunters who began entering from the
south and west around 10,000 B.C. They were armed with
Clovis fluted-point projectiles similar to those being used over
most of North America by Paleo-Indians hunting the big mammals. The archaeological evidence indicates that the newcomers
found the environment and resources of New England sufficiently congenial to establish patterns of subsistence, settlement, and social organization that became increasingly stable
over time. Central camps, such as the one found at the Bull
Brook site, near Ipswich, Massachusetts, appear to have been
occupied by whole bands or lineages of up to twenty-five related individuals. These sites show evidence of such communal
activities as tool-making, ritualized inter-band exchanges that
probably included women, and other non-hunting activities.
Smaller sites, such as "Wapanucket no. 8" in southeastern Massachusetts, represent hunting camps probably occupied occa-

---

Indian ethnic-linguistic boundaries in New England and
surrounding areas, *ca.* 1600, and major European outposts
established, 1600–1615.

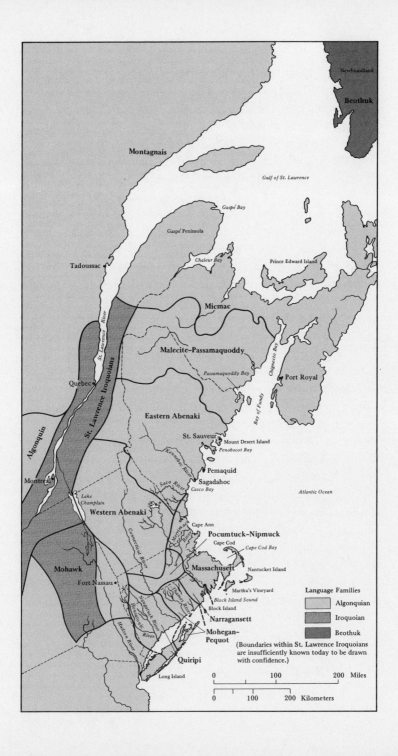

Newfoundland

Beothuk

Montagnais

Gulf of St. Lawrence

Gaspé Bay

Gaspé Peninsula

Tadoussac

Chaleur Bay

Prince Edward Island

Micmac

Chignecto Bay

Malecite–Passamaquoddy

Passamaquoddy Bay

Port Royal

Quebec

Bay of Fundy

Eastern Abenaki

St. Sauveur *Mount Desert Island*

Penobscot Bay

Algonquin

Kennebec River

Pemaquid

Sagadahoc

Montreal

Saco River

Casco Bay

Atlantic Ocean

Lake Champlain

Western Abenaki

Connecticut River

Cape Ann

Pocumtuck–Nipmuck

Cape Cod

Cape Cod Bay

Mohawk

Massachusett

Nantucket Island

Fort Nassau

Merrimac River

Martha's Vineyard

Block Island Sound

Block Island

Narragansett

Naugatuck River

Thames River

Mohegan–Pequot

Hudson River

Housatonic River

Quiripi

Long Island

Language Families

Algonquian

Iroquoian

Beothuk

(Boundaries within St. Lawrence Iroquoians are insufficiently known today to be drawn with confidence.)

St. Lawrence River

St. Lawrence Iroquoians

| 0 | | 100 | | 200 | Miles |

| 0 | 100 | 200 | Kilometers |

sionally by one or two families within a lineage as they followed the movements of their prey. The co-existence of the two kinds of camp suggests that their occupants had established seasonal patterns in their annual subsistence rounds, along with some degree of territoriality and residential stability.[2]

As the post-glacial warming trend continued, the great mammals died off and the big-game hunters turned their attention to deer, elk, moose, and caribou. By around 8000 B.C. the spruce-lichen forest had largely been replaced by one of pine and hardwoods, and a wider range of flora and fauna had been established. As a result, the choice of foods was considerably increased and the Paleo-Indian era gave way to what archaeologists call the Early Archaic (ca. 8000-6000 B.C.). Though hunting remained the principal subsistence activity and was indeed refined by technological advances, increasing attention was given to wild plant products and fish. In time, the inhabitants came to anchor themselves at particularly convenient locations, usually on the shores of rivers, lakes, or bays for access to fish, during most of the non-hunting phases of their cycles. Subsistence activities became increasingly specialized along lines of family, age, and sex. Material artifacts of the Early and Middle Archaic (ca. 6000-4000 B.C.) were heavily influenced by developments in the southeastern and midwestern parts of North America. Early Archaic projectile points, unlike those of the Paleo-Indians, are generally stemmed, barbed, or notched for more effective, specialized hunting. In the Middle Archaic appeared millstones for processing the widening range of foods, particularly plant products, and grinding stones for perfecting these and other increasingly specialized tools. In New England and throughout the northeast, Early and Middle Archaic cultures were marked by a pronounced shift away from the relatively undifferentiated economies and societies of the Paleo-Indians toward greater stability and complexity in social organization, and greater sophistication and specialization in the manufacturing of tools.[3]

By 4000 B.C. the last effects of the Ice Age had been felt. A predominantly oak-hemlock forest prevailed, and the full range of modern flora and fauna was established on both land and water. The Late Archaic cultures of eastern North America (*ca.* 4000-1500 B.C.) were built on this expanded range of food sources and constituted a nearly optimum adaptation to the environment. The availability of increased marine resources permitted the growth of larger, more dense populations along the coast, where people made especially heavy use of shellfish in the south and seals and other mammals in the north. These developments marked an important step toward the economic and cultural patterns, including the distinctions between northern and southern New England, that Europeans would eventually encounter.[4]

Several remarkable sites illustrate the cultural accomplishments of the Late Archaic. The Boylston Street Fishweir, built about 2500 B.C. in what is now Boston, covered approximately two acres and consisted of some 65,000 stakes between which brush was inserted to trap fish. Such weirs were still in use along the Atlantic coast of North America when Europeans began arriving. The construction, maintenance, and use of this elaborate structure suggest the high degree of inter-band coordination and residential stability that eastern Archaic bands achieved. Another site, "Wapanucket no. 6," dates to about 2300 B.C. It features an extensive array of stone objects, including tools, weapons, and vessels, but even more remarkable are the circular lodges—six dwellings plus a ceremonial lodge, the latter measuring 65 feet in diameter. It also includes a large number of ceremonial burials. Like the fishweir, this village reflects a degree of communal organization and material comfort that in turn suggests a very secure relationship with the physical environment.[5]

The burials at Wapanucket no. 6 and other archaeological sites illuminate some of the spiritual dimensions of Late Archaic culture. Above all they indicate an intense concern for the relationship between the worlds of the living and the dead. While some Archaic peoples cremated their dead before burial, others buried the corpses in a flexed, fetus-like position and smeared them with a red ocher substance which produced a placenta-like effect. This practice suggests that death was regarded as a kind of rebirth.[6] Such burials were not confined to New England but appear throughout the northeast in sufficient numbers for some archaeologists to speak confidently of a regional "cult of the dead" in which a single set of beliefs was incorporated within local traditions.[7]

From about 1500 B.C., this and other Late Archaic tendencies toward cultural uniformity were more than counterbalanced by others reflecting regional specialization, such as the new maritime orientations in northern and southern New England. Archaeologists once posited a distinct "Woodland" culture, introduced from without and characterized by ceramic pottery, elaborate burial mounds, and maize agriculture, as having succeeded the Archaic in eastern North America. Though "Woodland" as a term still enjoys currency, most archaeologists now recognize that pottery, burial mounds, and agriculture were entirely distinct from one another in time and place of origin and diffusion. Mortuary ceremonialism grew from an indigenous Late Archaic cult; ceramic pottery likewise appeared first in the Late Archaic, introduced into New England from the south; while maize agriculture did not become fully developed in southern New England before about A.D. 1000. Rather than constituting a single, great cultural leap, the phenomena once characterized as "Woodland" represent a series of separate developments that spread widely, further differentiating the Late Archaic cultures upon which they were built.[8]

The Archaic cultures of much of eastern North America finally disappeared under the impact of what archaeologists call the Mississippian cultural complex, which dominated much of the midwest and southeast from the eighth century to the eve of European contact. The principal features of this complex were systematic agriculture, hierarchical social and political structures, elaborate exchange networks, and clusters of large, pyramidal mounds.

The North Atlantic coast, however, remained beyond the reach of direct Mississippian influence. Many of the new ideas and techniques were introduced there, but gradually enough that the inhabitants incorporated them within their existing cultures. The spread of the most important of these developments—the combined cultivation of maize, beans, and squash—was restricted to climatically favorable areas, with the region south and west of the Saco River Valley supplementing hunting, gathering, and fishing with agriculture and, as a result, developing higher population densities. (Successful crops were occasionally produced in the Kennebec River valley.) Yet while domesticated plants increased in economic and dietary importance from about A.D. 1000, Mississippian influence in southern New England, on the margin of the agricultural zone, was strong enough only to modify, rather than transform, the patterns established during and after the Late Archaic. Like their fellow Algonquian speakers just to the north of the zone, the natives here approached the European contact era in autonomous village-bands that were optimally "fitted" to the food-producing capacities of their local environments.[9]

The economic and cultural patterns that characterized northern and southern New England when first encountered by Europeans, then, reflected not only the specialized adaptations that had developed since the Late Archaic but the earlier unity from which these adaptations had emerged. That unity was most apparent in language. Linguists have established that the Eastern Algonquian languages, spoken along the Atlantic coast from the Maritime Provinces to North Carolina at the beginning of the colonial period, constituted a distinct sub-group of

the Algonquian language family. The ancestors of Eastern Algonquian speakers are assumed to have spoken a single "Proto-
Eastern Algonquian" language, but when and how they sepa-
rated from the ancestors of Algonquian speakers around the
upper Great Lakes and in the northern Plains remains uncertain.[10] What is more certain is that, as numerous colonial
observers attested, the Eastern Algonquian languages formed
a kind of spectrum along the coast in which the speakers of
one language were conversant with their nearest neighbors but
spoke with decreasing fluency as the distance from home
increased.[11]

Within this spectrum, language and dialect boundaries
tended to conform to the same river drainage systems, bays,
and other natural features around which the Eastern Algonquian bands of New England and elsewhere had structured
their subsistence cycles and settlement patterns since Archaic
times.[12] Northernmost was the Micmac language, spoken by
seven bands that occupied the river systems emptying from
New Brunswick into the Gulf of St. Lawrence and Chignecto
Bay plus all of Prince Edward Island and Nova Scotia. Sharing
the Bay of Fundy with some of these Micmac bands were the
Malecite of the St. John River in New Brunswick and the Passamaquoddy of the St. Croix, now the United States-Canada
boundary. Malecite-Passamaquoddy is considered a single language with only minimal dialect differences distinguishing its
two components. Further south and west were the Eastern and
Western Abenaki languages of upper New England, of which
only the speakers of the former—often referred to collectively
as "the Abenaki"—figure in our story. As with the Malecite-
Passamaquoddy, their three dialects corresponded with river
drainage systems—in this case, the Penobscot, Kennebec, and
Androscoggin of central Maine.[13]

The coast-dwelling agriculturalists of southern New England
were so severely depopulated by epidemic diseases before the

beginning of extensive contact with Europeans that little linguistic evidence on them is available. But enough survives to
indicate that there were four distinct languages, each with several dialects. Massachusett was the language of the coastal and
island bands between the lower, agricultural portion of the
Saco River Valley in southern Maine and the eastern shore of
Narragansett Bay in Rhode Island. Among its speakers were
the Pawtucket, whose bands were clustered on the lower Merrimack and adjacent coast; the Massachusett themselves, around
Massachusetts Bay and its tributaries; the Pokanoket (or Wampanoag) of southeastern Massachusetts and the eastern side of
Narragansett Bay; as well as bands on Cape Cod, Martha's
Vineyard, and Nantucket. Narragansett was spoken along the
western shore of Narragansett Bay by several bands, including
the Narragansett themselves, and on Block Island. Mohegan-
Pequot was spoken in eastern Connecticut, between the Pawcatuck River and Thames River systems, by the Mohegan, Pequot, Niantic, and others, and in eastern Long Island by the
Montauk. Quiripi was spoken by numerous bands in western
Connecticut, between the Connecticut and Housatonic systems,
and in central Long Island. To the extent that pre-contact dialect boundaries can be discerned within each of these language
areas, they appear, like the northern languages, to follow geographic lines.[14]

Though more precise connections between pre-contact dialects and post-contact communities cannot be established,
other kinds of links between the two worlds can be. Through
scrutiny of the early colonial sources for data on population,
economics, and politics, we can obtain a general picture of native life at the beginning of the European invasion. Such a picture enables us to connect "prehistoric" Indians, as understood
through archaeology, and "historic" Indians, as recorded in
European documents.

Numbers

Despite the cultural continuity which preserved their links to the north, southern New England Algonquians had diverged in significant ways from their neighbors by the dawn of the European era. Most apparent and most fundamental was the demographic departure that resulted directly from the adoption and intensification of agricultural food production over the preceding four to six centuries. It is of course virtually certain that the southern portion of the region had always supported a larger population density than the north. More favorable climatic conditions and a wider range of food sources within smaller territories would have made this possible. The archaeological record supports this supposition. Northern New England has thus far yielded no sites to match the scale of the Boylston Street Fishweir or the lodge at Wapanucket no. 6. But the gap widened even further after agriculture took hold in the south, as written accounts of population before the catastrophic epidemic of 1616-18 make clear.

To raise the question of pre-contact native populations, much less to suggest some tentative orders of magnitude, is to enter a statistical wilderness. Until recently, all questions relating to pre-contact populations in North America were ritually referred to James Mooney's *Aboriginal Population of America North of Mexico,* published in 1928. For each region of North America, Mooney made a few general remarks and then presented a population breakdown by tribe or group of tribes based on his reading of estimates recorded by observers. Uncritically accepting his calculations for nearly half a century, ethnologists and historians advanced estimates of approximately 25,000 for the population of New England as of 1600, all but 3000 in the region from the Merrimack River southward.[15]

The undermining of this demographic orthodoxy has begun

only recently as the impact of European epidemic diseases on native populations in the Americas has been fully understood. Demographic and medical historians now realize that at the beginning of European contact the peoples of the entire Western Hemisphere had been, as it were, hermetically sealed from the immunities that had been established in the Eastern Hemisphere over the previous 40,000 years. As such, they constituted a vast "virgin soil" for such infectious diseases as smallpox, plague, and measles, resulting in epidemics of unprecedented scale, even by European standards.[16] Though work on the problem of Indian depopulation from disease began in the 1930s, it was only in the 1960s that enough data had been collected to call into question the figures advanced by Mooney and his counterparts elsewhere in the Western Hemisphere. Demographers, historians, anthropologists, and others differ widely in their own figures, but most now agree that Mooney's estimate of just over 1,000,000 for America north of Mexico in 1600 is only 10 to 25 percent of the actual total.[17]

Because of the abundant evidence in European sources that epidemic diseases severely reduced the native population of New England, the revised estimates have sparked new investigations of the problem there. One result is the discovery that here, as elsewhere, Mooney and his followers underestimated the extent of early, post-contact depopulation and consistently ignored or rejected evidence indicating larger pre-epidemic figures. They overlooked important evidence for both north and south, particularly an anonymous description of upper New England written in 1605 and included by Samuel Purchas in his *Hakluytus Posthumus* (1625) and pre-epidemic estimates for southern New England obtained by Daniel Gookin in the 1670s and first published in 1792. "The description of the Countrey of Mawooshen," as the document published by Purchas was entitled, locates villages, identifies their leaders, and estimates the number of adult males and houses in each.

Dean R. Snow has carefully correlated this information with
that provided in other pre-epidemic accounts and concluded
that about 11,900 Eastern Abenaki inhabited the river drainages from the Union River to the Saco in what is now the state
of Maine. This represents a significant increase over Mooney's
figure of 3000, based on figures given the Jesuit missionary
Pierre Biard by various Indians between 1611 and 1613. The
discrepancy is due to one of two factors—depopulation resulting from European contact between the times of the two estimates, or the possibility that Biard was unknowingly referring
only to adult males. The latter is reinforced by the facts that
the total number of men in the Mawooshen account—2930—is
almost identical to Biard's figure, and that every known population estimate by a New England Indian refers to adult males.
In any event, the description of Mawooshen is the far more
precise and detailed survey of the two. Using an adult male-
to-population ratio that obtained in the eighteenth century,
Snow offers his revised figure of 11,900 Eastern Abenaki.
Though this estimate may still be too low if the Eastern Abenaki
suffered the kind of post-contact decline in family size we shall
find in southern New England, it can be considered standard
until further evidence is uncovered.[18]

Moving south to the cultivated portions of New England, we
encounter an entirely different order of population magnitude.
Here again, Mooney's figures can no longer be considered reliable. Daniel Gookin's brief but systematic study, written in
1674, accounted for the central role of disease in native depopulation. Dividing the Indians from the Saco to the Quinnipiac into five great "nations," Gookin learned from older Indians that these groups counted about 18,000 adult males
among them before the first great epidemic. Mooney disre-
garded these figures as grossly exaggerated. His own estimates
totaled 23,900 individuals in all for the same area. Yet Gookin's
pre-epidemic totals and those he collected for surviving Indi-

ans in 1670 suggest the 90 percent depopulation rate proposed
by some present-day ethnohistorians and demographers, led
by Henry Dobyns, for the hemisphere as a whole since 1492.
Reviewing Gookin's figures as the most reliable evidence available, historian Francis Jennings has assumed an average of
four to five individuals per adult male and proposed a range of
72,000 to 90,000 persons between the Saco and Quinnipiac before the outbreak of the first great epidemic in 1616.[19]

As Jennings wrote, Sherburne F. Cook, a pioneer in assessing
the impact of disease on Indian populations, was taking a more
sustained look at southern New England demography. He
sought to assemble and coordinate documentary and archaeological evidence, to determine precisely which Indian group(s)
each piece of evidence concerned, and to translate figures for
adult males, families, or households (as such figures were usually given) into those for total populations. His work is especially valuable for the questions it asks and seeks to answer as
well as for the amount of evidence it assembles. But despite
his thoroughness and expertise, Cook's results were flawed by
his use of sources and his methodology. While he dismissed
four of Gookin's five estimates out of hand, calling one of them
"an apparent absurdity," he indiscriminately drew on virtually
every other author—primary and secondary—who ever ventured a guess.[20] And in addressing himself to the question of
the ratio of adult males to total population, Cook resorted to
several ahistorical, ethnographically invalid formulae that pre-
dated World War II.[21] Nevertheless, because of his awareness
of the impact of disease, Cook approached the order of magnitude suggested by Jennings, proposing a range of 60,000 to
80,000 and admitting that this may still have been too low in
light of recent findings elsewhere in the Western Hemisphere.[22]

Though far from abundant, evidence does exist for estimating the number of adult males per total population in pre-
epidemic southern New England. To begin with, we have one

estimate of family size from this period. After his fifteen-day
stay in Narragansett Bay in the spring of 1524, Giovanni da
Verrazzano reported that in each house "there lives a father
with a very large family, for in some we saw XXV to XXX people." Though Verrazzano did not make the connection, such
large families apparently resulted not only from a high fertility
rate, but from the low mortality rate he noted. "They live a
long life," he wrote, "and rarely fall sick; if they are wounded,
they cure themselves with fire without medicine, their end
comes with old age." Later accounts confirmed that the Indians
were strikingly healthy when they avoided European-induced
epidemics, while other reports commented on the mildness of
warfare before the introduction of guns and shrinking of resources due to colonization.[23] Let us assume, as Verrazzano
implies, that his figure is a maximum one and settle for an
average of just fifteen persons per household. Let us also assume, to be on the safe side, that there were two families in
most of them, as there were in the late 1630s when Roger Williams noted that two families would share "a little roundhouse
of some fourteen to sixteen feet over and so more and more
families in proportion" in those houses which were larger.[24]
The result is an average of 7.5 persons per family. Since marriage marked the end of the rites of passage into manhood in
southern New England, we can assume that the number of
men and number of families were about the same.[25] Applying
the factor of 7.5 individuals per family to Gookin's total of
18,000 fighting men, we get a total of 135,000 for the region
between the Saco and the Quinnipiac.

Yet to advance so precise a figure on the basis of existing evidence would be misleading. All we can really hope to obtain
is a range of figures with which existing estimates are consistent.[26] By converting our formula of 7.5 individuals per adult
male to one expressing a range from 7 : 1 to 8 : 1, we obtain a
reasonably narrow range for total population of 126,000 to

144,000 with which we can approach and test the evidence. Gookin's five "nations" and the figures he recorded for each provide us with a convenient baseline with which other, more localized estimates can be correlated.

One of Gookin's "nations" consisted of the numerous Pawtucket bands occupying the Merrimack drainage system as far inland as present-day Nashua, as well as the coast from the Saco River to Salem harbor. He estimated that before the epidemic they numbered about 3000 men. Beside this figure, we have the general testimony of Samuel de Champlain and John Smith as to the dense population of the coastal Pawtucket, as well as specific identification of three major communities—Smith's "Aggawom" (modern Ipswich) and "Naemkeck" (Salem) and Champlain's "Le Beau Port" (Gloucester).[27] The most useful information comes from Champlain's 1606 visit to Le Beau Port; upon arriving, he saw "two hundred [adult male] Indians in this place." But these were only the tip of the Pawtucket iceberg; during the days that followed the Indians claimed that 600 and, later, 2000 men were on their way to trade. It was the apparent populousness of the area that made the French fear for their safety and move on.[28] In 1614, John Smith learned that "at least" thirty villages were to be found along the Merrimack, and an archaeological survey conducted early in this century confirms that this figure is not unrealistic. Gookin's figure of 3000 men is thus quite compatible with what Champlain and Smith saw and heard, though it may have included many or all of the Western Abenaki of the upper Merrimack, rather than just the coastal Pawtucket as he thought. Multiplied by our factor of seven to eight, the resulting range of 21,000 to 24,000 is not unrealistic for this region.[29]

Aside from the virtually inaccessible inland areas, the most difficult section of southern New England to reconstruct is the coast and contributing drainage systems around Massachusetts Bay from modern Swampscott to Scituate. This area was in-

habited, according to Gookin, by around 3000 Massachusett
men. Champlain and Smith both noted not only the solidly
populated and cultivated coastline of this region, but the fact
that many of the islands in Massachusetts Bay were also settled. Smith heard, but did not take the time to confirm, Indian
claims that "there be neer three thousand people upon these
Iles," that thirty or more villages "doe possesse this Countrie,"
and "that the [Charles] River doth pearce many daies journie
the intralles of that Country." Gookin's reconstruction of early
seventeenth-century Indian groups suggests that Smith misun-
derstood the length of the Charles but not the extent of the
Massachusett system of alliances. For "the old men of Massachusetts affirmed" to Gookin that "their chief sachem held dominion . . . as far as Pokomtauke" on the Connecticut River.
Champlain found six "chiefs and tribes" along the Bay shore
alone, and Edward Johnson, an English colonist, later reported
that there had been seven. The pre-1616 observers left no estimates of single community sizes that might be correlated
with this regional one, but a clue from neighboring Plymouth
Bay suggests an applicable order of magnitude. Writing in
1623, an English trader there noted that "in this bay . . . in
former time hath lived about 2000 Indians." Assuming that
Massachusetts Bay's villages were about equal in size to Plymouth's, just the thirteen communities whose names Smith
learned (aside from the seventeen about which he was more
vague) brought the Massachusett beyond the 21,000 to 24,000
range suggested by Gookin's figure.[30]

Gookin also estimated that the Pokanoket—whose territory
he saw as extending from south of Massachusetts Bay to the
east side of Narragansett Bay, including offshore islands—
numbered 3000 men before the first epidemic. Several hints
exist in the literature as to the population size of individual
villages within this area. At Brant Rock, Champlain was met
by "fifteen or sixteen canoes," some of which held "fifteen or

sixteen Indians," whose village was probably near modern
Marshfield.[31] As we have just noted, the Plymouth colonists
were told (undoubtedly by their ally Squanto, who had lived
there) that their bay once held 2000 inhabitants. Champlain
and Smith both refer to three villages on Cape Cod. At the first,
Nauset, near what is now Orleans, the French were met in 1606
by "some 150 Indians," probably not an entire village or band; a
second village, Monomoy, near Chatham to the south, was inhabited by 500 to 600 men. The last figure suggests a particularly high village population of 3750 to 4500 individuals. And
this village was not drawing from its neighbors: the French
would have commented upon the presence of any of their
Nauset friends, with whom they had just renewed an alliance
established the year before, while their native harbor guide
left them when the French insisted upon sailing too close to
his enemies at a third village in the other direction.[32] We have
less evidence on Pokanoket groups farther to the west except
that we know of population centers at Buzzards Bay and at
Pokanoket itself, or Sowams, near present-day Bristol, Rhode
Island.[33] As for Martha's Vineyard and Nantucket, even the
conservative Cook estimates 3500 and 2500 respectively.[34] For
the Pokanoket, as for the Massachusett and Pawtucket, a range
of 21,000 to 24,000 is by no means unreasonable.

Besides the three "confederations" principally oriented toward the coast of what is now Massachusetts, Gookin identified two that faced the several island sounds directly south of
New England—the Narragansett and the Pequot. He saw the
Narragansett as dominating the bay of that name, except for
the Pokanoket village on the eastern shore, as well as the territory to the west to, but not including, the Pawcatuck drainage system. He also ascribed to them Block Island, the east
end of Long Island, and the Blackstone River drainage system. His figure of 5000 men multiplies to a range of 35,000 to
40,000 individuals, which is hardly too conservative, since the

trader Richard Smith estimated that there were 30,000 people
in the mainland and Narragansett Bay portions alone in 1641,
eight years after the tribe's first encounter with smallpox.[35]

Gookin included with the Pequot the Indians of the present
state of Connecticut as far west as the Connecticut and the
Quinnipiac rivers. His figure of 4000 fighting men translates to
28,000 to 32,000 individuals for this vast region. Though no
other early estimates exist against which to match it, this order of magnitude is entirely consistent with those found elsewhere in southern New England.[36]

It should be apparent by now that Gookin's estimates—or
rather those of his elderly native informants—do not vary
greatly from more direct pre-1616 observations, as Cook and
others have maintained. The range of 126,000 to 144,000 suggested here, however, represents no more than a proposed order of magnitude from which to continue research and discussion. Much work remains to be done, particularly in correlating
archaeological and documentary evidence. But we should now
have a more accurate sense of how densely southern New England was populated, particularly on the coast. Whereas the
11,900 Eastern Abenaki calculated by Snow had a population
density of just under 20 per 100 square kilometers, that for
southern New England farmers was nearly ten times as great.[37]
That was the demographic difference agriculture had made between these post-Archaic peoples.

Economies

Agriculture, then, was the key to southern New England's departure from the Archaic patterns that still prevailed to the
north. By the seventeenth century Indian women from the
Saco River southward had developed a variety of crops, including several types of maize, beans, and squash, as well as
pumpkins, cucumbers, Jerusalem artichokes, and tobacco. A

single field was planted with all these crops, and the most prominent feature was the regularly spaced mounds or "hills" in which several corn and bean seeds were planted. One effect of these hills was to strengthen the plants against winds and birds by allowing the roots to intertwine. The combination growing also resulted in higher concentrations of nitrogen in the soil and thus had a fertilizing effect. And when eaten together, the maize-bean combination, as grown throughout pre-Columbian America, provided more protein than the two would have separately. Beans contain an amino acid, lysine, which releases much of the corn's protein, zein. Maize contains an insufficient quantity of its own lysine to release the zein.[38]

After planting, Indian fields required constant attention. They were literally kept clear of all weeds, according to English accounts, and domesticated hawks were employed to reduce depredations by birds. By midsummer the Indians could begin consuming squash and green corn, but the major harvest came in September. Roger Williams observed that "the woman of the family will commonly raise two or three heaps of twelve, fifteene, or twentie bushells, a heap, which they drie in round broadheaps; and if she have helpe of her children or friends, much more." Much of this harvest was boiled, dried, placed in woven sacks, and stored in underground pits, where it was available for use during the winter.[39]

As the descriptions imply, agriculture had replaced hunting as the principal source of food for Indians in southern New England by the seventeenth century. In the villages, corn provided the basis for a stew or porridge to which was added whatever meats were available. When hunting or traveling, the Indians carried dried cornmeal. M. K. Bennett has attempted to reconstruct their annual diet from European accounts of subsistence activities and meals. He has produced a food balance sheet and estimated an average daily intake of about 2500 calories, on a par with that of Americans in the mid-twentieth century. Grain products, primarily corn, account for up to 65 percent of this figure. Animal and bird carcasses, fish and shellfish, and nuts and leguminous seeds follow, but are far behind at around 10 percent each. Though these figures are only rough calculations, they suffice to indicate the economic and dietary primacy that agriculture had attained.[40]

Nevertheless, agriculture's effects on the economic patterns established in southern New England during and after the Late Archaic were gradual and limited rather than revolutionary. Despite the impact of agriculture on population size and settlement patterns, the annual subsistence cycle in the south was still timed to coincide with the appearance of favored wild food sources. William Wood, who lived in Massachusetts Bay in the early 1630s, reported that hunters maintained huts "where they know the deer usually doth frequent." Wood also noted that in fishing the natives were "experienced in the knowledge of all baits, and diverse seasons; being not ignorant likewise of the removal of fishes, knowing when to fish in rivers, and when at rocks, when in bays, and when at seas." During these seasonal phases, related inland and coastal bands gathered at the appropriate sites, where they combined fishing with festivities and rituals. The movements of bird species were also closely observed, and specific seasonal schedules for gathering a wide variety of wild plant products were followed.[41]

Variation in food sources aside, Wood's description is not so different from that of Pierre Biard, written in 1616 and based on his observations of the Algonquian hunters of the Maritimes and (to a lesser extent) northern New England. Like Wood, Biard carefully recorded a cycle marked by fall and winter hunting, spring stream fishing, and summer sea fishing, involving specialized exploitation of innumerable minor species of mammals, birds, and fish. The one substantive difference between the two accounts is that whereas Biard's acquaintances "do not till the soil at all," Wood's spent half the year oriented toward agriculture. Yet the phases of cultivation, like any other subsistence activity, were carefully timed and coordinated with other activities in order to maximize yields.[42]

We have seen how an increase in subsistence choices lay behind the cultural changes of the Archaic period. Similarly, choice is central to the southern New England Indians' incorporation of a radical change such as agriculture into the existing subsistence system without disruption. Archaeologist Kent Flannery, in discussing the origins of maize cultivation in Mesoamerica, sees each subsistence activity as a separate "system" governed simultaneously by seasonal change and by human choice. The seasons regulate the food supply, and thereby a people's food-gathering activities, and thus have important social and cultural implications by providing the basis for a rudimentary but regular annual cycle. Human choice comes into play when people make decisions between two or more seasonally available food sources that cannot be exploited simultaneously. Post-Archaic bands in New England continued to refine their specialized subsistence activities, gradually centering them on river drainages or similarly diverse biological environments that allowed maximum choice. Then, through a myriad of decisions, southern New England Indians gradually shifted their priorities away from traditional food sources toward domesticated plants as the latter became available and proved preferable. In this way, agriculture was incorporated into existing patterns of subsistence, settlement, and territoriality.[43]

The continuity that the Indians maintained in their agriculture was ecological as well as cultural. The most drastic landscape change to accompany agriculture was the result of clearing the land by burning. This method of cultivation, known as "slash-and-burn" or "swidden," is one of the world's oldest agricultural techniques, confined today to certain tropical areas.[44] Often assumed to be an example of Indian carelessness and waste,[45] swidden agriculture is actually less disruptive of forest ecosystems than more intensive methods. Clifford Geertz, in a study of Indonesian agriculture, gives two examples of swidden's ecological advantage over wet-rice fields which apply in a general way to comparisons of Indian agriculture with the more intensive methods succeeding it in the temperate deciduous forests of New England. First, swidden maintains the diversity of a generalized ecosystem and thus preserves a large number of species, each represented by relatively few individual members, rather than making a selected group of species grow to large numbers and drive out the rest. Geertz's second point is that burning continues the forest's practice of supplying to the soil rich nutrient materials which are then returned to the biotic community.[46]

Besides its use for domestic cultivation, swidden aided more traditional subsistence activities as well. For this reason the underbrush was burned not only in spring but also in November after the larger trees had been cut for firewood; the semi-annual burning was thus an integral part of the subsistence cycle and marked two important phases of it. Burning off the dead undergrowth encouraged the live flora, and more deer entered the area to graze. The absence of dry twigs facilitated tracking and stalking them and other animals. Gathering wild plants was made easier, particularly because the fires had little effect on nut- and acorn-bearing trees and blueberry heaths, and so was movement about the countryside. There is no doubt that burning altered the physical environment and was the cause of the park-like appearance of much of the New England forest when the early Europeans encountered it. But with their burning the Indians maintained a functioning, diversified ecosystem that was, in Geertz's words, a "canny imitation" of its predecessor.[47]

The Indians also maintained continuity with the pre-agricultural past through their religious beliefs. They saw themselves as members of a larger system, their relationship to which was expressed in the idea that the fruits of nature, including the land itself, were gifts to be used with care and reciprocated for, and were not the exclusive possessions of human beings. Roger Williams noted that "if they receive any good in hunting, fishing, Harvest &c. they acknowledge God in it." One purpose of the festivals commemorating the phases of the annual cycle was to acknowledge such gifts through sacrifices of material goods. Rituals were conducted at the time of planting, at the appearance of green corn, and at completion of the harvest. Special rain dances were performed in times of drought. The southwest was considered the home of the paramount deity, Cautantowwit, or Kiehtan, because corn and beans had come from that direction and because it was the source of good weather. The Indians held the crow to be a sacred bird, not to be harmed, for having brought the grains to them.[48]

These agriculture-related beliefs and rites supplemented others whose origins long preceded the domestication of plants. John Josselyn, an English writer, described the capture of a moose in which the animal's heart, left rear foot, sinews, and tongue were removed before the venison was prepared. These and other taboos were common among the hunters of northeastern North America. They originated in beliefs that the animals had to be respected as sources of spiritual power who could withhold their gifts if not properly addressed and treated. One effect was to discourage the excessive killing of game, thereby encouraging the utilization of other food sources; a second was the crisis in belief undergone by some northern Algonquians when they began participating in the European fur trade.[49] In these practices we see the belief that the consumption of food, whether from domesticated plants or from wild animals, had to be accompanied by a gesture of reciprocity toward the powers responsible for supplying it. A balanced dependency relationship existed between humans and non-humans that neither could afford to break except at their peril. In this sense, agriculture had been fully integrated with the older hunter world-view.

Yet, though the Indians of southern New England were dependent on supernatural powers for a successful harvest, they do not appear to have been under the kind of restriction on the amount of corn produced that existed for the capture of wild animals. Corn was inanimate and so possessed no spiritual power of its own. Instead, it was the gift of Cautantowwit, who could withhold it if he were not properly worshiped but otherwise placed no limits on its production by humans. Unlike the animals, corn was regarded as an infinitely abundant source of food so that southern New England Indians not only stored corn for wintertime consumption but readily produced surpluses.[50]

The changes in lifeways resulting from agriculture led southern New England Indians to new perceptions of time, space, and climate which further differentiated them from their northern neighbors. Whereas the Micmac and Abenaki, according to Biard, identified the months in terms of currently available food sources, a calendar recorded in the seventeenth century indicates that farmers in southern New England identified each month—with the notable exception of the spring fish runs—by its relationship to the planting cycle.[51] Gluskap, the culture hero and transformer of Micmac and Abenaki mythology, fought a constant battle with, and was frequently outwitted by, winter; his experiences obviously mirrored those of his adherents.[52] In southern New England the meteorological emphasis had shifted away from the perils of winter toward obtaining conditions required for a successful harvest. The Indians here had elaborated the worship of Cautantowwit in the various rituals associated with the phases of the agricultural cycle and accorded him a position of pre-eminence among their deities. Indeed he had become the sustainer of individuals after life as well as during it; the souls of all good persons were

thought to proceed to his house in the southwest, there to re-
pose forever in sensual delight.[53] While the southwest was the
principal locus of spiritual power for southern New England
Indians, the Abenaki looked primarily to their own Mt. Katah-
din, which they frequently personified in myths.[54]

Despite these important differences, the religion of the southern New England Indians remained rooted, to a significant
degree, in pre-agricultural traditions. Like many of their Archaic ancestors, the dead were smeared with ochre, placed
in a fetal position, and buried facing the southwest (see fig. 1).[55]
Continuity was also reflected in the many similarities to native religion in northern New England. Indians in the two regions shared a wide variety of beliefs and rituals surrounding
hunting, healing, fortune, and other concerns. Their world was
inhabited not only by humans but by a wide variety of animals
and other beings who combined human-like modes of expression with supernatural powers.[56] Though agriculture and its
effects bestowed prominence on Cautantowwit in southern
New England, the Indians there were anything but mono-
theists. Like their northern brethren, they respected and feared
sources of power according to their demonstrated strengths
and benefits. Roger Williams learned the names of thirty-seven
"Gods" from the Narragansett, but it was apparent that the
number was infinitely flexible:

> There is a generall Custome amongst them, at the apprehen-
> sion of any Excellency in Men, Women, Birds, Beasts, Fish,
> &c. to cry out *Manitoo*, that is, it is a God, as thus if they see
> one man excell others in Wisdome, Valour, strength, Activity
> &c. they cry out Manitoo A God: and therefore when they
> talke amongst themselves of the *English* ships, and great build-
> ings, of the plowing their Fields, and especially of Bookes
> and Letters, they will end thus: *Manitowock* They are Gods:
> *Cummanittoo*, you are a God, &c.[57]

As Williams's own account indicates, the "manitou" which he
translated as "God" (meaning "god") actually referred to the

Figure 1. Skeleton of a Narragansett Indian, probably a male about 30 years old, buried in a cemetery in Jamestown, R.I. While the fetal, southwest-facing position of the body accords with traditions and beliefs dating back many centuries, the remains of personal possessions made of iron, copper, and brass near the ribs indicate that this person (like others at the site) was buried after the beginning of contact with Europeans, probably in the mid-seventeenth century. *Courtesy of the Sydney L. Wright Museum, Jamestown Philomenian Library, Jamestown, R.I.*

manifestation of spiritual power, a manifestation that could occur in almost any form. Belief in manitou was found, with variations, throughout the Algonquian-speaking world of central and eastern North America.[58] It enabled its adherents to accommodate traditional religion to changing circumstances. For, as Williams put it, they attributed to manitou "every thing which they cannot comprehend."[59] Rather than rejecting that which was unknown, they welcomed it and sought to come to terms with it. Thus Algonquian horticulturalists had made the transition from a hunting-oriented culture without experiencing a radical discontinuity in world-view, and thus hunters and farmers alike would seek in the same way to accommodate themselves to the more abrupt changes accompanying European colonization.

Polities

Social and political arrangements in southern New England reflected the cultural continuity that facilitated while controlling economic change. Nowhere was this more apparent than in that most fundamental of economic distinctions—the sexual division of labor. In northern Algonquian bands, men did the actual hunting while women took the game home and prepared it. Women also set up and broke camp and procured wild plant products and fish—not to mention bearing and doing most of the rearing of children. Southern New England women performed all of these tasks as well as planting, maintenance, and harvesting of their families' crops. The lives of the men, on the other hand, continued to revolve around hunting.[60] To the extent that economic and demographic change had an impact on male roles, it was to heighten the importance of warfare, diplomacy, and trade—activities which called on the same survival skills as hunting. Thus young men underwent rigorous tests to prove their manhood. According to a Dutch observer in the early seventeenth century, young Pokanoket men were left alone in the forest for an entire winter. Upon returning to his people in spring, a candidate was expected to imbibe and vomit bitter, poisonous herbs for several days. At the conclusion of his ordeal, he was brought before the entire band, "and if he is fat and sleek, a wife is given to him."[61]

The different economic roles of women and men were part of a larger pattern of sexual segregation that long preceded the rise of agriculture. In both southern and northern New England, male activity was political while female activity (including the maintenance of family garden plots) was domestic. This segregation was reinforced by taboos and other social rules. Women ate separately from men and were confined to isolated huts during menstruation. Female sexual and social modesty was, according to European observers, strictly observed by the women and enforced by the men. Girls wore small aprons almost from birth while, according to Roger Williams, boys went naked until they were ten or twelve.[62] The earliest explorers noted that they rarely encountered Indian women and that when they did, a safe distance was maintained from the strangers.[63]

Because of the blindness of European observers, the beliefs underlying these practices are lost to us. We can be reasonably certain, however, that they were rooted in understandings of the meaning of sexual differences. We can be even more certain that the social and economic conditions in which these beliefs were rooted no longer held in southern New England. Whereas men killed the game that provided most of the food in northern New England, it was the agricultural and other activities which men disdained that fed Indians in the south. M. K. Bennett's estimates of calories consumed daily show that nearly 90 percent were the direct result of female labor. Only meat products and some fish were the result of male labor, and even these were procured with the assistance of the women.

As Judith K. Brown has pointed out, women's economic roles in tribal societies tend to vary according to the compatibilities of those roles with child-rearing. Agriculture, like gathering and fishing, was carried out near the village, was not physically dangerous, and could be performed effectively in spite of frequent interruptions. Such was not the case with hunting, warfare, and diplomacy. Indeed, agriculture produced even greater segregation between the sexes than prevailed among hunters and left women, because of the more sedentary nature of their activities, as the source of group continuity. Many eastern North American horticulturalists addressed the tension between women's actual and recognized importance by adopting a system of matrilineal kinship reckoning and matrilocal residence in which women were accorded a degree of political power, albeit largely behind the scenes.[64] However, although the evidence is inconclusive, such an institutionalization of the collective position of women does not appear to have been made in southern New England by the early seventeenth century, even though women occasionally assumed band leadership.[65] In the case of sex roles, the economic changes of the previous six centuries had scarcely even modified the structure and world-view of pre-agricultural hunters.

If sex was the basic distinction within New England Indian societies, kinship was the basic bond. Individuals identified themselves in terms of lineage and their multiplicity of relationships to others. According to a knowledgeable Dutch trader, the natives of New England and New Netherland "reckon consanguinity to the eighth degree." Indeed, the village-bands in which Indians grouped themselves were primarily collections of extended lineal families. Because marriages were exogamous, the bond of kinship crossed band lines so that individuals dissatisfied with one band could join their relatives in another. Loyalty to kin, more often than to band, induced individuals to participate in retributive violence.[66] Just as it widened the gap between the sexes, agriculture reinforced the autonomy of individual families. Though inter-familial cooperation was frequent, garden plots were assigned to and managed by individual families. Men occasionally married more than one woman to increase their agricultural income.[67]

Kin loyalty could either strengthen or weaken a band, depending on circumstances and, above all, the band's cohesion. The task of solidifying the band's strength and integrity fell primarily to one or, in some cases, two individuals, usually called sachems in the south and sagamores in the north, who gained their positions through inheritance but retained them by keeping the respect of the community. The sachem's principal responsibilities were quite simply to carry out or coordinate those activities and functions that were the concern of the group as a whole rather than of families or individuals—hunting, inter-band trade and diplomacy, and the administration of intra-band justice. Careful European observers were virtually unanimous in remarking that the sachems depended on the consent of their people, relying more upon leadership ability and charisma than family names in securing popular loyalty. "Their authority is most precarious," remarked Biard of the Micmac and Abenaki sagamores, "if indeed, that may be called authority to which obedience is in no wise obligatory."[68] And though agriculture had brought larger populations to the south, the leaders' powers were similarly circumscribed. "Although they have an absolute Monarchy over the people," wrote Roger Williams of the paradox that continually baffled Europeans, "they will not conclude of ought that concerns all, either Lawes or Subsidies, or warres, unto which the people are averse, and by gentle perswasion cannot be brought." And William Wood noted that although inheritance rules were generally observed, an occasional "usurping intruder" was not unknown. If a sachem's "fair carriage bear him not out the better," Wood added, "they will soon unscepter him."[69] The key to the seeming paradox was the principle of reciprocity, mentioned above, which also underlay the relationship between leader and follower. Sachems assigned garden plots to families, and received portions of each harvest in return. English observers noted that these sachems and their counselors enjoyed a distinct social status and lived quite ostentatiously off the tribute collected from their followers. Yet these same leaders were careful to present gifts regularly to those followers, upon whose support they ultimately depended. Far from being kings, lords, or even "chiefs," the sachems of southern New England, as well as the sagamores to the north, were coordinators and ceremonial leader-representatives of their people.[70]

Underlying personal leadership, a band maintained its integrity through good collective relationships with those spiritual forces capable of affecting its fate. It was thus heavily dependent on individuals who had proven themselves capable of communicating with such forces. Some sagamores, such as Membertou of the Micmac and Passaconoway of the Pennacook, a Pawtucket band, augmented their positions by assuming shamanistic powers. "And then," in Biard's words, they were "greatly dreaded."[71] Further south, religious power was not generally linked to inherited political leadership. The sachems here surrounded themselves with an elite corps of counselors (called *pnieses* by the Pokanoket) chosen because of their ability to visualize or incorporate the deity Hobbamock and hence to utilize his powers for the good of the group. Sachems were also careful to maintain good relations with their groups' shamans, or *pow-wows*. Like the pnieses, the pow-wows were considered invulnerable in battle and served as political and military advisers to the sachems. They conducted large-scale séances during which they invoked spirits whose counsel was desired for critical decisions. They also conducted collective sessions to heal individuals. Band members gathered in the home of a sick person to assist the powwow in exorcising the destructive spirit which had lodged in the victim's soul.[72]

Reciprocity among humans, as well as between humans and non-humans, was maintained through a complex sequence of rituals. These rituals were especially elaborate and critical in southern New England, where the system of family agriculture might otherwise have increased the potential for an unequal distribution of wealth within the group. Thus redistribution of familial wealth was one function of the annual round of festivals. At one festival, the Nickòmmo, according to Williams, the host or hostess presented a gift of money and goods "(according to and sometimes beyond their Estate) . . . to the value of 18 pence, 2 shillings, or thereabouts to one person." The recipient then "goes out and hollowes thrice for the health and prosperity of the Party that gave it, the Mr. or Mistris of the Feast." At the Keesaqúnnamun, a harvest festival, certain males danced before the large singing audience and gave away their wealth to a poor Indian who had to beg for it as part of the ritual. At other rituals, material possessions were sacrificed to deities. With productivity of family garden plots varying as widely as it must have, the rituals served to restrain desires for material and social superiority. Before extensive English settlement, southern New England Algonquians do not appear to have thought themselves poor, and except during the Keesaqúnnamun ritual, no one begged. They neither secured their wigwams nor concealed their personal possessions, and had no laws against theft.[73]

Certain ceremonial games also appear to have redistributed wealth and otherwise reinforced social cohesion. Here again the limitations of English observers limit the evidence available to us. Particularly unfortunate is their overlooking of the results of such events. Such information would enable us to distinguish, in Lévi-Strauss's terms, between games and rituals. Rituals are structured so as to produce results which maintain equilibrium among the players and those they represent. Games, on the other hand, start from a structure but produce results that are contingent upon events and can be attributed to such factors as chance or individual talent. This distinction enables us to see farther than did the colonists. Their descriptions reflected hostility toward gambling and assumed that the giving away of money or other possessions by a loser meant that the Indians were strictly game-players. For example, William Wood observed that the Massachusett Indians "are so bewitched with these two games [Puim and Hubub], that they will lose sometimes all they have . . . all is confiscate by these two games." In light of the Indians' wealth-distributing mechanisms, Puim and Hubub may well have been rituals on at least some occasions.[74]

Wood was also highly amused by a sport that resembled English football:

> There are rich goals all behung with wampompeag [wampum], mowhachies [?], beaver skins, and black otter skins. It would exceed the belief of many to relate the worth of one goal, wherefore it shall be nameless.

Again a redistribution of wealth is suggested, the more strongly because of the way the game was played:

> Their goals be a mile long placed on the sands. . . . Sometimes . . . it is two dayes before they get a goal. Then they mark the ground they win, and begin there the next day.

The Indians may in fact have been engaging in a social equilibrium ritual similar to that of the Gahuku-Gama of New Guinea who, having learned football, "will play, several days running, as many matches as are necessary for both sides to reach the same score." This, concludes Lévi-Strauss, "is treat-

ing a game as a ritual." Wood provides still further evidence
for such an interpretation:

> Before they come to this sport, they paint themselves, even as
> when they go to war, in policy to prevent future mischief be-
> cause no man should know him that moved his patience or
> accidentally hurt his person, taking away the occasion of study-
> ing revenge. Before they begin their arms be disordered, and
> hung upon some neighboring tree, after which they make a
> long scroll on the sand over which they shake loving hands, and
> with laughing hearts scuffle for victory. While the men play,
> the boys pipe and the women dance and sing trophies of their
> husbands' conquests. All being done a feast summons their
> departure.[75]

In this ritual the Indians appear to have gone to great lengths
to emulate the ceremonies associated with revenge, while
scrupulously avoiding any occasion for its realization. Such a
ritual may have been useful in maintaining equality and peace
where population growth, increased agricultural activity, and
political centralization heightened the potential for male violence within and between groups.

The sachems too played the games and lost. The most richly
bedecked sachem was often left "in mind and riches equal
with his naked attendants, till a new taxation furnish him with
a fresh supply."[76] In such cases the sachem was fulfilling a ritualized role that reminded everyone that he was one band
member among many whose dependence on the rest equaled
their dependence on him. As with the mechanisms of political
organization, these games served to counter the centralization
of authority in the sachems' hands.

The essential interdependence of band members was enforced through rules that governed personal conduct in communal settings. At council meetings, the men would sit smoking
their pipes in deep silence so as to concentrate on each other's
words. According to John Josselyn these speeches rhymed and

were replete with physical gestures that supplied more specific meanings to certain words.[77] This was one of a number of
situations in which the band required the collective emotional
commitment of all its members. While their culture provided
ample outlet for emotional expression, both convivial and vio-
lent, the famous "stoic" personality of the Algonquians served
to suppress any such expressions that posed dangers to the
group. The repression of pain was deemed a virtue which was
cultivated from youth and which met its supreme test when
prisoners defied the tortures of their captors. Fear was also
proscribed, not simply for being unseemly but because it
could endanger the whole group. Roger Williams "once trav-
elled with neere 200 who had word of neere 700 enemies in
the way, yet generally they all resolved that it was a shame to
feare and goe back." Europeans never ceased to be alarmed by
the boasting that Indian men engaged in among themselves
to fortify their courage during times of tension. While fear
was to be suppressed in times of danger, personal anger also
had to be minimized within the group. Wood reported that in
all his contacts with Indians, he never saw "any falling out
amongst them, not so much as cross words, or reviling speeches
which might provoke to blows." Though some modern observers have suggested that physical and psychological "stoicism"
among Eastern Algonquians denoted a psychology of individ-
ualism, the evidence from early colonial New England suggests
that its function was originally communal.[78]

Rituals not only reinforced equality and communalism within
bands but served to regulate inter-band relations as well. Lin-
guistically related bands sharing rivers or bays generally allied
for purposes of conducting exogamous marriages and exchanging material goods. These relationships were reaffirmed at the
festivals accompanying the spring fish runs and at others in
which games, giveaways, and religious invocations served
functions that were political as well as religious and economic.

Such alliances frequently united bands of two or more adjoining river systems, especially with the advent of the European fur trade. Biard described the annual summer gatherings of northern hunters at which sagamores renewed their ties with one another. On New England's south coast, the Narragansett, Pequot, Mohegan, and other groups were linked by a complex network of marriages.[79] Inter-band alliances were frequently dominated by single individuals, such as Miantonomi, through the force of their personalities plus the demographic, geographic, and other advantages enjoyed by their bands. But while they might be widely revered and/or feared, they had no institutionalized authority over other bands. When two or more bands were united, it was by ritualized exchange rather than by centralized authority. Under post-contact conditions, such exchanges frequently took the form of tribute paid by members of disadvantaged bands to the sachems of stronger ones. Such arrangements led many Europeans (and subsequent scholars) to assume that leadership was permanently and hierarchically arranged with "highest *Sachims*" and "under *Sachims*."[80] Though the Europeans never quite unlearned this notion, their own accounts of Indian politics in actual operation indicate a quite different arrangement; a band's perception that an alliance was no longer reciprocal (in these cases, that it was no longer receiving an adequate return on its tribute) could lead it to withdraw its loyalty and direct it to another partner. The "chiefdom" and "tribe" of political anthropology were not to be found in southern New England; the only permanent, supra-familial organization was the band.[81]

The purposes of inter-band exchanges were manifold. They facilitated exogamous marriages and the distribution of material resources that bands could not have obtained on their own. But these functions were embedded in a deeper purpose: exchange—not just of goods but, to quote the classic study of the subject, of "courtesies, entertainments, ritual, military assistance, women, children, dances, and feasts"—was the means by which a normative social and political equilibrium was maintained.[82] Underlying it was the same principal of reciprocity which informed religious worship and other rituals among New England Indians. To fail to reciprocate appropriately in such a system was to upset the balance of the universe and was, therefore, virtually unthinkable. Yet to judge from the early colonial evidence, genuine enthusiasm, even a kind of cosmopolitanism, was at least as important as fear of adverse consequences in motivating Indians to enter into exchanges. The desire to gain access to new sources of spiritual power as well as, perhaps, to discover a new food or tool, led to the diffusion of items over long distances via both exchange networks and direct contact.[83] Even utterly alien strangers, like the Europeans who appeared with increasing frequency over the sixteenth and early seventeenth century, might be approached—unless or until experience deemed otherwise.

In short, to exchange goods or otherwise interact socially was, like the forms of interaction with non-humans, part of keeping oneself and one's world in balance. Life had always proceeded this way in New England, despite the radical transformations that had occurred, especially in the south. As a result, Indians had never gone hungry or otherwise wanting. It was this world which Miantonomi recalled, and to which he juxtaposed the non-reciprocating English, when seeking to galvanize the natives in 1642.

two

HUNTERS and TRADERS

THE COMING OF Europeans irrevocably altered the cultural systems that had developed over the previous millennia in North America. The delicately balanced, self-sufficient, kin-based communities with their ritualized reciprocal exchanges and their Neolithic technologies had been reached by the expanding nation-states of Europe, with all their instability and upheavals as well as their organizational and technological accomplishments. "Never in the history of the world," writes Charles Hudson, "have cultures so different and so unprepared for each other come into such ineluctable collision."[1]

The first stage of Europe's conquest of northeastern North America was, to use T. J. C. Brasser's term, "the traders phase."[2] Casual contacts and exchanges with visiting explorers and fishermen began, when not marred by hostile or otherwise strange behavior by the Europeans, on a basis that was not unfamiliar to the Indians. Metal, glass, or cloth items were exchanged for furs in a setting that was unprecedented only in the strangeness of the visitors and their wares. But as casual exchanges became systematic, natives began altering their subsistence and residential patterns in order to obtain more furs. As a result, they grew dependent on their European trading partners while frequently entering into competition with one another. In the end, the principles of reciprocity and equality had been substantially undermined by the ethics and imperatives of the traders.

The brief traders phase in southern New England began not as a result of Europeans sailing directly there and establishing contact with the Indians, but through the gradual expansion into the region of trade activity originating on its periphery. To get at the real beginning of the traders phase in southern New England, then, we must first examine its antecedents to the north and west.

The Trade Begun

Regular contacts between Indians and Europeans in northeastern North America were initiated not by publicity-conscious explorers but by anonymous fishermen who wished to keep the locations of rich grounds to themselves. For this reason, the details of the beginnings of contact are largely obscured by a lack of documentation. We do know that, under the pressures of increased competition and expanded markets, western European fishermen working the North Atlantic had gradually ventured more widely during the late fifteenth century. It is virtually certain that Bristol men fishing off Newfoundland made contact with the North American mainland before John Cabot's "discovery" of it in 1497, and possibly before Columbus'; there is fragmentary but suggestive evidence to indicate that they were fishing regularly in Newfoundland waters as early as 1480 or 1481.[3] Cabot's voyages inspired a series of commercial exploring ventures around Newfoundland and the Gulf of St. Lawrence, but by 1510 these efforts had been abandoned. Meanwhile the Bristol men had been joined by ships from Portugal, Brittany, and the Basque country, so that the area was teeming with several hundred fishermen and a few whalers annually.[4]

Though Cabot reported sighting natives on shore and returned with some material evidence of human activity, he made no direct contacts with Indians. Recorded contacts began shortly thereafter. Between 1501 and 1509 at least four kidnappings involving several dozen Micmac were carried out by European explorers.[5]

With the advent of routinized fishing, regular contacts between specific groups of Europeans and natives were established on an annual basis, and procedures for trade were developed. Some sense of these procedures, and of their geographical distribution, can be obtained from the accounts of explorers Giovanni da Verrazzano and Jacques Cartier. Sailing north from Carolina in 1524, Verrazzano and his crew encountered Indians who were interested in "trinkets," earrings and necklaces similar to the ceremonial and decorative objects that comprised the bulk of their own trade. At Narragansett Bay the natives scorned all utilitarian objects like silk cloth and metal tools, as well as gold. Guns were of interest for their workmanship, but not for their practical application. For Verrazzano, "these people are the most beautiful and have the most civil customs that we have found on this voyage." Refugio, as he called Narragansett Bay, was to him a utopia peopled by noble savages.[6]

Proceeding northward, Verrazzano found at Casco Bay Indians of a very different kind, Abenaki who obviously had traded with Europeans and insisted on defining sharply the terms of their meeting:

> If we wanted to trade with them for some of their things, they would come to the seashore on some rocks where the breakers were most violent, while we remained on the little boat, and they sent us what they wanted to give on rope, continually shouting to us not to approach the land; they gave us the barter quickly, and would take in exchange only knives, hooks for fishing, and sharp metal. We found no courtesy in them, and when we had nothing more to exchange and left them, they made all the signs of scorn and shame that any brute creature would make.[7]

The difference between the attitudes of the Indians in the two areas is clear. In southern New England, trade was still primarily a means of establishing or maintaining alliances based on reciprocity. As such it consisted primarily of non-utilitarian objects. The natives at Narragansett Bay approached the sailors with these assumptions. This is not to say that they were unacquainted with European goods; the "many sheets of worked copper" that Verrazzano saw being worn as jewelry had certainly come from European pots rather than from American mines, suggesting the extent to which European goods were diffused and adapted beyond areas of direct contact.[8] However, the Abenaki at Casco Bay, obviously experienced in dealing directly with Europeans, sought metal utilitarian objects rather than "trinkets." Even so, these objects were no more than technological improvements on existing stone tools, and were easily adapted to the existing culture; no wholesale transformation was entailed in their occasional acceptance and use. The Abenakis' behavior also suggests a recent unhappy experience. Perhaps, as Dean Snow suggests, it was at the hands of the Portuguese explorer João Alvares Fagundes three years earlier, or was similar to the fate of several dozen Penobscot Abenaki kidnapped the following year by the Spanish explorer Esteban Gomez.[9] But the recent visitors here could also have been fishermen-traders.

That not all such early contacts were unfriendly is indicated by Jacques Cartier's experiences as he explored the Gulf of St. Lawrence in 1534. In Chaleur Bay, between New Brunswick and the Gaspé Peninsula, he met a party of about three hundred Micmacs who displayed the same kind of friendliness that Verrazzano had encountered at Narragansett Bay. But unlike the natives at the latter, the Micmac knew how to trade with Europeans. After holding up their furs on sticks to attract the ship's attention, they had to pursue the hesitant French in their canoes in order to get the latter to trade. In the ensuing exchange the Micmac traded their stock of furs for the same sorts of utilitarian items that the Casco Bay natives had obtained from Verrazzano.[10]

Proceeding around the peninsula, Cartier and crew next put in at Gaspé Bay, where they met another party of 300. Not only did this group differ from the Micmac in language and customs, but they were, in Cartier's words, "the sorriest folk there can be in the world, and the whole lot of them had not anything above the value of five sous, their canoes and fishing nets excepted." The vocabulary compiled by Cartier and other evidence make it clear that these Indians were Iroquoian speakers from the village of Stadacona, some 32 miles above the present site of Quebec City, who migrated to the seashore each summer to fish and hunt seals. Again the reception accorded the French was enthusiastic, though the Stadaconans as a group appear to have been unacquainted with Europeans. Their willingness to trade suggests prior knowledge, however, perhaps acquired through their seal hunters or their hostile Micmac neighbors.[11]

Whereas Verrazzano's account might suggest that Indian attitudes toward Europeans were naïve and friendly until experience dictated a more hostile posture, what Cartier's shows was probably more typical—at least near the center of European fishing activity where he was exploring.[12] Both Indian groups he encountered were eager for trade relations regardless of prior experience, and displayed the cordiality generally shown to visitors, the Micmac having forgiven or forgotten the kidnappings of twenty years earlier. One dimension of the trade's rapid expansion is suggested by the fact, not discovered by Cartier until his return a year later, that the Stadaconans had recently suffered heavy losses at the hands of some Micmac who disputed their presence at Gaspé. The latter were apparently attempting to extend their hunting activities as well

as increase their contacts with European visitors. They probably benefited from their possession of a few iron axes and
knives.[13] Here was where the contributions of European technology became critical for Indians. The possession of such
weapons constituted an advantage which, when the fur trade
drove bands beyond their customary territories and into competition with one another, eventually obliged all Indians in the
vicinity to participate as a matter of survival.

Despite the rapid expansion of the trade in furs, the accounts of Verrazzano and Cartier reveal how limited it remained through the first third of the sixteenth century. These
limitations were dictated by the dynamics of codfish production and trade. European fishermen initially opted for deep-
water banks where the larger varieties of cod were available
in such quantities that they could be quickly obtained and
returned to Europe for profit. For this kind of "wet" or "green"
fishing they generally did not leave their boats. But eventually
the area became sufficiently crowded so that some fishermen,
especially Bretons and Basques, moved closer to the nearby
shores. Soon after, sporadic trading between coasting vessels
and Indians began.[14] By the time Verrazzano and Cartier
passed through, the Indians knew that to trade they had to
gather on the shore and signal. The process was especially
familiar to the Micmac, who appear to have had a surplus of
furs ready for Cartier.[15]

The fur trade was bound to remain a casual appendage of
cod fishing so long as it was conducted from coasting boats.
But around mid-century the ever-increasing demand for fish
and competition for profits led merchants to develop regular
drying stations on the Labrador, Newfoundland, and Acadian
shores as a means of maximizing cargoes and profits. This
facilitated regular contacts between Indian hunters and European merchants and led to an upsurge in the trade in beaver
pelts. The permanent opening of the St. Lawrence in the

1580s hastened the process. As a result, the price of furs dropped, and the beaver hat, formerly a luxury good, became more widely available in western Europe. It quickly became an item of fashion, the demand for which produced a distinct, specialized fur trade.[16]

A Nexus Established

While the trade in furs and fish never lost its international character, the predominance of the French within the Gulf of St. Lawrence and along the Acadian coast increased as the century wore on. Even before the advent of drying stations, Basque and Breton fishermen were garnering most of the furs of the Micmac, the Malecite, and the Passamaquoddy as well as of the Algonquian-speaking Montagnais north of the St. Lawrence.[17] By the end of the sixteenth century, the culture and institutions of these groups had been profoundly affected.

There is no doubt that the Micmac responded to the trade in terms of their traditional culture and values. The prestige customarily associated with successful hunting was reinforced by the new material rewards. The goods themselves were accorded the treatment proper to any objects possessing sacred powers. When valued as possessions, they often served as burial goods, to the dismay of the French. French alcohol was added to the traditional festivals celebrating the completion of successful hunting seasons and trading rounds. French clothing and jewelry enabled the Micmac to elaborate their traditional styles of bodily adornment. Iron arrowheads, axes, and knives gave their possessors important advantages not only in hunting but in avenging insult or injury.[18]

These incentives, and the steady proliferation of French traders, led the Micmac to become specialized laborers in an economic nexus. As French tools, utensils, and other items replaced their aboriginal equivalents altogether, the time for-

merly spent manufacturing them was devoted to the hunt.
After a couple of generations, the old skills were forgotten.
No longer able to supply themselves with these items, the
Indians had become economically dependent on the French
trade. Full-time hunting also deprived them of their subsistence autonomy. Concentrating exclusively on the hunt,
they abandoned other food-producing activities of the winter
months while over-killing the formerly adequate supply of
fur-bearing animals. By the beginning of the seventeenth
century, they were leading a precarious existence every winter, relying on the French and other outside sources of food
for survival.[19]

The trade also affected the structures of native politics and
diplomacy. Within bands the sagamores' position was strengthened as increased hunting led to increased wealth through
receipt of their traditional portion of each hunt. Intensive
hunting also led to increased competition with neighboring
groups, such as the Stadaconans and Malecite, for territory. In
these conflicts the Micmac generally prevailed because of their
European weapons.[20] Further, the trade created competition
for access to French traders and their goods. The impact of
regular trading centers, such as drying stations and, later,
colonial outposts, is apparent from what happened when the
French established one of the latter at Port Royal in 1605. As
we shall see, the local Micmac under Membertou became the
dominant power among Indians trading with the French because of their proximity to Port Royal.

Such advantages could not, however, conceal more fundamental processes of decline among the Micmac. Membertou
told Marc Lescarbot in 1610 that in his youth his people had
been "as thickly planted there as the hairs upon his head," but
that since the French had come their numbers had diminished
radically under the impact of disease. French observers like
Lescarbot and Pierre Biard identified disease and depopula-

tion with the changes in Micmac life wrought by the trade.
They argued that the new seasonal cycle of summer idleness
and indolence near the French posts followed by hard work
outdoors in autumn and winter left the Indians vulnerable to
disease. Yet the Micmac traditionally enjoyed sedentary,
abundant summers while fishing, moving inland to hunt and
gather during winter. In terms of movement and labor time,
the cycle had not changed so radically. The Indians themselves
may have been closer to identifying at least one source of ill
health when they blamed the quality of the French food upon
which they had come to depend. The blatantly moral judg-
ments of the French are opened to further question by the example Biard used to illustrate his case. He noted that 60 members (a majority) of a Micmac village had perished during a
single season while none of the French had even become ill.
Biard was surely witnessing a "virgin soil epidemic," in which
an immunologically vulnerable population is in large part
destroyed after contact with outsiders—a pattern repeated
many times during the European conquest of the Americas.
Biard's estimate of 3000-3500 Micmac living in 1611 represents, according to Dean Snow's estimate, about one-fourth
of the population a century earlier.[21]

Micmac demoralization in the face of these changes is un-
deniable. As Calvin Martin has noted, European diseases
undermined the powers of shamans to heal or explain the
plight of the sick. This meant an undermining not only of traditional values related to religion but of Micmac self-confi-
dence.[22] Yet the degree of demoralization should not be
exaggerated, for the Micmac possessed a rich store of cultural and communal resources upon which to draw in coming
to terms with the crisis that so suddenly confronted them.
For the most part, they continued to perceive and act in traditional Micmac ways. Thus they saw their connection with the
French as a relationship between equals. Trading sessions

were conducted as traditional ritualized exchanges, as can be
seen from Biard's description:

> And they set themselves up as brothers of the King, and it is
> not to be expected that they will withdraw in the least from
> the whole farce. Gifts must be presented and speeches made
> to them, before they condescend to trade; this done they must
> have the Tabagie, in other words, the banquet. Then they will
> dance, make speeches and sing *Adesquidex, Adesquidex.*
> That is, that they are good friends, allies, associates, confed-
> erates, comrades of the King and of the French.

And the Micmac considered themselves braver, more peaceful
with each other, and more ingenious than the French, which
Biard found laughable.[23] The most visible signs of change and
decline were understood as the work of outside sources. We
have seen that diseases were attributed to the quality of the
food purchased from the French, which some Indians charged
was spoiled or counterfeited.[24] Finally, as we shall see, the
trade-inspired causes of warfare were not incompatible with
the traditional ethic of revenge.

It is easy to dismiss these Micmac beliefs as naïve forms of
self-deception and rationalization. To do so, however, is to
overlook the phenomenon of cultural persistence and adaptation in the face of crisis, as well as the lack of choices actually
available to Indians in situations like that of the Micmac.[25]
The long-range, destructive effects of the European trade were
not apparent at first; the Indians saw only goods which made
traditional activities somewhat easier and more efficient. Later,
when dependence was a reality, they strove to maximize their
advantages within the limitations imposed by that reality. Although there was no precedent in Indian experience for change
of such magnitude and rapidity, the new lifeways were largely
assimilated within native belief systems.

Awareness of the conditions under which Indians were introduced to the trade should also alert us to the fallacy of the

traditional idea that a blind Indian "demand" for European goods was the fundamental and driving force behind the fur trade.[26] To the extent that "demand" was a factor, it was that of European merchants and their hat-wearing customers which impelled the trade and turned formerly self-sufficient hunters into specialized producers dependent on conditions and decisions over which they had no control. And it was this demand, along with related economic and diplomatic imperatives originating in Europe, that soon turned trade activity into outright colonization on an expanded geographic scale.

French-Micmac Expansion

As the sixteenth century drew to a close, France increasingly felt the pressures of imperial rivals—England, the Netherlands, Spain—on its previously uncontested claims to northeastern North America. Recognizing that occupation rather than legal pronouncement was the way to enforce these claims, Henry III and Henry IV authorized several unsuccessful attempts to establish trade monopolies by means of colonies during the last quarter of the sixteenth century. In 1603 Henry IV made yet another try. He named Pierre de Gua, sieur de Monts, vice-admiral and lieutenant general of Acadia and the St. Lawrence Valley. De Monts's obligations were to expand French interests through further exploration for fur trade routes and minerals, to establish alliances with the natives and bring them to Christianity, and to finance the operation. His rewards included a ten-year monopoly on the fur trade and the power to grant lands in seigneurial tenure.[27] The following year a few dozen men, led by de Monts and several associates, including Jean Biencourt de Poutrincourt and Samuel de Champlain, established an island post at the mouth of the St. Croix River.

De Monts immediately sent Champlain to explore the coast southward. The explorer-cartographer's principal stop was at the Penobscot, where he met with the sagamore Bashaba. Champlain offered the Penobscot Abenaki not only friendship but reconciliation with the Micmac and Montagnais, who were their enemies, the prospect of regular trade, and the presence of French settlers who would introduce agriculture "in order that they might no longer lead so miserable an existence as they were doing." Bashaba replied that the offer was satisfactory, and that French settlement and peace with the Abenaki's enemies were desirable "in order that in future they might hunt the beaver more than they had ever done, and barter these beaver with us in exchange for things necessary for their usage." Champlain departed, assuming that the vast fur resources of the Penobscot drainage system had been secured for the French.[28]

Besides establishing trade relations, the expedition was to locate a site for a permanent French post on the Maine coast. But de Monts was attracted by Port Royal, on the Bay of Fundy coast of Nova Scotia, for its superiority as a year-round shelter—and, most likely, by the entrenched, productive fur trade that had flourished on the Bay for decades. In 1605 he moved his post there. The principal beneficiaries of this decision were the inhabitants of the nearby Micmac village and their remarkable sagamore, Membertou.[29] Like other northern Algonquian sagamores, Membertou was the principal religious as well as political figure in his band. As prophet, healer, and warrior he was renowned, though in the last role he had apparently made many enemies and was, in Lescarbot's words, "well content to keep close to the French, in order to live in safety." This did not mean that Membertou acknowledged a dependency relationship between his people and the French. As we have seen, the Micmac saw themselves and the French as equals, and Membertou considered himself "the equal of the King and all his lieutenants."[30]

The intrusion by the French into native politics was no accident. As Marcel Trudel has shown with reference to the St. Lawrence area, once the French undertook a serious colonial policy they realized that the continued flow of furs depended on direct political control of participating Indian groups.[31] Having secured the loyalty of the Port Royal Micmac and of the Oüigoudi, or St. John, Malecite directly across the Bay, de Monts proposed to extend this new alliance to the south, among the Abenaki. The first step had been Champlain's 1604 agreement with the influential Bashaba. Subsequent steps were taken during voyages made in 1605 and 1606, each of which surveyed topography, natural resources, and Indian communities as far south as Cape Cod. On the Kennebec in 1605 the French, led by de Monts, were able to secure only a minor sagamore, Menthoumermer, having missed two more important figures. One of these, Marchin, allied himself the next year with Poutrincourt, who commanded the 1606 expedition, but the other, Sasinou, continued to elude the French.[32]

Like the Micmac and other allies of the French, the Abenaki were primarily hunter-gatherers whose small, highly mobile bands sparsely populated the land. From the Saco River southward, the French encountered a different kind of Indian. Champlain repeatedly remarked upon the density of the region's population, the size and layout of its villages, and the extent and productivity of its agriculture. He also noted that these "Armouchiquois," as the French called them, possessed few furs for trading. Nevertheless the French explored this coast in both 1605 and 1606, attempting to establish good relations with the various Indian groups while considering the desirability of locating a colony there to contain Spanish expansion northward from Florida.[33]

Though the reception accorded the French by the Pawtucket, Massachusett, and Pokanoket was generally friendly, hostilities arose on several occasions. In Nauset harbor in July 1605 an Indian, perhaps unsatisfied with the "trifles" to which the French were restricting the agricultural Indians, walked away with a French kettle. The Europeans opened fire with their muskets, and the natives responded with arrows. When the air had cleared, one Frenchman was dead and one Indian had been captured (see fig. 2). After being assured by the local Indians that the offenders were from a different band, the French released their prisoner and friendly relations were resumed.[34]

A more serious conflict erupted the following year at the neighboring village of Monomoy, near Pleasant Bay. The French were commanded this time by Poutrincourt, more suspicious and given to retribution in his dealings with Indians than de Monts; just before its arrival, the expedition had narrowly avoided violence at Gloucester harbor when Poutrincourt had become uncomfortable over the number and conduct of the Indians.[35] The French recruited a harbor guide at Monomoy in an effort to establish contacts along the south shore of Cape Cod; but he abandoned them when they insisted on coasting westward into territory controlled by his enemies. When the French realized that Monomy held between 500 and 600 adult males, they attempted to defuse what they saw as a potential threat with a demonstration of their guns and swords. On top of this arrogance and insensitivity, the French erected a large cross in the harbor. In reaction to these acts (and perhaps to the incident at Nauset a year earlier), the Indians dismantled their wigwams and moved their village inland to the woods. Poutrincourt, fearing that the withdrawal meant that an attack was imminent, ordered all his men on board. But unknown to him, five of them remained ashore for the night. At dawn they were attacked; one died instantly and the others were wounded, three of them mortally (see fig. 3). The French drove the attacking party back into the woods and buried their dead man. As they withdrew from the harbor, the Indians re-emerged on the

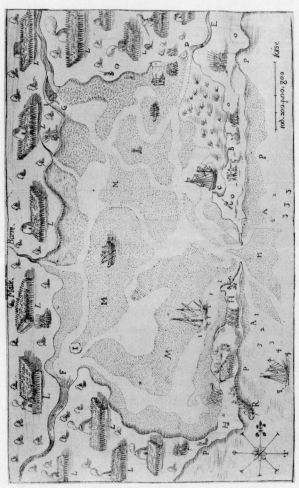

Figure 2. Samuel de Champlain's map of Malle Barre (Nauset harbor, Cape Cod), one of a series based on his explorations of the New England coast in 1605 and 1606. Note the fish trap at the mouth of a stream (G); the large number of family garden plots (L), a feature that would disappear from Cape Cod and the coast northward a decade later; and the French-Indian skirmish (B) in which one Frenchman was killed. *Les Voyages de Sieur de Champlain Xaintongeois* (Paris, 1613). *Courtesy of Chapin Library, Williams College, Williamstown, Mass.*

Figure 3: Indian attack on Champlain's party at Port Fortuné (Monomoy, Cape Cod), 1606. This last and most serious conflict with Indians during the voyages of 1605-1606 helped persuade the French to concentrate their colonial activities further north. The several hundred Indians were angered by the cross the French had erected and, perhaps, by the skirmish in Fig. 2. *Les Voyages de Champlain Xaintengeois* (Paris, 1613). *Courtesy of Chapin Library, Williams College, Williamstown, Mass.*

beach, dug up the corpse, tore down the cross, and jeered the French by turning around, "taking sand in their two hands and casting it between their buttocks, yelping the while like wolves."[36] The message of this "sign language" was unmistakable.

The French concluded that "Armouchiquois" country was no place to colonize, at least for the moment. Not only were its harbors hazardous for large vessels, its Indians were too thickly populated and too hostile to risk placing a small outpost there. Moreover these agricultural Indians were less dependent on the hunt than Indians to the north.[37] Despite these negative factors the French did enjoy amicable relations with most of the seven or eight groups they contacted. These, plus Champlain's detailed maps of the harbors at Gloucester, Plymouth, Nauset (fig. 2), and Monomoy, would assist other French in extending the coasting trade southward during the ensuing decade.[38]

One agricultural group remained important in the thinking of the French, apparently contrary to their original intentions. In 1605 the French had treated the Indians at Chouacoet, at the mouth of the Saco River, as they had other "Armouchiquois" farther south, that is, by presenting them with gifts and proclaiming themselves friends but without establishing firmer political or economic commitments. Like the other horticulturalists, these Indians had nothing to barter that interested the French. In Champlain's words, "they make no provision of furs except to clothe themselves."[39] Yet by the following year the French had changed their minds, returned to Chouacoet, and affirmed an alliance with the Indians and their sagamore, Olmechin, a close ally of Marchin on the Kennebec.

The presence of two important native figures on the 1606 expedition—Chkouden, sagamore of the St. John Malecite, and Messamouet, a Micmac ally of Membertou—helps explain the return of the French.[40] (A second factor—an English voyage up the Kennebec—is discussed in the next chapter.) It is clear from the accounts of Champlain and Lescarbot that hostilities between the Micmac and the Malecite on the one hand, and the Abenaki on the other, had intensified during the early 1600s, and that two alliances, more or less along regional lines, had begun to form. Thus in 1604 Champlain's Malecite interpreters were unwilling to accompany him to the Kennebec, and in the following year the French rescued some Malecite captives there. In 1606 they returned a Micmac being held at Chouacoet.[41] The alliances were by no means clear-cut or formal, however, for rivalries and friendships continued to be determined by individual bands. When battle lines were drawn in 1607, for instance, the elusive Sasinou of the upper Kennebec sided with the northerners against his nearer neighbors. Though traditional motives of revenge undoubtedly fueled these rivalries, an underlying economic pattern is apparent. Champlain was told that corn had formerly been grown at the mouth of the Kennebec, but that the Indians who produced it had been forced inland "on account of the war they used to wage with others who came and seized it." The Chouacoet Indians had remained on the coast but made frequent use of the palisaded fort at their village to protect and defend themselves.[42] When we recall the winter food shortages experienced by the Micmac and other Indians engaged in intensive hunting for furs, their deeper motives for conducting such raids and for participating in the French diplomatic thrust become apparent.

These motives are further clarified by the results of the extraordinary meeting at Chouacoet in 1606. According to Lescarbot, who remained behind at Port Royal, the session was opened by Messamouet, who offered to trade "kettles, large, medium, and small, hatchets, knives, dresses, capes, red jackets, peas, beans, biscuits, and other such things." While presented in the traditional mode of a ritual exchange, the

items included were not those customarily associated with such
exchanges. Here was a proposal to a well-provisioned agricultural people that they purchase European goods—including
food—from a hunting people who were their enemies. The
Chouacoet response might have been predicted. Messamouet's
proposal was met by the sudden appearance of "12 or 15 boats
full" of Olmechin's people, heavily painted and armed. Recognizing the need for greater persuasiveness, Messamouet em-
barked upon a long speech in which he reminded his skeptical
hosts "how of past time they had often had friendly intercourse
together, and that they could easily overcome their enemies if
they would come to terms, and make use of the friendship of
the French . . . in order in future, to bring merchandise to
them and to aid them with their resources." He boasted that
having visited France and resided in the home of the governor
of Bayonne, he knew more than they of the potential benefits
of the trade for all Indians. He then flung into Olmechin's
canoe "all his merchandise, which in those parts was worth
more than three hundred crowns in cash." With this insistent
gesture Messamouet indicated that he expected Olmechin and
the people of Chouacoet to accept an inferior position in a
political-economic nexus with the French and the Micmac.[43]

Olmechin salvaged his dignity in the best way he could.
Instead of following protocol by immediately accepting the
offer with a speech and the ceremonial presentation of gifts
of equal value, he simply had a canoe full of "corn, tobacco,
beans, and pumpkins" delivered to the overweening Messamouet as he departed the following morning. With this act
Olmechin was demonstrating his own wealth, returning Messamouet's insult in kind—and repudiating his proposal. He
then concluded his own treaty with the French, a move he
probably thought would discourage Micmac retaliation.[44]

Meanwhile a separate sequence of events reinforced the
resentments created at Chouacoet. In the fall of 1606, a Male-

cite or Micmac party led by one Ioucaniscou carried out raids
on the Penobscot and the Kennebec. Several Abenaki at each
location were killed, including some women. In retaliation a
group of Micmac was attacked near the Penobscot by members of Olmechin's and Marchin's bands, and a Micmac sagamore, Panoniac, was killed.[45] Panoniac's death brought cries
of mourning and revenge from Indians on both sides of the
Bay of Fundy. As the dead man was buried, Membertou
called for retaliation against the followers of Olmechin, Marchin, and Bashaba (on whose territory the murder occurred)
during the following spring, and vowed to lead the 250-mile
sea expedition himself.[46] The two motives for Micmac revenge
became fused to include as targets the three most powerful
groups of potential French allies among the Abenaki. By the
following June, Membertou's coalition included Micmac,
Malecite, and Montagnais, plus Sasinou of the Kennebec.[47]

The invaders met their enemies at Chouacoet. In his poetic
celebration of the decisive Micmac-Abenaki battle there, Lescarbot enumerated the weapons possessed by each side. The
list tells the whole story. Though the Abenaki had some
French knives, they relied principally on "bows, arrows . . .
picks, shields, and wooden maces." The northerners' arsenal,
on the other hand, included "spears, daggers, and cutlasses,"
and "axes, knives, bows, arrows, swords, picks, and darts."
The Abenaki's casualties were greater

> . . . because their arrows
> With heads of bone, do not make as mortal a wound
> As those used by the Neighbours of the French
> Which have steel tips at the ends of their wooden shafts.

When even this arsenal proved insufficient for carrying the
day, Membertou and Chkouden distributed several muskets
which, Lescarbot asserted, the French "had lent" them. Lescarbot's implication that the Micmac did not, as a matter of

course, handle guns is hard to reconcile with his statement that ten of their foes, including Olmechin and Marchin, were immediately cut down and that the remainder thereupon beat a hasty retreat.[48]

What Alvin Morrison has termed "the Micmac sack of Saco" is a classic illustration of the ways in which some Indian groups contributed, albeit on their own terms, to the course of European expansion. It is clear from Champlain's visit to Bashaba in 1604 that the French initially envisaged a direct trade relationship with each of the Abenaki hunting groups. The French would furnish European goods for furs and would oversee a peace with the Micmac. Such a peace was essential to the realization of the plan, but the French lacked experience in diplomacy with Indians. They discounted both the importance of revenge as a traditional motive for warfare, and the sagacity of Indian leaders in perceiving how to maximize their advantages within the restrictions of a colonial system. The Micmac were correct in one sense when they asserted their equality with the French, for they recognized the interdependence of the two peoples. As a price for their loyalty they insisted that French hegemony over the Indians to the south be a French-Micmac hegemony, and that it be extended to include horticulturalists with whom the Micmac, but not the French, needed to trade.

Were the Micmac motivated by traditional desires for revenge, or was their addiction to trade goods so strong as to determine all their motives and actions? Clearly they were no longer living the autonomous existence they had known before European fishermen began plying their shores. Nevertheless they continued to perceive and define their actions in traditional terms. The quarrel with Olmechin began ostensibly when he refused their offer of peace and trade. Then Olmechin and his allies permitted the murder of a beloved Micmac sagamore. Panoniac's funeral was accompanied by

ritual mourning and the traditional vows of revenge. Before
setting out the war party engaged in a mock battle with the
women of the village, the outcome of which was assumed to
foreshadow that of the real event. When the two groups met
prior to combat, they engaged in the ritual exchange of goods
that customarily preceded such encounters. And the victors
celebrated their triumph in traditional fashion, returning with
the heads of their dead enemies plus live prisoners for tor-
ture.[49] Though the fact of the battle itself indicated the extent to which Europeans had intruded into indigenous political processes, nothing had happened which the Indians could
not comprehend and explain in traditional terms.

Yet the autonomy of the Micmac was severely circumscribed by the nature of their colonial relationship with the
French. This became apparent soon after the battle of Chouacoet when financial pressures forced the French to withdraw
temporarily from Port Royal. During the next year the Indians ate the pigeons and harvested the grain that the French
had left behind. That they sorely missed their trading partners was indicated by the desperately enthusiastic receptions
accorded a delegation sent from France by Poutrincourt (who
had been charged with reviving Port Royal) in 1608, and one
led by the commander himself on his return in 1610. But now
Poutrincourt maintained his distance. He understood that
Port Royal's special relationship with Membertou had alienated the Abenaki, thereby threatening French control of
northeastern North America. After checking on Port Royal,
the 1608 expedition under Angibault de Champdoré hastened
to Chouacoet to make a separate peace with Poutrincourt's
recently defeated allies there. Olmechin's successor, Asticou,
was skeptical about French intentions and suggested the need
for an intermediary. Oagimont, a Passamaquoddy sagamore
on the St. Croix River, was chosen. After lengthy negotiations
and many French presents, the Indians of Chouacoet agreed

to a new peace.[50] Seldom are losers treated so royally, but Poutrincourt recognized that his goal of securing the furs and loyalties of all Indians in the region required such diplomatic repair work. The French had discovered the difficulty of controlling relations among Indians who were otherwise loyal and dependent. For their part the Micmac had come to understand both the advantages and disadvantages of their special relationship with the French: they possessed European weapons, boats, and tools while lacking adequate food supplies and full autonomy. This peculiar juxtaposition continued to prompt raids on their southern neighbors until the 1630s, when the latter acquired powerful European allies of their own.

Jesuit Colonialism

Poutrincourt himself returned to Port Royal in 1610 to renew his political and economic offensive among the Indians. In its second incarnation, Port Royal emphasized missionary activity, not only to secure more funding from the Crown but to extend its political control over Indian allies and trading partners. Lescarbot was certain that the Port Royal Micmac had been favorably disposed toward Christianity under de Monts, but claimed that the French decided not to baptize the Indians when they realized that their stay was not permanent. He undoubtedly exaggerated the degree of missionary zeal at the first Port Royal. For while a few temporary conversions had been effected, the Catholic priest and Huguenot minister in residence appear to have expended most of their energies quarreling with each other rather than ministering to either French or Indians.[51]

The executor of the new strategy was a secular priest, Jesse Flesché, who began at once to work among Membertou and his people. Within a matter of weeks the sagamore and twenty of his relatives had been baptized. Within the year their example was followed by about a hundred more Acadian Micmac. This wave of conversions is striking, especially because Flesché did not wait to learn the Micmac language but worked through an interpreter.[52] One factor most certainly in his favor was the Indians' economic dependence on the French, which meant that the conversions carried certain political implications. In criticizing Flesché, the Jesuit Biard, who arrived the following year, asserted that the converts "accepted baptism as a sort of sacred pledge of friendship and alliance with the French," but had no notion of its deeper theological meaning. One group understood the term "baptized," but not "Christian."[53] It was the political meaning that was important to the Indians, who saw baptism as a ritual sealing of their bond with the French. Again they maintained a posture of equality with the French and avoided confronting some of the harsher realities of their position in that relationship. And as before Membertou's favorable location near Port Royal brought him extra benefits. For it was around the time of his baptism that he was elected "Grand Sagamore" of all the Micmac, an office for which there was no recorded precedent. Membertou also wanted to become a preacher; if this desire had been realized, his religious and political roles would have continued to carry equal prestige.[54]

Poutrincourt's publicizing of these conversions got him more than he bargained for. Following Henry IV's death in 1610, the Queen Mother, Marie de Medici, acceded to the request of the Society of Jesus that its missionaries be permitted to work in Acadia. Despite his distaste for Jesuits, Poutrincourt was obliged not only to go along but to accept as financial partners the two missionaries delegated. The Society hoped that in this way its operation would become self-supporting. After delays and bickering over these and other conditions, Fathers Pierre Biard and Enemond Massé arrived in the spring of 1611.[55]

The two Jesuits set about their work with characteristic vigor and devotion. Massé made an effort to "live as a nomad" by embarking upon a long journey with one of Membertou's sons, and nearly died from exposure and the Indian diet.[56] Thereafter the two missionaries stayed closer to their countrymen. They quickly assessed the religious condition of the natives, in the wake of Flesché's conversions, and found it badly wanting.

In Biard's opinion, Flesché lacked two skills essential to missionary work—a knowledge of the natives' language and the ability to cure illness. The first would take time, as the misisonaries quickly realized, and yet it was necessary. They vowed that no adults would be baptized before being thoroughly catechized in their native languages. Until then they were content to allow Indians to attend French services at Port Royal, and to baptize children and dying adults.[57] Biard also recognized that "he who would minister to their souls, must at the same time resolve to nourish their bodies." During his first summer he presided over the recovery of one of Membertou's sons, whom the Indians had given up for dead, with the aid of some holy relics and spoken vows. Later, arriving among the Abenaki during an epidemic, he recited the gospels and gave each of the sick a cross to wear.[58] Among Indians whose lives had been substantially affected by the French, Biard appeared as a shaman with access to sources of power not available to traditional healers. His ability to assume the ritualistic roles and medical functions of the shamans demonstrates his recognition of one of the more important criteria for missionary success in North America.[59]

In supplanting the shamans, the two Jesuits were not simply offering a Catholic façade to cover traditional religion, as the Puritans later charged. Indeed they were, in James Ronda's words, as much "cultural revolutionaries" as the Puritans' own missionaries.[60] In their view Indian religion was fundamentally devil-worship and the Indians themselves lived like animals.[61] During the illness of Membertou's son and the fatal one of the sagamore himself in 1611, they strongly denounced Indian treatment of the sick and the dead. They took the two men in after the Indians had given them up for dead. The priests were aided by Membertou's insistence that he be buried as a Christian and that, contrary to Indian custom, his relatives visit his grave. After his death the missionaries went further in reforming burial customs. They banned all sacrifices, dances, and death-songs, and permitted only the somber feast to continue—provided it was held away from the French fort.[62]

Among the Micmac at Port Royal, the Jesuits could afford such drastic measures from the outset, for the Indians' economic dependence on the French was complete for much of the year, and they were in and about the fort except when hunting. Among Indians farther away, especially enemies of the Micmac, the missionaries proceeded more cautiously. In 1611 Biard traveled with Poutrincourt's son, Charles de Biencourt, to the Kennebec and Penobscot to trade for some badly needed corn. In each case the Jesuit made effective use of rituals and icons and successfully employed his shaman-like healing techniques. The Indians had little corn, but Biard appears to have facilitated a trade in furs at each stop and to have helped smooth political relations between the Indians and the colony. Religious conversion was not discussed even obliquely, though Biard felt he had made an important first step in that direction; it was the political results that were most important.[63] The Port Royal colony had now established independent relations with each of the losers in Membertou's raid.

The potential impact of the misionaries as colonial agents in Acadia was enormous, but went largely unrealized. Tensions between the Jesuits and Poutrincourt, plus the con-

tinued precariousness of Port Royal's finances and food supplies, led to a move to form a separate French colony with
royal and Jesuit Society backing. Biard and Massé joined in
establishing "St. Sauveur" on Mount Desert Island in June
1613.[64] One month later an English warship under Captain
Samuel Argall, operating out of Jamestown, took the outpost
by surprise and captured or drove away all its inhabitants.
Massé and several others were placed in a small boat which
eventually reached Acadia safely. Biard remained an English
prisoner for nearly ten months before he was finally released.
In the interim he had to watch while Argall administered the
same treatment to the post and residents at Port Royal, ending for two decades the political and religious—but not the
economic—presence of the French in Acadia and New England.[65]

Between New France and New Netherland

Though delaying French efforts to colonize, Argall's attacks
did little to discourage the steady increase in French trading
activity in Acadia and its expansion southward. When John
Smith explored the coast from the Penobscot to Cape Cod
between April and June 1614, he found that the trading season was virtually over and that, apart from a lone English
ship, the traders were all French. To the north, he learned,
French traders maintained their monopoly by continuing to
use the undefended, abandoned fort at Port Royal as a post.
He found that two large vessels had scoured all the harbors,
spending six weeks in Massachusetts Bay alone. The better-
endowed northern trade had yielded 25,000 skins that year,
according to Smith's estimate, and he judged the south capable of producing 6000 to 7000 skins annually.[66]

Underlying the nascent southern trade was a striking degree of unity among the Indians, based in part on economics.

Smith reported that southern farmers were supplying corn to Abenaki hunters. At least part of the return for this corn was presumably European goods which the Abenaki, far less populous but vastly richer in furs, were beginning to acquire. Though built on pre-contact patterns of exchange, such a trade had revolutionary implications once Europeans were involved. By obtaining corn from their southern neighbors, the Abenaki could intensify the specialized hunt for furs while averting the perennial food shortages suffered by the Micmac. At the same time, farmers as well as hunters would be making greater use of European metal and cloth goods. We have no way of knowing how solidified these patterns had become during the half-decade or so of French trade before Smith's visit. But it is clear that an indigenous pattern of reciprocal exchange by self-sufficient peoples was being transformed into one in which groups engaged in specialized production were dependent on outside sources for at least part of their food supplies (in the case of the Abenaki), tools, and clothing. The potential for, if not the actuality of, colonial dependence had been established.[67]

These economic considerations were closely related to issues of defense for the Indians. By eliminating the French colonial effort in Acadia, Argall had removed the one restraint on Micmac raids to the south for corn and other items of tribute. These raids had resumed and, as a result, the economic alliance of Abenaki and southern New England Indians was politicized by the threat of a common enemy. Moreover, the historic French-Micmac relationship and the continued French solicitation of Micmac furs kept the alliance members wary of French motives.[68]

Smith's description of the political and linguistic boundaries within this grand alliance is noteworthy for its approximation to that of Daniel Gookin, as learned from Indian informants sixty years later. Taken together, the two accounts tell us something about the patterns of alliance and trade that prevailed briefly in New England during the early 1610s. Smith distinguished three groupings of autonomous bands on the Maine-to-Massachusetts coast, each grouping united by "language, humor, and condition." One, for which Bashaba was a prominent spokesman, ranged from the Penobscot to Salem harbor and another from Nahant to Plymouth Bay, while a third covered Cape Cod. Smith further divided the first group into two parts, separating those north of the Saco River from the rest. Though he did not explain it, this division corresponds to that between farmers and hunters.[69]

Focusing on the farming peoples from the Saco southward, Gookin likewise noted the existence of three groupings on the eastern coast and the fact that they "held amity, for the most part, with each other." His Pawtucket constituted precisely the southern, agricultural half of the most northerly grouping identified by Smith. His Massachusett likewise coincided with Smith's middle grouping except that Gookin excluded the Patuxet of "Accomack" (later Plymouth) and placed them with the Pokanoket. Gookin also included all the Cape Cod Indians in this most southerly group, as did Smith, plus several additional groups that Smith did not observe—those of Martha's Vineyard, Nantucket, and the territory between Buzzards Bay and Plymouth Bay on the east and Narrangansett Bay on the west.[70] Because of the tendency among scholars to enshrine these groupings as tribal and therefore permanent, it is important to recognize that each consisted of numerous autonomous village-bands. Though clusters of village-bands were united by "language, humour, and condition," to use Smith's words, they were not irrevocably bound to one another, as subsequent events demonstrated.[71]

With one arm, as it were, extending south along the Atlantic coast, the French directed another west through the

St. Lawrence Valley. French whalers had begun trading at the post of Tadoussac, where the Saguenay flows into the St. Lawrence, as early as 1550, and established a firm alliance with the local Montagnais. But as trade moved westward it generated intense conflict among Indian groups for hunting territories and for direct access to the French. Champlain discovered the results of this competition in 1603 when he ascended the St. Lawrence above Tadoussac. He found that the Montagnais were afraid to accompany him into that region and that the populous Iroquoian-speaking villages of Stadacona and Hochelaga, contacted and described by Cartier seventy years earlier, had utterly disappeared. The source of the fear and destruction, he learned from the Montagnais, was the Mohawk, who lived on the river of that name and were the easternmost members of the League of the Iroquois. Geographically disadvantaged by a lack of direct access in any direction to European traders, the Mohawk appear to have undertaken a new type of warfare which sought the complete destruction, if necessary, of those who stood in their way. As a result, the once fruitful St. Lawrence River Valley had been rendered a virtually abandoned arena of terror.[72]

Though the Mohawks' successes in scattering their enemies undoubtedly satisfied psychological and cultural imperatives to avenge wrongdoings and to perform valiantly in battle, their economic goals continued to elude them. For the French retained firm control of the principal depot at Tadoussac and of the loyalties of the Indians who traded there, principally the Montagnais. In 1609 Champlain and two other Frenchmen accompanied a joint Huron-Algonquin-Montagnais war party against a group of Mohawk at what is now Lake Champlain. The latter were routed when the French opened fire with their muskets (see fig. 4). In the following year the same parties met on the Richelieu River and the Mohawk suffered an even more decisive defeat.[73]

Figure 4. Champlain and French guns aid New France's Indian allies in routing the Mohawk at Lake Champlain, 1609. As a result of this battle and another the following year, the Mohawk turned to the Dutch on the lower Hudson as a trade partner. The inaccurate depictions of Indian dress and boats and the palm trees in the background suggest that this drawing was not made by Champlain himself. *Les Voyages de Sieur de Champlain Xaintengeois* (Paris, 1613). *Courtesy of Chapin Library, Williams College, Williamstown, Mass.*

Effectively excluded from the St. Lawrence, the Mohawk directed their attention southward, where an alternative to the impenetrable French trade had presented itself. The year before, sailing up the river that would soon bear his name, Henry Hudson had entered the Dutch in the rapidly escalating competition among Europeans for furs. Hudson's reception in the Manhattan area varied from one band to another, probably depending on previous trade experiences and/or local rivalries. But his real discovery lay further north near modern Albany, where he encountered the Mahican, a larger, more cohesive group than those at the coast. During the nine days that his ship, the *Half Moon*, remained at anchor, the Indians brought food and furs and received in exchange "trifles," as well as some knives and hatchets. On one occasion some Indians were introduced to alcohol. In all the trip was a great success, terminated only as the supply of trade goods ran low and hostilities between Dutch and English crew members erupted.[74]

By the following year Dutch private merchants were plying the Hudson, inaugurating a new sphere of trade that would expand rapidly. Indeed the only factor inhibiting the flow of furs from "New Netherland" was the conflicts among rival traders and within their crews. The number of vessels increased each year, until in 1614 no less than five ships from four companies met on the Hudson. One supercargo defied his captain and went looking for furs on his own with part of the crew, while three other crews mutinied and seized one of the ships for themselves. Though the four companies agreed on a division of the 2500 skins they obtained, the ramifications of the chaos echoed in the Amsterdam courts for several years. Meanwhile the Estates General moved quickly to squelch the now-dangerous competition and chartered the New Netherland Company as a three-year monopoly.[75]

Though the monopoly was not renewed in 1618, the inter-

val enabled the Company to bring a measure of organization
to the trade. Fort Nassau, at the present site of Albany, became the principal depot and the Mahican the principal Dutch
clients. Furs flowed in not only from the Mahican's own lands
but from Indians occupying adjacent territories, including the
Mohawk and those of western New England.[76]

For the Mohawk, the Dutch presence offered a more ac-
cessible source of European goods than the French, and
probably at a better price. On the St. Lawrence their pelts
were less desirable than the thicker coats coming from the
north. On the Hudson theirs were the thicker coats. Though
conflict with the more favorably situated Mahican would
erupt in the 1620s, the Dutch initially allowed them free and
equal access to the post.[77]

While consolidating the Hudson River trade, the New
Netherland Company extended its activity along the coast in
both directions. As one group moved into the Delaware River
Valley, Adriaen Block led an expedition in 1614 which initiated contacts with Indian groups as far eastward as Buzzards
Bay, on Long Island, and on the Connecticut River as far
north as modern Windsor. Out of these contacts, a series of
new trade nexuses would soon arise.[78]

The findings of the Block expedition provide our only
glimpse of the south coast of New England on the eve of intensive Indian-European trade relations there. Throughout
the area they explored, the Dutch found Indians like those at
Buzzards Bay—"shy [and] not accustomed with strangers,"
and no evidence of the trade activity that Smith was discovering that same year to the east. In Narragansett Bay they
found two distinct groups—the Wampanoag, or Pokanoket,
"in the lower part" and the Narragansett on "the west side."[79]
Further west, the Dutch identified the Pequot on the Mystic
River and the Mohegan on the Thames.[80] Finally, they identified three Connecticut River groups—the "Sequins," the

"Nawaas," and the "Horikans"—plus the Quinnipiac near what became New Haven.[81]

These political identifications and relationships are striking for the contrast they present to those of two decades later, the more so because it is the later configurations which writers since 1637 have assumed reflect the pre-contact period. The Dutch identified the Narragansett and Pokanoket as two strong groups centered on Narragansett Bay, whereas the latter would later be seen as a group whose principal interests lay in the Plymouth area. Dutch references to the Mohegan and Pequot are even more remarkable. Instead of the traditional picture of a single Pequot "tribe" with a Mohegan branch that had recently "invaded" the lower Connecticut River Valley from the west, they describe two distinct groups located well to the east of that river. Indeed, the Pequot's only rival at the time of Block's visit was not on the Connecticut at all but was rather the Pokanoket located even farther to the east. The Dutch sketched not the fierce rivalries and upheavals engendered by Pequot expansionists found in histories written since the arrival of the English, but rather a series of autonomous bands enjoying, relative to the ensuing quarter-century, a stable existence.[82] But the voyage itself, and the map and written accounts that resulted, occasioned the beginnings of active Dutch trading on the south coast and on the Connecticut River as far north as modern Enfield. By the time additional European accounts were written, the south coast had been transformed beyond recognition. Even more than that of the coast north of Cape Cod, this section's history on the eve of the traders phase is virtually unknown.

By 1614 the incidental trading begun on the shores of Newfoundland more than a century earlier had evolved and expanded to encompass all of New England. While French traders on the Atlantic and the St. Lawrence drew furs from the east and north, the Dutch drew pelts from the west and south to the Hudson and to their floating posts in and around Long Island Sound. To the trade in furs on the east coast the French had added a trade in corn. Had subsequent history unfolded as the traders hoped, the Indians would have moved gradually toward the kind of economic dependency being experienced by the Micmac and other eastern Canadian groups. But the appearances of Argall and Smith signaled that the region was increasingly attractive to English entre-preneurs with interests very different from those of their French and Dutch counterparts. Though scarcely noticeable at the time, the preparation for southern New England's trans-formation from an arena of trade into one of settlement had already begun.

three

HOSTS and VISITORS

W<small>HILE</small> MERCHANTS FROM France and the Netherlands were amassing respectable profits in and around New England during the first two decades of the seventeenth century, English adventurers were approaching the region with different goals and achieving different results. The French and Dutch sought to establish permanent trading posts for obtaining furs, a goal which required that they maintain friendly relations with stable Indian groups. Colonies as such would grow out of the posts and would not supersede the economic nexuses established with Indian bands. The English on the other hand were, with one notable exception, less interested in trade. They saw furs as at best useful by-products of expansion and showed more interest in exploiting resources such as fish and sassafras that did not require native cooperation. Moreover, in response to economic and demographic upheavals at home, they thought in long-range terms of making Indian land available to Englishmen for farming. Understanding that this goal virtually guaranteed eventual conflict between the two peoples, the various colonizers generally sought to establish their political, military, and cultural superiority. They cultivated Indian allies, but only to obtain assistance in establishing themselves, and their methods were more coercive than those of the traders, who observed at least the outward forms of Indian reciprocity. As a result, the generally harmonious relations between Indians and traders were paralleled by hostility between Indians and colonizers. At the same time, the difference in their economic goals meant that the English focused on the very lands which de Monts had rejected for France—those supporting the larger populations engaged in intensive agriculture.[1]

For all their planning and effort, the English made no headway among the Indians during the first decade and a half of the century. Initial native resistance to colonization and settlement was broken here, as in much of the Western Hemisphere, not by superior numbers, enterprise, technology, or military skill but by that most lethal of Europe's weapons, its diseases.

Barricados and Captives

Though European contact with the coast between the Penobscot and the Hudson may even have preceded Verrazzano, there is little evidence of interest in, or familiarity with, the area before the late 1570s. To be sure, fishing and fur-trading voyages occasionally ventured that far south from Newfoundland and Acadia, undoubtedly adding European tools, clothes, and ornaments to those the natives were acquiring via their own trade networks. But for the most part, this region was overlooked. Because mariners preferred touching at Newfoundland or at the Canaries and West Indies rather than crossing the Atlantic directly, the New England coast was rarely glimpsed for most of the sixteenth century.[2]

It was would-be colonizers from England who showed the earliest interest in "Norumbega," as New England was then termed. In 1580 Sir Humphrey Gilbert began a project for the eventual colonization of the barely known region by dispatching a ship which made contact with Indians at Narragansett Bay. But on a colonizing voyage in 1583, Gilbert was diverted to Newfoundland, where he went down with his ship.[3] Interest was revived in the early 1590s when Edward Hayes assessed colonial prospects on the coast between 40° and 44°N. for Lord Burghley (Sir William Cecil). Based on reports of fishermen and traders returning from the region, Hayes proposed a settlement that would begin as a fishing station and later take up farming in order to support itself.[4]

Though Hayes's suggestions were not immediately adopted, they eventually inspired a more sustained English interest in the region. A series of expeditions between 1602 and 1611 surveyed the economic and colonial potential of several coastal sites. They remained for longer periods of time than their predecessors, sometimes camping on land, and increasingly alienating the natives.

In the spring of 1602 an expedition backed by the Earl of Southhampton and others sailed in the *Concord* under the command of Bartholomew Gosnold. The plan was to leave twenty of the 32 crew members behind for the winter to begin England's first colonial effort since the Roanoke failure a decade and a half earlier. As it approached Cape Neddick, off the southern Maine coast, the ship was met by a Basque shallop complete with mast, sail, oars, anchor, and six to eight occupants whom the crew members, in the words of one, "supposed at first to be Christians distressed." Upon closer approach, the strangers proved to be neither Christian nor distressed but native inhabitants of the adjacent coast who were considerably more at ease than their confused visitors. The Indians boldly boarded the ship, led by one who wore a black serge waistcoat and pants, shoes and hose, and a hat with a band. They spoke, according to *Concord* officer Gabriel Archer, "divers Christian words, and seemed to understand much more than we, for want of Language could comprehend."[5]

Undeterred by this sign of his country's late arrival in the region, Gosnold moved south, rounded Cape Cod, and coasted to the area of Martha's Vineyard and Buzzards Bay, where he remained for five weeks. The English used trade as a means of establishing initial contact with local Indians from both the islands and mainland, and found one group with a healthy surplus of furs, a sign of previous contact with Europeans. Relations began on a friendly footing as the natives offered food and tobacco and the English responded with knives and other implements (see fig. 5). But tensions rose when certain Indians took some English possessions, first a target and later some pothooks. The English attributed this failure to honor the idea of permanent, private possession to the natives' ignorance of good and evil.[6]

A week after their arrival the crew built on the island of Cuttyhunk a fortification from which they tried to keep the Indians, except when enlisting their assistance in harvesting sassafras, valued in Europe as a cure for syphilis. While the island was apparently unoccupied for the growing season, the English encountered ample evidence that it was used for hunting, fishing, and gathering at other times of the year. When Gosnold took the *Concord* to explore the bay, the remaining crew alienated themselves even further from the Indians by refusing to continue exchanging gifts. Though the first-hand accounts of John Brereton and Gabriel Archer omit details and forgo speculating on Indian motives, it is clear that the English cessation of trade, the symbol of friendship between peoples, heightened Indian suspicions to the breaking point. On June 11, two Englishmen scouting for food were attacked and one received an arrow in his side. The incident served to drive the expedition away and to preclude the establishment of a colony for the moment.[7]

Despite the circumstances surrounding their departure, Gosnold and at least some of his officers were optimistic about the area's resources and colonial prospects. John Brereton's promotional account omitted the Indian attack and

Figure 5. Bartholomew Gosnold trading with the Indians at Martha's Vineyard, Mass., 1602. Following promotional accounts, Theodore de Bry's illustration stressed the friendly beginnings of this would-be colonizing expedition (and added two extra ships) rather than the mutual suspicions that finally led the Indians to drive the English away. Thedor de Bry, *America* (pt. 13, Latin ed., Frankfort, 1634). *Courtesy of the Edward E. Ayer Collection, The Newberry Library, Chicago.*

concluded with glowing praise for the area and its inhabitants.[8] This enthusiasm led a group of Bristol merchants with similar interests to send two ships under Martin Pring to the same area in the following year. Landing at Provincetown harbor, Pring took no chances and built his fortress at the outset "to keepe diligent watch and ward in, for the adver-

tizement and succour of our men, while they should worke in
the Woods" gathering sassafras. Nevertheless the local Nauset
Indians continually approached them in a friendly manner
and were delighted by one sailor's guitar music. Whenever
they stayed too long or became otherwise too friendly, the
English turned their two large mastiffs loose on them.
Pring's account is uninformative on the sudden souring of the
Indians' attitude, but they were obviously disturbed by this
less than reciprocal conduct. One day, according to Pring,
"about seven score Savages armed with their Bowes and
Arrowes . . . environed our House or Barricado." The English drove them back with their muskets and dogs. A few
days later the Indians frightened the English by setting fire
to the forest. As the English began leaving the next day, the
Indians tried to persuade them to stay, but the crew "sent
them backe, and would [have] none of their entertainment."[9]

Pring's experiences with hostile Indians, like Gosnold's,
were not sufficient to discourage the most determined English
colonizers. In 1605, George Waymouth, backed by a coalition
of would-be Catholic colonists and Plymouth fishing merchants, sailed the *Archangel* into the Kennebec.[10] Friendly
contacts at the outset with Abenaki Indians from the Penobscot as well as the Kennebec came as a surprise where, in the
revealing words of James Rosier, the voyage's chronicler, "we
little expected any sparke of humanity." From Rosier's description of trading that followed in the next two weeks, it is
clear that Europeans were not unknown to the Abenaki but
trading had not been routinized. Yet the English repeatedly
spurned invitations from representatives of Bashaba to come
to the Penobscot to trade for furs and tobacco. Instead the
English grew suspicious that a Kennebec group was setting
a trap for them and devised one of their own. Luring five
Indians away from the others with trade goods, they seized
them and took them back to England. In his narrative Rosier

implies that the kidnapping was a response to Indian hostility. Yet he also notes that the English would have gone to even greater risks to capture some Indians, it "being a matter of great importance for the full accomplement [*sic*] of our voyage."[11]

This statement reveals the priorities of Waymouth and certain of his countrymen. They considered the capture of natives who would serve as sources of information for colonial planners and as emissaries, guides, and interpreters in the future more important than the establishment of immediate political and economic ties with potential Indian neighbors. Indians with experience and indoctrination in England, they assumed, would make better diplomats than the English themselves. The French had used Indians, as we have seen with Messamouet at Chouacoet, but they generally secured the consent of the Indians themselves before transporting them.[12] But consent presupposed the kind of reciprocal diplomacy in which the would-be colony-builders were unwilling to engage.

Yet by refusing Bashaba's invitations the English lost a major diplomatic and economic opportunity. As we saw in the preceding chapter, the Penobscot sagamore agreed in 1604 to trade directly with the French, but the latter did not follow up with him in the next year. It becomes apparent that in attempting to approach the English, Bashaba had decided to act on his own. Moreover the Abenaki with whom the Waymouth expedition dealt were among those who were to resist the 1607 Micmac raid on Chouacoet, with its tacit French support. Instead of exploiting these tensions to their own advantage, the English only earned a bad name for themselves. When Champlain stopped in at the Kennebec a few weeks after Waymouth's departure, he was told that a ship of strange men "under cover of friendship" had, as they then thought, murdered five Indians.[13]

Waymouth turned his captives over to Sir Ferdinando

Gorges, commander of Plymouth fort in England, then developing what would prove to be a life-long interest in dominating efforts to colonize New England.[14] Gorges sent two of
his captives, Manedo and Sassacomit, back to New England
with Captain Henry Challons in 1606. Along the way Challons
and crew were captured by the Spanish, and Sassacomit was
seriously wounded during the attack. Though Manedo's fate
is unknown, Sassacomit eventually escaped from a Spanish
prison, made his way to England, and returned to his home
with Captain Nicholas Hobson in 1614. His itinerary anticipated by a few years that of the more famous Squanto, the
Patuxet Indian who joined the Plymouth colony in 1621.[15]

Two more Waymouth captives returned home as part of a
plan by Gorges and his Plymouth Company to establish an
English colony near the Kennebec just as a rival company
was establishing Jamestown several hundred miles to the
south. Tahanedo, a Pemaquid River sagamore, was delivered in 1606, and his countryman Skidwarres accompanied
a colonizing expedition of 120 men under George Popham and
Raleigh Gilbert in the following year. Gorges's assumption
that the return of the two captives as prestigious emissaries
would allay any anti-English feelings among either them or
the other Indians proved to be naïve. Upon their arrival Gilbert had to force a reluctant Skidwarres to lead the expedition
to his village on the Pemaquid. When the unsuspecting residents saw the Englishmen entering their village late at night
they took to their arms until the voice of Skidwarres turned
the near-battle into a round of embraces. But then, instead
of preaching the virtues of England, Skidwarres and Tahanedo apparently counseled their people to be on their guard.
Moreover, the wary Skidwarres refused to remain with the
colonists and rejoined his people, though continuing to act
as an intermediary between the two groups.[16]

In this role, he promised to guide and introduce Gilbert to

Bashaba, the most powerful and revered of the Abenaki, but Gilbert missed their appointment and tried unsuccessfully to find the Penobscot River himself. A month later Skidwarres and Tahanedo brought Bashaba's brother and another Penobscot River sagamore to Gilbert with offers to trade.[17] For Bashaba, who had always before waited for Europeans to come to him, the embassy represented a significant overture. As with the invitation to Waymouth two years earlier, his timing was significant. This offer came just three months after the battle of Chouacoet, when he had seen Membertou's muskets demonstrate that trade with Europeans was more than a matter of iron tools and brightly colored cloth, that it was the key to survival itself in an emerging colonial milieu.

Gilbert promised the emissaries that he would come soon, but he never did. The Sagadahoc colony, as it has come to be known, became bogged down with more pressing problems and was abandoned within months. Historians have generally followed the contemporary English accounts of Gorges and the colonial publicist, William Strachey, in ascribing the colony's failure to the losses of its principal leaders and to an unusually severe winter.[18] But these were promotional accounts whose authors (neither of whom was present) were eager to minimize factors that would discourage future backers and colonists. In particular they did not want to play up the ability of Indians to break up a colonial venture. Firsthand Kennebec accounts—Rosier's of the Waymouth voyage and James Davies's of Sagadahoc's first two months—stressed the ability of the English to control Indians through trade goods, guile, and, if necessary, violence, subjects which Gorges and Strachey omitted altogether. Yet Davies noted that the English had nearly fallen out with their Abenaki neighbors soon after establishing their colony site at Sagadahoc. And Gorges was considerably more candid in his pri-

vate correspondence than in his public relations. The colonists
had become bitterly divided into factions, he wrote to Robert
Cecil soon after the collapse. Moreover the fur trade had
come to a standstill because the Indians kept their stores concealed. If any attempted to trade with the English, Tahanedo
and Skidwarres "instantly carry them away, and will not
suffer them to com neere us any more." Clearly the Indians
around Pemaquid and Sagadahoc had found more congenial
trading partners. When Pierre Biard arrived at the Kennebec
three years later, he obtained an even more complete account. According to the Indians he met there, one leader,
George Popham, was favored by the local Indians but distrusted by those of Chouacoet, whose pow-wows even claimed
credit for his death. With Popham gone, the colony's relations with the local Abenaki deteriorated. After being driven
away from the fort several times with violence, some of them
attacked a group of colonists and killed eleven. The colony
was abandoned shortly thereafter. Once the official accounts
of the Sagadahoc venture are supplemented by those which
are more candid and more critical, it becomes clear that the
colony's failure was rooted in the larger failure of English
diplomacy toward Indians.[19]

These events cast additional light on the French solicitation of the Chouacoet Indians shortly after the latter's defeat
in 1608, as noted in the preceding chapter. It should now be
clear that Poutrincourt's action was a response not only to the
demise of his own colony and the effects of Membertou's ag-
gressiveness but to the simultaneous appearance of a European trade rival. But Gorges's complaints about Indian reluctance to trade with the English suggest that the French
had little to worry about as yet. Nor was the reputation of the
English enhanced in coming years. When Henry Hudson put
the *Half Moon* into the Penobscot in 1609, he found two separate parties of Indians who were obviously familiar with

Europeans. One transported itself in French shallops while the other filled the explorer's ears with tales of gold, silver, and copper mines "hard by us." One Indian even spoke some French. Mistrusting the natives from the outset, the mixed English-Dutch crew seized the goods of some and then took to fighting among themselves before finally departing.[20] Recent Abenaki experience with Europeans was confined to the French and English, and Hudson and half his crew spoke English. So although the *Half Moon* sailed under a Dutch flag, the incident could only have reinforced the natives' assumptions about English amiability.

Meanwhile Gorges had not abandoned his strategy of securing loyal Indian guides through kidnapping. An expedition dispatched by the Earl of Southampton and commanded by one Edward Harlow in 1611 sought to satisfy Gorges in this respect. At Monhegan Island, Harlow captured three Indians, one of whom escaped. The escapee, Pechmo, returned with a group of natives who wounded three crewmen and captured one of the ship's small boats. Proceeding southward in hopes of encountering less resistance, Harlow captured three more Indians, including Epenow, a sachem at Martha's Vineyard. Gorges spent three years grooming Epenow, assuming that more time was all that was needed to avoid the kind of uncertain loyalty that Tahanedo and Skidwarres had accorded the Sagadahoc colonists. He had every reason to be optimistic. Epenow showed himself, in Gorges's words, "a goodly man of brave aspect, stout and sober in his demeanour, and had learned so much English as to bid those that wondered at him, welcome, welcome. . . ." Epenow also filled Gorges's head with stories of fabulous gold mines on Martha's Vineyard, obviously a device to hasten his return. In 1614 an expedition to find the mines for Gorges set out under the command of Nicholas Hobson, who had been with Harlow in 1611 when Epenow was captured. As they approached the island,

Epenow leaped overboard. Observing the action, his country-men provided a cover in the form of a barrage of arrows directed at the ship. In effecting Epenow's escape, they wounded Hobson and a number of his crewmen. The vessel limped home, the expedition an utter failure.[21]

After twelve years of efforts, English colonizers had acquired a good deal of knowledge and experience along the coast from the Kennebec to Cape Cod. Though some still hoped to find gold or the Northwest Passage, the explorers' principal contribution was to accumulate specific information on the territory and its resources. But thus far they had been unable to establish an ongoing English presence or to secure the loyalty of the natives. Instead their blustering approach, particularly their violence and their unwillingness to enter into reciprocal relationships, was fanning Indian resentment toward their nation. Aside from Sir Francis Popham, who built on his brother George's friendship with the Indians near Sagadahoc to establish a regular trade at Pemaquid, English prospects in the summer of 1614 looked hardly more promising than they had at the turn of the century.

New England I

What cause for English colonial hopes that did exist lay less with the explorers of the New England region than with the Virginia Company's settlement at Jamestown, begun in the same year as Sagadahoc under conditions no more auspicious. But unlike the northern outpost, Jamestown survived its uncertain beginnings. By 1613, a reorganized Company and a new governor, Thomas Dale, were looking beyond the tiny settlement to their entire claim, which extended north to the 45th parallel. It was then that Samuel Argall, with a commission from Dale, effectively upheld that claim with his sacking of St. Sauveur and Port Royal.[22] Argall's action was the first by the English that seemed to transcend the unrealistic fantasies and the narrow particularism of the earlier adventurers, and to move a small but concrete step toward establishing a colony north of Cape Cod.

The elimination of the French colonial presence, however, did not mean the end of their trading presence and its effectiveness among the Indians. This fact was grasped by the man who was Virginia's second and greater, if unintended, contribution to New England colonization—John Smith. Coasting from above the Penobscot to Cape Cod in 1614, he found that French traders had largely exhausted the supply of furs at every harbor except Pemaquid, where Francis Popham had succeeded in trading (literally) on his late brother's good reputation. At Massachusetts Bay alone the French had remained "neere six weekes, [and] left nothing for us. . . ." Moreover they had overseen a peace among all the Indians of the region so that "now they are all friends, and have each [*sic*] trade with [the] other, so farre as they have societie on each others frontiers."[23] It was Smith who first recognized that for an English colony to succeed it would have to contend with native political structures, including the larger networks organized in the service of the French trade.

Smith sailed in 1614 in command of two ships and 45 men for a group of merchant adventurers headed by Marmaduke Rawdon. They headed for Monhegan Island to hunt whales and search for gold and copper mines. Should these more speculative ventures fail, the expedition was to collect fish and furs sufficient to cover the costs of the voyage. Nothing was said about exploring, mapping, or colonizing. The whales and mines indeed proved elusive, so Smith put most of the crew to fishing while he took eight or nine men ostensibly to hunt for furs. This small crew did trade, obtaining some 1300 pelts, mostly beaver, despite the lateness of the season and the earlier French sweep.[24] But Smith had other things on his mind.

Out of this cruise, he produced the most accurate map yet made of the coast (renaming its most prominent features) and a detailed description of the landscape, inhabitants, and colonial potential of the region.

Smith is generally associated with the colonization of Virginia and indeed spent more time there than in New England, remaining in the latter for less than three months. Yet after his visit New England became as important to him as Virginia and continued so until his death in 1631. He proclaimed himself the true discoverer and gave it the name "New England." And he publicized and celebrated its utopian qualities and colonial potential. Given a land "so planted with Gardens and Corne fields, and so well inhabited with a goodly, strong and well proportioned people . . . ," he asked, "who can but approve this a most excellent place, both for health and fertility? And of all the foure parts of the world that I have yet seene not inhabited," he concluded, "could I have but meanes to transport a Colonie, I would rather live here then [sic] any where."[25]

The immediate purpose of Smith's publicizing efforts was to secure financial backing for a colonizing expedition. He found it in the repeatedly frustrated but persevering person of Ferdinando Gorges. Obviously made for each other, Smith and Gorges began a collaboration during the winter of 1614-15. By summer they were ready to sail. Once again Smith would command two ships, most of whose crew members would devote themselves to fishing and whaling. There was no mention of mines. But this time Smith would carry the title "Admiral of New England," a lifetime commission, and he and seventeen others would winter on the Pemaquid. The key to the colony's success lay with Tahanedo, the sagamore upon whom Sagadahoc had depended. Despite his wavering loyalty eight years earlier, he was the one native leader with whom Gorges, through Francis Popham, had maintained contact. Unlike the

earlier colony, Smith's expedition would reside at or near Tahanedo's village, would ally with him and other New England
Indians against the French and Micmac, and would be sufficiently equipped with trade goods to establish a firm economic
connection. Having established a secure northern frontier,
Smith would then look toward colonizing among the "Gardens
and Corne fields" to the south.[26]

Smith's confidence in Tahanedo might appear to have been
misplaced, given the English record with Indian protégés. But
Smith was certain that his own experience enabled him to dismiss the mishaps of others. "The Warres in Europe, Asia, and
Affrica," he wrote with characteristic bravado, "taught me how
to subdue the wilde Salvages in *Virginia* and *New-England*, in
America." And his ruthless policy of controlling Indians by intimidating them had, he felt, paid off in Virginia. As Edmund S.
Morgan has noted, Smith's model in the handling of Indians
was Cortez: like the conquistador, he would use military repression in order to force the natives to work for their colonial
masters. Such a strategy was required where "there is for every
four or five naturall Spaniards, two or three hundred Indians
and Negros," and would be all the easier where the population
gap was narrower. Virginia had taught him, Smith said, that
psychology and experience, not numbers, were the critical factors in conquering Indians. By this he meant absolute self-
confidence plus the ability to employ the proper combination
of deception, intimidation, and brute force. Such were the resources with which to meet Indian "power, dexteritie, treach-
erie, and inconstancie." His countrymen who preceded him to
New England were basically fools for having been outwitted
and physically harmed by the natives. His own crew of nine
had skirmished with groups of Indians two or three times in
"silly incounters" during his visit of 1614 without suffering any
casualties and had ended up winning the friendship of their
opponents. Smith intended to apply the same psychology to

Tahanedo. As he later recounted, he would have used "this proud Salvage . . . to have gotte that credit with the rest of his friends and alliants [for] . . . any designe I intended."[27]

Military repression would be needed in Smith's New England not only to ensure the colonists' safety but to feed and otherwise support them during the early years. Until it was self-sufficient, Smith calculated, a colony of three hundred would require an armed force of thirty to forty men to ensure an adequate supply of corn from the natives. Moreover, natives could be employed nine months out of the year in a nascent fishing industry "till the rest provide other necessaries fit to furnish us with other commodities."[28] In Smith's eyes, Indian resistance to colonization originated in previous abuses suffered at European hands as much as in any inherent character traits. But whatever the reasons, coercion was now the only realistic possibility.

Smith's was a marked departure from previous English strategies to the extent that it accounted simultaneously for past colonial experiences, the strength and presence of both Indians and European rivals, and the economic realities of colonization. But if Smith's predecessors lacked his sagacity and boldness, they shared his fundamental recognition that Indians would not willingly accept subordination, rather than reciprocity, as the basis for a colonial relationship. And he was even less realistic than they in his expectation that the natives could be coerced into slavery. In bragging about his Virginia exploits, Smith overlooked the fact that, while intimidating some of the Indians there for periods of time, he had hardly succeeded in subjecting them to systematic English discipline. But Smith was a captive of the conquistador myth and thus of the dream that labor, as well as wealth, could be extracted from North America.[29] His vision of "New England," applicable to neither Algonquian nor English, went unrealized.

From Paradise to Golgotha

Though he continued to write about New England until his death in 1631, John Smith did not return there in 1615 or ever again. Through a series of mishaps arising from poor ship construction, pirates, and his own stubborn personality, his projected 1615 expedition fell apart; the "Admiral" was captured and remained a French prisoner for the rest of the year.[30] Had Smith returned he might have recognized that his dream had begun to unravel even in the wake of his departure the year before. Smith had left part of his crew behind under Thomas Hunt to finish up fishing operations and carry the catch to Malaga. Along with his fish, Hunt captured about twenty Indians from Patuxet (on the site of the future Plymouth colony), including Squanto, and seven from Nauset for sale into slavery. Coming as it did in the long sequence of English kidnappings and other hostile actions—most recently, Smith's three skirmishes and the return of Epenow—Hunt's action indelibly marked the English as an enemy of the New England natives, a reputation that survived the epidemic to greet the first Plymouth colonists six years later.[31] In the meantime New England's northern frontier was severely weakened by a new war between the Micmac and the Abenaki in which the latter were routed and Bashaba and many of his followers killed.[32] But the real destruction of Smith's New England came during the ensuing three years. From 1616 through 1618 the Indians were subjected to an epidemic, or series of epidemics, of catastrophic proportions. Attempts by medical historians to diagnose the malady have floundered on the inconclusive nature of surviving descriptions. The only first-hand European witnesses whose observations survive, Richard Vines and Thomas Dermer, agents of Gorges, both referred to the disease simply as "the plague," and the remaining evidence likewise supports the conclusion that the epidemic represented a strain of plague.[33]

European immunity to the disease was confirmed at the epidemic's outset when Vines and his party, in Gorges's words, "lay in the Cabbins with those people" during an expedition to Chouacoet and "not one of them ever felt their heads to ake while they stayed there." Several parties of French captives lived among the stricken Indians during these years, one even marrying an Indian woman and fathering her son. Though most of these died before 1619, the epidemic was apparently not responsible. The immunity and the staggering Indian death toll make it clear that a virgin soil epidemic of massive proportions had occurred.[34]

Though the specific European carrier cannot be identified from among the scores of unknown traders and others who visited New England during the late 1610s, the geographic and demographic outlines of the epidemic are distinct enough to narrow somewhat the range of possibilities. Vines reported that most of the coastal Abenaki had perished, and Dermer confirmed this report for those south of Monhegan Island. The epidemic's other coastal extremity is quite abrupt—the Pokanoket on the eastern and northern shores of Narragansett Bay were struck but the Narragansett on the west side were not. The disease likewise spared those inland groups just to the north of the Bay who were in a position to avoid contact with the Massachusett.[35] In the absence of a definite diagnosis, no final explanation of this peculiar outline can be expected. However, one cannot help but be struck by its spread among precisely those coastal groups which Smith observed trading heavily with the French and which, according to Gookin as well as Smith, were closely allied to one another before the outbreak. As Smith's description implied, exchanges among these groups had become increasingly active and specialized in the five or so years before the epidemic's outbreak in re-

sponse to the French trade. Especially striking is the fact that
it did not spread from the east coast to inland groups who
could trade with the Dutch on the south coast, or from the
Abenaki to their Micmac enemies. Thus the very source of
the Indians' momentary prosperity and harmony—the French
trade—apparently brought about their subsequent impoverish-
ment and destruction as well.[36]

The affected region was a vast disaster zone, comparable to
those left by modern wars and other large-scale catastrophes.
Hardest hit was the coast from Massachusetts Bay, which
Smith had called "the Paradise of all those parts," to Plymouth
Bay, a stretch which Champlain and Smith had described as
under virtually complete cultivation and habitation. Below the
Neponset River, the three villages recorded by Smith had utterly disappeared. The most notable of these was Squanto's
Patuxet, estimated as formerly numbering 2000 persons. More
than a decade after the disaster, the English colonist William
Wood noted the underbrush that had overtaken the fields. And
an earlier English observer, Thomas Morton, remarked that
when he arrived in 1622, the "bones and skulls" of the unburied
dead "made such a spectacle . . . it seemed to me a new found
Golgatha [sic]."[37] The Pokanoket on Narragansett Bay fared
only slightly better. Thomas Dermer wrote in 1619 that they
had fifty men, and the Plymouth colonists counted sixty when
they signed a treaty with the group two years later, their figure
including the village of Nemasket near modern Middleboro.
Here, as on the coast, the overgrown fields were readily apparent to the newcomers.[38] The three villages of Cape Cod included only one hundred men in 1621, compared with the 650
to 800 that Champlain had seen in two of them in 1606.[39] Dermer found the coastal Massachusett even "less to be feared"
than the Pokanoket, and accounts by English settlers from the
1630s suggest why. The largest of their three remaining villages, on the Neponset River near modern Quincy, numbered

only fifty to sixty inhabitants. The accounts make no mention at all of most of the others noted by Champlain and Smith, including those on the islands in Massachusetts Bay.[40] Among the Pawtucket, villages near modern Medfield and Saugus numbered about fifteen persons each in 1631, according to Thomas Dudley, while Naumkeak consisted of but two or three families. The later accounts make no mention of the villages at Nahant and Gloucester which Champlain had visited. The impact was somewhat less severe on the Merrimack, where 400 to 500 men lived in 1630, according to information reaching Dudley.[41]

A quick comparison of these figures and descriptions with those recorded before the epidemic conveys some sense of the devastation. Most of the villages seen or listed by Champlain and Smith had utterly vanished, and the remaining few numbered at most in the dozens rather than the hundreds or thousands. Some sense of the numerical impact can be obtained by recalling Gookin's figures for adult males prior to the outbreak. For his Pokanoket, we have no record for Martha's Vineyard immediately after the epidemic. But we can certainly assume that a majority of the 3000 men reckoned for all the Pokanoket before the epidemic lived on the mainland, where about 150 survived. Though Gookin's 3000 Massachusett men included many inland natives, who probably escaped the epidemic, the vast majority certainly inhabited the now-barren coast where fewer than 100 remained. For the Pawtucket, Dudley's upper figure of 500 in 1631 represents only 17 percent of the 3000 men reckoned by Gookin's informants. More precise mortality and depopulation rates are, of course, impossible to calculate. Not only are most figures only rough approximations, but further fluctuations and movements occurred before most Indian communities, especially those inland, were described in writing. And we have no sense of the epidemic's impact on family size and proportion of adult males to total population beyond

Massachusetts Bay colonist Edward Johnson's assertion that the plague swept "away whole Families, but chiefly yong Men and Children, the very seeds of increase," a statement that accords with modern observations of such epidemics. Sherburne F. Cook has proposed a decline of 75 percent, largely on the basis of the guesses and estimates of contemporaries and later writers. But many of Cook's sources were not present both before and after the epidemic if at all, and he did not utilize some of the direct sources cited here. Moreover, as we have seen, his pre-epidemic figures are almost certainly too low. More recently, Alfred Crosby, a medical historian, has suggested a decline of 90 percent. On the basis of the fragmentary, impressionistic data reviewed here, this figure does not appear unrealistic for the Massachusett and mainland Pokanoket.[42]

Some of the political implications of the catastrophe are clearer. Many survivors left their villages to combine with relatives elsewhere, undoubtedly accounting for some of the abandoned villages. Their numerical weakness made the survivors more vulnerable than ever to their stronger neighbors, especially the Micmac and the Narragansett. The former stepped up their raids, resulting in widespread fear along the coast. In one such raid, they apparently killed a major Pawtucket sachem, Nanapeshamet, at his village just north of Massachusetts Bay.[43] The Pokanoket sachem Massasoit and ten of his pnieses humbled themselves before the Narragansett, agreeing that they and their people would evacuate their position at the head of Narragansett Bay and settle for the Taunton River drainage system.[44] Their post-epidemic weaknesses prompted the survivors to form composite villages and bands and affected political alignments by enabling those sachems able to gather the largest numbers around them to influence weaker neighbors requiring their protection. Thus, as we shall see, the Neponset band led by Chickataubut was predominant at Massachusetts Bay, while Massasoit remained the strongest among

the Pokanoket, his humiliation before the Narragansett not-
withstanding. Passaconaway, sachem of the Pennacook band
of the Pawtucket, combined shamanism with his inherited position to dominate the village of the lower Merrimack.[45]

Passaconaway's position illustrates another dimension of the
epidemic's aftermath—the spiritual deprivation experienced by
its survivors. To their stricken neighbors, the Narragansett's
good health appeared to result from their faithful sacrifices to
Cautantowwit of material goods. This was the only explanation
for a catastrophe in which even the pow-wows succumbed.
(The usual practice whereby family and friends gathered with
the pow-wow in a sick person's wigwam could only have
served to spread the disease more rapidly.) The Indians further alienated themselves from important sources of supernatural power by abandoning their burial rituals. Archaeologists
have uncovered several multiple grave sites around Massachusetts Bay, dating from the seventeenth century, with few or no
burial goods. And Morton and William Bradford testified that
the unburied remains of people in the Plymouth area were
still quite visible several years afterward.[46]

The fear that they had been rendered spiritually powerless
was one response which enabled the survivors to understand
their plight in familiar terms. Another was to look to recent
and contemporary events for signs. A French captive's proclamation in 1615 that his God could destroy the Massachusett
was afterward recalled as a prophecy of the epidemic.[47] Seen
as a manifestation of French spiritual power to which the Indians had best align themselves, the epidemic reinforced native hostility toward the English enemies of the French. The
brunt of this hostility was borne by Captain Thomas Dermer
when he visited the area for Ferdinando Gorges in 1619 and
again in 1620.

In these expeditions, Gorges characteristically pinned his
hopes of planting a colony on the loyalty of an Indian anxious

to return home. His hopes might have seemed more firmly grounded this time, however, in that he was not linked with the Indian's seizure. Thomas Hunt had taken his captives, including Squanto, to Spain in 1614 in the belief that he could find a ready market for them as slaves. Several had been sold when, according to Gorges, "the Friers of those parts took the rest from them, and kept them to be instructed in the Christian faith." Hunt left Malaga a disappointed profiteer. How Squanto, in Bradford's words, "got away" from that city and his Catholic mentors is unclear. We know only that by 1617 he was residing in the London home of John Slany, treasurer of the Newfoundland Company, and that a year later he was in Newfoundland itself where he met Dermer, a former associate of John Smith. Dermer in turn took Squanto to England to meet Gorges, who saw in him the key to countering French successes and his own and England's failures among the natives. For his part Squanto knew, as had Epenow, how to tell the would-be founder of "New England" what he wanted to hear in order to secure his passage home. In March 1619 Dermer and Squanto set sail for the Patuxet region with yet another Gorges commission.[48]

Moving in the circles he did, Squanto undoubtedly knew something of the epidemic which had ravaged the New England coast in his absence. But whether or not he was prepared to find his own village completely vacated is less certain. At first, Squanto's presence and diplomatic skill enabled Dermer to break through anti-English sentiments at Nemasket and Pokanoket proper and to establish friendly contacts. For once an Indian guide was performing as Gorges had hoped. But as Dermer returned to his ship and prepared to sail around Cape Cod, Squanto took his leave in order to search for surviving Patuxets. On his own, Dermer was unable to persuade the Indians of Monomoy of his good intentions. Here, where Poutrincourt's crew had suffered casualties thirteen years earlier, he

108   MANITOU AND PROVIDENCE

was captured and barely succeeded in escaping. He then met
Epenow on Martha's Vineyard and left thinking he had as-
suaged the latter's hostility toward Gorges and the English for
his earlier captivity. Off Long Island Dermer was again attacked but escaped and made his way to Virginia.[49]

When Dermer returned to southeastern New England in the
summer of 1620, he found that another English crew had just
visited the area, invited some Pokanokets on board, and then
shot them down without provocation. The incident revived the
resentment that had prevailed before Squanto's return. Dermer was taken prisoner at Nemasket and only released after
Squanto interceded on his behalf. Proceeding to Martha's
Vineyard, Dermer, Squanto, and company were attacked by
Epenow and his followers. Most of the crew died at the scene;
Dermer himself escaped with fourteen wounds to Virginia,
where he soon died. Squanto was apparently taken captive, for
it was in this condition that he was living with the Pokanoket
when the Plymouth settlers met him in March 1621.[50]

Though Dermer's voyage had ended in tragic failure and
though the Indians' anti-English sentiment had reached a new
intensity, Gorges was more optimistic than ever about realizing
his colonizing ambitions. For what Vines and Dermer had conveyed above all was the utter weakness of the surviving coastal
Indians, especially their vulnerability to European microbes
and power. Vines had been dispatched, probably late in 1616,
to do what Smith had intended in 1615—test the harshness of
the New England winter and the feasibility of year-round settlement. With the aid of the epidemic, he succeeded with an
ease far beyond the expectations of Smith, Gorges, or anyone
else. Though Dermer never returned home, he sent at least two
letters detailing conditions among the coastal natives.[51] Even
before the second letter had arrived, Gorges was developing a
design more grandiose than the small outposts he had previously envisioned. He now sought a royal patent for the territory between Virginia and New France which would include

a liquidation of all Virginia Company claims in the region. The territory would be governed by a "Council of New England," based in England. After a long delay, the charter was finally sealed on November 3, 1620.[52] Eight days later, the *May-flower*, carrying just over a hundred prospective settlers from England, arrived at Cape Cod. Though ostensibly bound for the Hudson River or some other location within the Virginia Company's patent, their leaders were well aware of Gorges's pending charter, and probably had tacit approval to settle within his domain. They also carried a copy of Dermer's last letter, dated just four months earlier, recommending the de-populated site of Squanto's Patuxet, "which in Captain [John] Smith's map is called Plymouth," as the place to begin English colonization. By the end of the year, they had followed this advice and, in so doing begun the settlement of the land now officially called "New England."[53]

The reciprocity that Indians sought to maintain in economic, political, and spiritual relationships was seriously undermined in southern New England by the sequence of English actions and the plague epidemic. The propensities of English visitors (with the limited exception of the Pophams) toward violence and kidnapping, and their refusal to enter into and maintain reciprocal relationships, finally succeeded in arousing the hos-tility of most coastal Indians from the Penobscot to Cape Cod. Then the epidemic so reduced the coastal peoples in numbers and strength that their ability to maintain autonomy and, thus, real reciprocity with outsiders was largely lost. The once-powerful Pawtucket, Massachusett, and Pokanoket were re-duced to terror and humiliation before the numerically tiny Micmac as well as the formidable Narragansett, who now en-joyed important advantages in the competition for trade with Europeans. Even more critically, the epidemic enabled the hitherto inept English to establish a foothold for settlement.

four

SURVIVORS and PILGRIMS

SOUTHERN NEW ENGLAND during the early 1620s was a study in contrasts. North of Massachusetts Bay, where the rivers reached far inland, parties of English traders dealt from vessels and, increasingly, from land-based posts with Pawtucket and Abenaki epidemic survivors. Though their positions as middlemen helped, to some extent, to shore up these bands, the unpredictable nature of such a casual trade kept them vulnerable to attack or exploitation. On the coast of what is now Rhode Island and Connecticut, on the other hand, where the epidemic had not struck, large quantities of furs and European goods flowed between native groups and Dutch West India Company traders. Between these two areas, a third scenario was being played out. Though not uninterested in trading for furs, the leaders of the tiny Plymouth colony first sought reliable sources of food as well as physical and psychological security for their group. And they endeavored to establish the political and ideological legitimacy of the colony and of their own leadership. Translated into policies and actions, those imperatives led them to seek the domination of the territory and native inhabitants within a radius of about fifty miles of their settlement, and the suppression of competing modes of Indian-European interaction.

New England II

Since Gosnold's expedition nearly two decades earlier, the various attempts to establish settlements, temporary and permanent, in New England had been executed by crews of male laborer-soldiers. Smith and Gorges did envision settlement by English families, but only after a colony had established its productive potential and, hence, its future. The *Mayflower* expedition represented a radical departure from this precedent. Its 102 passengers arrived not as indentured or hired employees of an English enterprise but as members of economically self-sufficient households—husbands, wives, children, and servants—seeking to locate permanently. Moreover, some of them had just ended nearly a decade of self-imposed exile in the Dutch city of Leyden as members of a congregation of English Puritan Separatists. Finding themselves economically straitened and fearing that their children were abandoning the national and religious identities of their parents, about thirty of the Leyden Separatists, or "Pilgrims," as they became known, formed a settler vanguard seeking a new home for the group in North America. Traveling to Southampton, England, they finalized a partnership agreement with a group of London-based "Adventurers," who provided the bulk of the capital for the undertaking, and recruited about seventy non-Separatist "Strangers" to strengthen their ranks. Ordinary planters received one share each and a few leading "Planter-Adventurers" each invested in an additional share. All capital and profits would belong to the joint-stock company for seven years, at which time they would be divided proportionately among the partners on both sides of the Atlantic.[1] Thus alongside the familiar expectations of investors for fish and furs, the *Mayflower* bore those of the voyagers who sought homes and a measure of material prosperity. In addition, a minority of the passengers, including the expedition's organizers and leaders, were continuing a quest for control of their religious, political, and cultural environment.

This diversity of motives raised a potential for conflict that was heightened by the ambiguity of the group's political status. Having headed for territory in which there was no legally

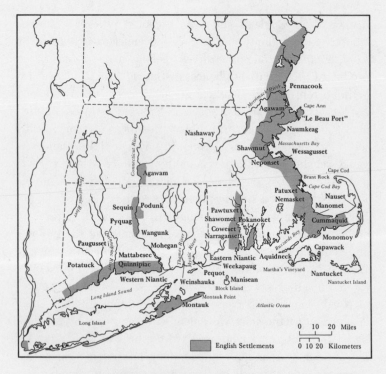

Areas of English settlement as of 1643 and known pre-contact locations of affected Indian bands.

constituted local authority to enforce the Crown's proclaimed sovereignty, the individual settlers would clearly be on their own once they disembarked. Yet it is apparent that the leaders of the Separatists, such as William Bradford, Edward Winslow, and Isaac Allerton, who were both Adventurers *and* settlers, presumed all along to govern the entire body. Accordingly they had recruited Miles Standish, a soldier of fortune fresh from the Dutch wars, to be the group's military commander. Then, while riding within sight of their destination, they secured the *"Mayflower* Compact," whereby all the passengers did "Covenant and Combine ourselves together into a Civil Body Politic." As explained by Bradford, the later governor and historian of Plymouth colony and a principal advocate, the measure was necessitated once it became clear the settlers were not going to live in Virginia. There had then arisen "the discontented and mutinous speeches" of some of the Strangers, who proclaimed themselves independent of any authority. Bradford did not say what alternatives to signing the dissenters were offered. The Compact served a second critical purpose as a legal claim by the body, "as firm as any patent, and in some respects, more sure," to represent the Crown in exercising local sovereignty over the land and its native inhabitants.[2] The shipful of passengers that had left England with diverse expectations of the New World arrived there as a covenanted, civil community under firm Separatist control. Its leaders considered themselves legally and militarily prepared to exercise authority over the remnant bands of Indian survivors around Patuxet which Thomas Dermer had enumerated for them.

Even before the *Mayflower* reached Patuxet, Standish had given shape to the colony's Indian policy during the stopover at Cape Cod. Though Bradford protested that the colonists hoped to trade with the Indians, he was also "sure that it was God's good providence that we found [some of their] corn . . . for we knew not how we should find or meet with any Indians, except it be to do us a mischief." Expecting "mischief," Standish's troops maintained an armed bearing as they "found" and rifled food, personal possessions, and burial goods and even uncovered what were apparently Martin Pring's 1603 "barricado" and the body of one of Dermer's crew from the year before. The colony's posture hardly seems to have been calculated to foster amicable trade relations. The natives kept their distance for three weeks, finally attacking Standish and his men one day with a volley of arrows and then retreating into the woods. Though Bradford thought that it had "pleased God to vanquish our enemies and give us deliverance," the visitors took no chances and left Cape Cod the same day.[3]

At Patuxet/Plymouth the colonists likewise stirred native suspicions by their aloofness during the first four months of their stay. But their situation grew desperate over their first New England winter. They lost half their number to starvation and disease, and they were ill-prepared for the approaching planting season. Under these conditions, they were no longer in a position to alleviate their shortages through pilferage with impunity. Clearly Standish's policy had to be modified enough to allow for some kind of contact, however restricted, with the natives. Nevertheless the impasse was not broken until the beginning of spring, and then by an Indian initiative.[4]

The Pokanoket had been watching the struggling colonists throughout the winter, their understanding of what they saw immeasurably aided by the presence of Samoset, an Abenaki from Pemaquid whose people had been trading with Sir Francis Popham for more than a decade, and their captive, Squanto. With these men offering advice and experience, the Pokanoket concluded that the time was ripe to befriend the settlers instead of maintaining a hostile distance. An alliance with Plymouth would enable them to break from the hold of the Narragansett, whose haughty demeanor stung even more than that of the English. Nevertheless the decision was not one to be taken lightly. Bradford wrote that, before approaching the English, the Indians gathered "for three days . . . to curse and execrate them with their conjurations." But this description betrays his fear of witchcraft as it was understood by Europeans rather than a comprehension of Indian beliefs and customs. More likely the Pokanoket were ritually purging themselves of their hostilities toward the English as a prelude to their diplomatic reversal.[5]

Samoset and Squanto arranged the meeting in March 1621 between the Pokanoket and Plymouth colony that resulted in their historic treaty. This treaty has been hailed ever since by historians and others as reflecting the good intentions of both

parties, and particularly the fairness of the colony. In it each
side agreed to aid the other in the event of attack by a third
party, to disarm during their meetings with each other, and to
return any tools stolen from the other (already a sore point
with the English). But in addition to these reciprocal agreements, several others were weighted against the natives. Massasoit, the Pokanoket sachem, was to see that his "neighbor
confederates" observed the terms, and the Indians were to
turn over for punishment any of their people suspected of as-
saulting any English (while no English had to fear being tried
by Indians). In other words, Massasoit's esteemed position
among the natives was to be the basis of Plymouth's projected
political control which, as we shall see, included trade relations. He would serve, in effect, as the colony's Indian agent.
In return, the treaty concluded, "King James would esteem of
him [Massasoit] as his friend and ally." The meaning of this
last honor was made explicit by the colony's annalist, Nathaniel
Morton, who wrote that by the treaty Massasoit "acknowledged himself content to become the Subject of our Soveraign
lord the King aforesaid, His Heirs and Successors; and gave
unto them all the Lands adjacent, to them and their Heirs forever." Also noteworthy is the fact that while the contemporary,
public account of the treaty stated that both sides would disarm during their meetings, Bradford's private history and
Morton's official account (which, for the most part, follows
Bradford's verbatim) omitted the passage pertaining to English disarmament. As future events would make clear, inclusion
of this clause would have revealed an ongoing treaty violation
on Plymouth's part. These discrepancies between the private
and public accounts indicate that among themselves the English regarded the treaty as one not of alliance and friendship
between equals but of submission by one party to the domination of the other.[6]

For the Pokanoket, on the other hand, the meaning of a political relationship was conveyed in the ritual exchange of speeches and gifts, not in written clauses or unwritten understandings based on unknown and alien concepts such as sovereignty. From their standpoint the English were preferable to the Narragansett because they demanded less tribute and ritual humiliation while offering more in the way of gifts, protection, and prestige. In place of their pre-eminent position on Narragansett Bay, they gained a strong ally in Plymouth as well as access to the territory formerly hunted on by the Patuxet. Before the epidemic, the latter had been, according to John Smith's report of his visit there in 1614, of the "language, humor, and condition" of the Massachusett.[7] Ignoring this earlier history, the treaty of March 1621 reinforced Pokanoket expansion into the region. The treaty also strengthened Massasoit's tribute-collecting powers among Plymouth's neighbors. By shifting their power base away from Narragansett Bay toward Plymouth Bay and Cape Cod, the Pokanoket could easily reconcile the agreement with both their traditions and their interests.

The treaty also brought a change in status for Squanto. According to Thomas Morton (no relation to Nathaniel), an English trader and astute observer of Indian politics who first visited New England the following year, Squanto was "freed and suffered to live with the English." And so the widely traveled captive finally resumed residence at Patuxet to serve its new occupants as guide, interpreter, diplomat, and general adviser on the perplexities of the land and its native inhabitants. Among his first services was the securing of corn seed and instruction in its planting, including the use of fish fertilizer, a practice that one scholar now claims he learned from the English during his stay in Newfoundland rather than from his own people.[8]

While a first step, Squanto's advice hardly freed the colonists from the danger of another "starving time." For the next three years, Plymouth relied principally on corn supplied, sometimes willingly, sometimes under threat of coercion, from the Pokanoket and their tributary allies. Some corn was apparently obtained at the treaty-signing, for three months afterward the colony claimed that its supply was running low. Edward Winslow, Stephen Hopkins, and Squanto were dispatched to Massasoit to trade seed for some of the Pokanoket's corn and to convey Plymouth's desire to compensate the victims of Standish's pilfering expedition on Cape Cod during the previous November. The emissaries also sought furs from the Pokanoket so as to begin the colony's effort to turn a profit for the Adventurers. To all these requests, Massasoit responded favorably.[9] Henceforth, corn and furs would be the principal objects exchanged by the Indians for Plymouth's protection from other enemies—and from the colony itself.

By themselves, Plymouth's trade-related requests suggest that the colony had come to recognize the degree of its economic dependence on its neighbors and the fallacy of its earlier arrogance on Cape Cod. But this suggestion is offset by a second set of requests arising from the two parties' differing understandings of the treaty. The Pokanoket viewed the colonists as fellow members of a regional social network whose members cemented their ties through giving and receiving hospitality. Even before the treaty-signing ritual had concluded in March, the colony ejected two Pokanoket who wanted to stay overnight. Soon, Pokanoket families passing near Plymouth began stopping by the village for meals. For the Separatists, who had found their sense of spiritual and communal integrity being undermined even by Dutch Calvinists, such casual conviviality undermined all the boundaries—political, cultural, and psychic—upon which their collective existence and, hence, their pretensions of sovereignty depended. For this reason, Plymouth also charged Winslow and Hopkins with clarifying to Massasoit the colony's understanding of their alliance. Presenting him with an English coat, the emissaries claimed that their short corn supplies precluded the continuation of such social visits. From then on they would receive only the sachem or his designated representative. The relationship was to be not between peoples but between political units as represented by their leaders.[10]

In the hospitality accorded them throughout their journey, Winslow and Hopkins found only reinforcement for the English desire to restrict social contacts between the two peoples. All along the way they were invited to eat and drink with each party of Indians they met. When they reached the village of Pokanoket, or Sowams, Massasoit invited them to spend the night. This meant sleeping on a plank bed with the sachem, his wife, and two other men. The next day Massasoit begged his guests to stay another evening, but they declined. "We desired to keep the Sabbath at home," Winslow commented, "and feared we should either be light-headed for want of sleep, for what with bad lodging, the savages' barbarous singing (for they use to sing themselves asleep), lice and fleas within doors, and mosquitoes without, we could hardly sleep all the time of our being there; we much fearing that if we should stay any longer, we should not be able to recover home for want of strength." Clearly, receiving Indian hospitality was as great a burden as bestowing it.[11] Thus to political subordination Plymouth added social segregation as a component of its relationship with its "ally." The key to the need for segregation lies in Winslow's phrase "want of strength." By it he inadvertently suggests the extreme psychic discomfort, as well as the economic or physical effects, that led the English to eschew relationships of mutual obligation in favor of those in which they could maintain firm control.

The treaty soon brought new surprises to each side. Having supposed Massasoit to be a "king," the English assumed that the agreement gave them sovereignty over a tributary network extending from Massachusetts Bay to Narragansett Bay to the tip of Cape Cod.[12] Besides exaggerating the extent of Massasoit's influence, they overlooked the fact that Indian sachems did not possess the authoritative powers of European monarchs even within their own bands, much less others. They "ruled" only by satisfying their "subjects." Massasoit's regional esteem derived from his having established a successful alliance among a group of neighboring bands. But the members of these kin-based, face-to-face communities were under no obligation to "obey" him or to assume that any agreement he made with an outside party bound them, especially if they doubted the wisdom of the agreement. Such was the case in the spring and summer of 1621, as many of the Indians hitherto loyal to Massasoit now rallied around Corbitant, a sachem at Nemasket, and sought a rapprochement with the Narragansett. At a time when Standish and other Plymouth leaders and troops were away on Cape Cod, a Narragansett contingent attacked Massasoit and drove him from his village. Corbitant then kidnapped Squanto and Hobbamock, Plymouth's two trusted Indian advisers, and a third Indian friendly to the colony. But Hobbamock escaped and alerted the returning Plymouth troops, who hastened to Nemasket with sufficient speed and force to rescue Squanto and to extract (indirectly) a statement of contrition from the safely hidden Corbitant.[13]

The Nemasket incident prompted Plymouth to strengthen its proclaimed sovereignty through direct treaty relationships with its neighbors.[14] In the resulting treaty of September 1621, unlike that signed with Massasoit, the Indians' political status was made clear—at least to those who could read English and could understand the meaning of the terms. The signers acknowledged themselves "to be the Loyal Subjects of King James." The list of names suggests how widespread native discontent and factionalism over Plymouth's conduct had become. Most prominent were Corbitant and Quadaquina, Massasoit's own brother, whose suspicions of the English had first been voiced at the earlier treaty-signing when he asked them, in keeping with that treaty, to put away their guns. The list also included Canacum of Manomet. Located near the site of modern Sandwich, his was the closest village to Plymouth and therefore of special concern. Another signer was Epenow of Martha's Vineyard, Dermer's nemesis of the year before, whose presence among the dissidents is less surprising than his apparent deference to English authority thereafter.[15]

As with the first treaty, Nathaniel Morton's rendering reveals some interesting insights into Plymouth's use of treaties. Besides the names noted above, he also included those of Obbatinewat and Chickataubut, two Massachusett sachems from Shawmut (later Boston) and the Neponset River respectively. Unfortunately the only copy of the treaty is that in Morton's official colony history, published in 1669. It is dated September 13, 1621. Yet according to William Bradford, an expedition for Massachusett country departed on September 18 of the same year—five days later. And according to Winslow's account, it was this expedition which established Plymouth's first contact with Obbatinewat and "told him of divers sachems that had acknowledged themselves to be King James his men." Obbatinewat, whose people had been subjected to "Tarrentine" (Micmac) raids for corn several times since the epidemic, was persuaded of the benefits of a Plymouth alliance and added his name to the list. While this conflict in chronology is relatively minor, Morton's document is more seriously suspect because it includes the name Chickataubut, an appellation which the Neponset River sachem Obtakiest did not assume until two years later.[16] The inclusion strongly suggests that Morton or an earlier hand added the two sachems' names to the document after the fact so that the conflicts which later ensued between Plymouth and the Neponset Massachusett would appear as treaty violations by the latter rather than as invasions by the former. It should be noted that Morton is the only source for any agreement or treaty between Obtakiest/Chickataubut and Plymouth.[17]

Though it was concerned with establishing a relationship with Obbatinewat, the expedition's larger purpose was to extend Plymouth's political and economic influence north of Massachusetts Bay to include the "Squaw Sachem" of the Mystic River Pawtucket. This sachem had succeeded her husband, the prestigious Nanapeshamet, who had apparently died at the hands of Micmac raiders in 1619.[18] Since then the band, like others around Massachusetts Bay, had taken to shifting its village site frequently in order to avoid further attacks. It had also sought to avoid contact with Plymouth, whose presence likewise induced suspicion and fear. Upon reaching the Mystic, the Plymouth troops succeeded only in finding some of the band's women members, whom they persuaded to cook for them, and one frightened man. After persuading the women to trade even "their coats from their backs," after which the women "tied boughs about them[selves], but with great shamefacedness," the English departed with promises to return for more trade. Yet there was little in Plymouth's approach to inspire confidence. Its emissaries entered Pawtucket territory accompanied by Obbatinewat, a proclaimed enemy. Then they violated native religious taboo by spending the night in the abandoned home of Nanapeshamet. Finally, in their abuse of Indian notions of female modesty, they expressed a contempt that could not have been lost on the Indians. Even in recounting the incident, Winslow admitted that "native women are more modest than some of our English women are."[19] Yet we can imagine the reaction if a group of Indian men had so obtained some English women's clothing. The significance of Plymouth's posture on this occasion would become apparent in its subsequent checkered relations with the natives around Massachusetts Bay.

For the moment, however, the colony's ascendancy was unchecked. It even succeeded in temporarily neutralizing the most dangerous source of hostility, the Narragansett. Having escaped the plague epidemic, this powerful band now dominated trade relations between Europeans (generally Dutch by now, with some French remaining) and natives in and around Narragansett Bay. Whatever the loss of the Pokanoket to Plymouth's sphere of influence meant to the Narragansett in terms of traditional prestige, it was most certainly a material loss. Moreover, Plymouth was now a rival in Massachusetts Bay, where the Narragansett were also expanding their hunting and trading activities. It was in the context of this competition that the Narragansett (perhaps with Dutch support) sent Plymouth a snakeskin containing several arrows in January 1622. With Squanto and Standish advising, Bradford, as governor, returned the skin filled with powder and shot. Canonicus, leading sachem of the Narragansett, refused to receive the response. According to Winslow, no Indian at Narragansett or elsewhere would have it, "and having been posted from place to place a long time, at length [it] came whole back again." By this action or lack thereof, the Narragansett renounced their claim to the tribute of the Pokanoket and related bands.[20]

Yet even while extending its influence outward, Plymouth had difficulty controlling its supposedly loyal Indians closer to home. Soon after the snakeskin incident, the enmity between Squanto and the Pokanoket resurfaced. Each began playing on the colonists' greatest fear by alleging that the other was fomenting a major conspiracy of the Narragansett and Massachusett against Plymouth. While the rivalry between Squanto and the Pokanoket pre-dated the *Mayflower*'s arrival, it was intensified by the jealousy each felt over the other's influence with the colony. Squanto had secretly begun to reconstitute the Patuxet from their dispersed remnants under his leadership in hopes of both challenging the Pokanoket's prestige and reducing his own dependence on Plymouth. The plot failed but, while Plymouth's leaders expressed their anger at Squanto for acting behind their backs, they protected him from a vengeful Massasoit in order to be able to continue playing the two off against each other. The result was to introduce tensions into the Plymouth-Pokanoket relationship that were not allayed until after Squanto's death the following summer.[21]

The increasing tension felt by the colony vis-à-vis Indians both near and far, friendly and hostile, brought an even greater militarization of the tiny settlement. Following the snakeskin incident, Standish organized the male population into a militia of four squadrons and supervised construction of a defense pale around the village. Later in the year, as relations with the Pokanoket soured and news of a massive Indian uprising in Virginia arrived, work was begun on a fort atop an adjacent hill.[22] At the same time Standish began introducing Plymouth's allies to some of the finer points of English morality and justice. While his troops sought corn at Nauset and again at Mattachiest in winter 1623, some of their beads and other "trifles" were stolen. On each occasion Standish threatened to wipe out the entire band if the "trifles" were not returned at once. In each case the colonists left satisfied after the sachem managed to recover the objects and administered a beating to the suspected offender.[23] In these incidents, Standish attempted to tighten discipline within the alliance by seeing that sachems executed punishment for offenses against the English. He was careful not to undermine the authority of the sachems and the internal organization of the band. Nevertheless the intent of Plymouth's colonial policy was to undermine band autonomy by enforcing direct political and economic subordination to the colony. As in Smith's vision of New England, military coercion was the basis for trading with Indians and extracting military assistance from them. The similarity is not surprising.

Standish, like Smith, was a military man with experience in the Netherlands.[24] But Smith's conquistador model was based on the pre-epidemic assumption of an extreme English numerical inferiority to the natives that no longer held while, for Standish, the military imperative remained paramount despite the weakness of his foes/subjects.

The purpose behind Standish's actions was, of course, to inspire terror and submission rather than harmony and the mutual respect of equals. Not surprisingly, many Indians noted a contradiction between Plymouth's militarism and its professions of Christian love for the Indians. Quadaquina's discomfort at the treaty-signing of March 1621 was only the first example of this. Corbitant, the ever-wary Nemasket sachem, questioned Edward Winslow sharply on this point in March 1623. He wanted to know: "if your love be such, and it bring forth such fruits, how cometh it to pass, that when we come to Patuxet, you stand upon your guard, with the mouths of your pieces presented to us?" Though Winslow tried to argue that such receptions were marks of respect, Corbitant could only shake his head and reply "that he liked not such salutations."[25]

Clearly, Plymouth's militaristic bearing toward the Indians was arousing both fear and hostility; it violated their concepts of reciprocity as well as their understanding of the first treaty. The Indians were still for the most part frightened of guns, especially since they did not have their own or know yet how to use them. Though Plymouth could extract deference (and corn) whenever its troops visited a village, resentments smoldered when they left and provided a grain of substance to English fears of conspiracy. But the role of their own conduct in fomenting native hostility was beyond the grasp or interest of the colony's leaders. For them it mattered most that they had succeeded in taking the first step toward realizing the Separatist ideal of exclusion from and domination over the economic, political, and cultural environment. What had eluded them in Holland now seemed possible in New England. Never-

theless it was only a first step—they still needed both their
native suppliers of corn and their English suppliers of capital
and credit more than either of these parties needed them.
Moreover, the process of western European expansion which
resulted in their own arrival might well bring others whose
presence would prove highly problematic.

Pilgrims and Paupers

Plymouth's recently acquired, still fragile hegemony was undermined in the fall of 1622 by the establishment of a second
group of English colonists at Wessagusset, near Obtakiest's
village on the Neponset. It consisted of sixty single men, mostly
indentured servants, who had arrived earlier at Plymouth without adequate provisions even for food and shelter. They had
been sent by Thomas Weston, a non-Separatist London merchant who had first brought the Leyden group and their
English backers together. Now mired in financial and legal
difficulties, Weston asked the Plymouth settlers to "lend or
sell" his destitute band some of their corn as repayment for
his earlier support. With such a start, Weston expected to establish a thriving colonial enterprise based on fish and furs.[26]
But to Plymouth, whose own lifeline of corn depended primarily on Massasoit's loyalty and Standish's terror, this sudden
intrusion of a second corn-consuming community lacking
means of payment could only be disruptive. Moreover, Weston's long-range plans made him an economic rival to the north
where, with Narragansett Bay closed to them, Plymouth's
leaders knew they must turn for furs. These anxieties were
reinforced by the warnings of Separatist friends writing from
England that the newcomers were untrustworthy and "base in
condition." One in particular, Robert Cushman, feared "these
people will hardly deal so well with the savages as they
should," and he suggested that Squanto inform Plymouth's
Indian allies "that they are a distinct body from us."[27]

The events of the next several months are by no means easy
to unravel, largely because the four extant accounts were each
written to present a different point of view. Edward Winslow's
Good Newes from New England (1624) was explicitly de-
signed to exonerate Plymouth of the charges against it that
some Wessagusset men later circulated in England. William
Bradford, whose account was later transcribed in Nathaniel
Morton's *New England Memoriall* (1669), likewise defended
Plymouth as part of his larger drama of the colonists' survival
in the face of obstacles imposed by all manner of persons and
circumstances. *A Declaration of the Affairs of the English
People that First Inhabited New England* (1662), by Phineas
Pratt, represented the anti-Indian faction at Wessagusset that
finally depended on Plymouth to rescue it, while Thomas
Morton's *New English Canaan* (1637) represented those who
sought an accommodation with the natives (though Morton
himself returned to England before matters had become this
serious). Of course the Indians are not represented directly
in the literature, though Morton partially fulfills that role in
his brief, incomplete account. Historians assessing Wessagusset's importance in the unfolding of Indian-English relations in New England have tended to accept the first three
accounts without criticism and to overlook or dismiss Morton's.
Less frequently, some have portrayed Plymouth's action as per-
fidious. Thus far none has fully considered the incident from
the perspectives of all its participants, particularly the natives'.[28]

From the new settlement's beginning, the warnings from
England appeared borne out. No sooner had Weston's group
established itself than the Massachusett were complaining to
Plymouth of the newcomers "for stealing their corn, and other
abuses conceived by them." Though Plymouth's leaders be-
wailed the "disorder [that] (as it seems) had made havoc with
their provisions," they wanted to control any exchanges of corn
that took place.[29] Thus representatives of the two colonies
conducted a joint expedition to Cape Cod after the fall harvest,

in a move that must have raised doubts in native minds about the seriousness of Plymouth's deploring of the newcomers' conduct. A Plymouth expedition to Massachusetts Bay the following month turned these doubts to convictions. Recently, wrote Winslow, the Indians had been ravaged by "a great sicknesse . . . not unlike the plague, if not the same." While they were in this condition, their stores of corn and fur had been pilfered by some Wessagusset men so that they had none to trade to Plymouth. Now, wrote Winslow, they would give "as much for a quart of corn as we used to do for a beaver's skin." But contrary to Cushman's advice, the Plymouth men made no public effort to restrain their fellow Englishmen and offered nothing more than sympathy to the natives.[30]

As winter set in, the balance of power between the newcomers and the natives shifted abruptly. The Massachusett recovered from the epidemic and acquired, presumably from other Indians, a supply of corn, while Wessagusset's own supply ran out. When the momentarily contrite Wessagusset leaders tried to trade for corn, the Indians refused. This repudiation of the role expected of all Indians residing near English colonies outraged many of the Wessagusset men, who called in March for an armed assault on the offenders to satisfy their wants. The colony's "governor," as Bradford styled its leader, John Sanders (Winslow preferred "overseer"), succeeded in convincing the men that Plymouth's advice should be sought before proceeding with such a drastic step. In a letter to Bradford, Sanders wrote that "he had used all means both to buy and borrow of Indians, whom he knew to be stored, and he thought maliciously withheld it, and therefore was resolved to take it by violence." When Bradford asked the Massachusett messenger who bore the letter about his people's corn supply "as if he had intended to buy of them," the latter answered that they had only enough for spring planting, "having already spared all they could." In other words, their supplies were at a level comparable with Plymouth's own. With this intelli-

gence, Bradford advised against violence on the grounds that
"all of us might smart for it."[31]

Bradford's reply presupposed that "Governor" Sanders actually governed Wessagusset. But a close reading of the
sources indicates that the little settlement was long since out
of Sanders's or anyone else's control. Sanders himself had departed hastily for Monhegan Island without even waiting for
Bradford's reply, ostensibly in search of more corn, but more
likely to escape a situation that was deteriorating rapidly. In
their desperate straits, the Wessagusset men had split into
several factions, each with its own approach to the problem
of procuring corn from the Indians. While one group simply
stole, another found it easier to get along with the Indians by
trading, working, and, in a few cases, living with them. Members of a third group, including (originally) Sanders plus
Phineas Pratt and several other leaders, did little more than
wring their hands in horror at the actions of the other two,
hoping that they would be rescued by Divine Providence,
Plymouth, or some other outside force.[32] The leaders also con-
tended with Massachusett hostility, expressed at times as
taunts and at other times as demands that the leaders control
and punish the thieving offenders. After repeated exchanges
over the punishment issue, Pecksuot, a Massachusett pow-wow,
lectured the leaders in their duty to restrain their men from
committing offenses against outsiders:

> All Sachams do Justis by thayr own men. If not we say the ar
> all Agreed & then we ffite, & now I say you all steele my Corn.

Though one Wessagusset man was hanged, the Indians remained unconvinced that the colony had experienced a real
change of heart.[33] It was at this point that the differences in
approach to the corn shortage between the leaders and the
thieves largely dissolved, leading to Sanders' letter to Bradford.

But as Sanders' query on the advisability of an outright attack went forth, the news of its contents reached the Massachusett, leading them to fear the intentions of Plymouth as well as of Wessagusset. At about the same time, the former received its first inkling that it too was suspect when Standish, on a mission to secure corn from nearby Manomet, was snubbed in favor of a Massachusett sachem, Wituwamet. According to Winslow, Wituwamet was recruiting at Manomet and elsewhere on Cape Cod in order to effect a general rising against the English on the grounds that Plymouth would defend Wessagusset. Soon after, Winslow cured Massasoit of an apparently fatal illness, finally ending the rift that had begun over the now-deceased Squanto's conduct. Expressing gratitude, the Pokanoket sachem described a massive Massachusett-led "plot" against Plymouth that included all its Cape Cod and Martha's Vineyard allies plus Agawam, north of Massachusetts Bay. Massasoit advised the colonists that by killing the Massachusett leaders, they could nip the entire scheme in the bud.[34] Finding Massasoit's story plausible and his proposed strategy acceptable, the Plymouth leaders resolved that Standish would take just eight men, so as not to alarm his targets, to Wessagusset as a kind of commando force of assassins. As the force was departing, Wessagusset's Phineas Pratt, supposedly leading in Sanders's absence, staggered into Plymouth after an exhausting overnight journey with the added intelligence that the Massachusett were awaiting only the melting of the snow and the construction of additional canoes before striking. To the Plymouth leaders, the evidence of an anti-English "conspiracy" was now overwhelming.[35]

Upon arriving at Wessagusset, the expeditionaries were appalled to find those colonists who had made their peace with the Indians casually gathering food outside the settlement without fear for their safety. To Winslow, a member of the expedition, these men were obviously "senseless of their own misery" in their insistence that "they feared not the Indians, but lived and suffered them to lodge with them, not having sword or gun or needing the same."[36] The Plymouth men were beyond considering the possibility that, left unprovoked, the Indians would be friends rather than foes. Standish soon located the leaders and thieves, whose enthusiasm for swift action was buttressed with the promise of a daily ration for all who would cooperate. With Pecksuot reminding the new arrivals that he knew why they were there and challenging them to initiate the violence when ready, Standish prepared to execute the strategy advised by Massasoit. The next day, unable to gather all of his targets into a single location, he unleashed a series of surprise attacks. First, Wituwamet, Pecksuot, and two additional Massachusetts were lured into a Wessagusset house on the pretext of a feast and slain with their own knives. In the next few hours, three more Indians died in similar fashion. Late in the day, Standish and his group met the vengeful Obtakiest and some of his followers. The hero of this battle was Hobbamock, the Pokanoket pniese, until then a passive observer of the day's events. He was doubly frightful to the Massachusett because their own supposedly invulnerable pnieses had been killed or wounded, so that by merely appearing on the field in a menacing fashion, he drove them away. The only casualty was Obtakiest's elbow, which was broken by a bullet. Wituwamet's head was then taken back to Plymouth and posted outside the newly completed fort as a warning to any and all Indians who sought to defy the colony.[37]

In his brief for the colony, Winslow adduced mountains of evidence to prove the existence of an Indian conspiracy against all English, thereby justifying Plymouth's intervention at Wessagusset. He noted the revelations of Massasoit and Pratt, as well as one by a brother of Obtakiest and a later "confession" by a captured Indian, along with the taunts and generally hostile actions of the Indians. The problem with these pieces of evidence is that each describes a conspiracy of different dimensions. The perpetrators range from Wituwamet and a few followers to a large collection of bands, including several of Plymouth's Cape Cod "allies"; while the targets range from Wessagusset alone to all the English. At the same time, Winslow and Pratt inadvertently presented evidence that throws into doubt the existence of a conspiracy. Despite their provocative behavior, the offending Indians were in a position to be drawn into Standish's traps. Moreover, it is clear that a substantial portion of the Wessagusset men were living outside the settlement and were unconcerned about the threat of Indian violence. Though three Englishmen living with the Massachusett were killed after Standish's action, this was in explicit retaliation for the murders of the seven Indians.[38] Thus it is unlikely that there was a conspiracy directed at *all* the English. As Pecksuot's exchange with the Wessagusset leaders indicates, it was primarily the issue of corn thieves and their punishment that aroused Massachusett hostility. If Plymouth was drawn in, this was because of its collusion with the offending party, as well as its own conduct toward the Indians on other occasions.[39]

Pratt also indicated that, aside from the theft of their corn, the Massachusett disliked and distrusted the militaristic bearing of the Wessagusset leaders.[40] From the reactions to Plymouth's military displays noted earlier, we know that Wituwamet would have had no trouble basing an appeal to neighboring bands on this issue. But how likely was it that such shared hostility was translated into conspiratorial action? Massasoit himself noted that Plymouth would relieve itself of danger by eliminating the Massachusett leaders. Now clearly the Massachusett were anything but a power in southeastern New England at the time. What appears to have been the case is that a single band was responding to a series of provocations and that the support they gathered from others was little more than moral. As we have seen, concerted action by several bands was not characteristic in southern New England, where bands were autonomous and revenge was largely a matter of personal and familial concern. In short, a specific grievance of a few Indians against a few Wessagusset men dovetailed with a less focused anti-English resentment among a larger number of Indians. the result was the *appearance* of a conspiracy that Massasoit exploited to regain his position as Plymouth's only dependable Indian friend and that Plymouth itself used for conducting its armed intervention.

Plymouth intervened in order to reassert and expand its control of the surrounding territory and its inhabitants, English as well as Indian. Standish's action was deemed a success not only for having cowed the Indians but for having eliminated Wessagusset altogether. For besides threatening Plymouth's hegemony over the Indians, Weston's colony revived the threat to its ever-precarious communal boundaries and the official Puritan morality which they enclosed. For this reason, Plymouth's leaders condemned not only those who stole from the Indians but also those who lived with them. As products of artisan backgrounds and idealizers of economic self-sufficiency, they had no patience with those who could not obtain their corn honorably and conserve their supplies rationally. As Puritans seeking to maintain a covenanted community, they could not tolerate neighbors who lacked even the rudiments of law and order. As products of the English lower classes, on the other hand, the Wessagusset servants sought to relieve their misery either by theft or by cooperating with the Indians. A few even found the Indian way of life preferable to being indentured to a starving colony. To the Plymouth leaders, who worried constantly about the loyalty and spiritual condition of many of their own colonists, this willingness on the part of some Wessagusset men to abandon their countrymen in favor of the natives was even more threatening than the thievery of the others. Bradford reported that even Sanders "was taxed by some amongst them for keeping Indian women, how truly I know not." By their examples such men suggested that, in interacting with Indians, English people could abandon the self-discipline of the Puritan and the artisan as well as the policy of coercion, social exclusivity, and proclaimed sovereignty upon which the Plymouth enterprise rested. And so after subduing the Indians, they "rescued" the Wessagusset men, offering them food and shelter at Plymouth. While Phineas Pratt and a few others accepted the invitation, most showed their gratitude toward their "rescuers" by sailing toward the fishing grounds off the Maine coast, preferring to take their chances that employment and passage home could be found there to an uncertain future as soldier-servants under Miles Standish.[41]

Plymouth's sudden outburst of violence provoked reactions of incredulity from various quarters. Among Indians they took the form of hostility or panic. "The Salvages of the Massachussets," reported Thomas Morton, ". . . could not imagine from whence these men should come, or to what end, seeing them performe such unexpected actions; neither could [they at first] tell by what name, properly to distinguish them; [but] did from that time afterwards, call the English Planters Wotawquenange, which in their language signifieth stabbers or Cutthroates." Though Obtakiest (known after 1623 as Chickataubut) and the Massachusett welcomed English settlers to Massachusetts Bay seven years later, they remained resentful of Plymouth.[42] Among the Massachusett's Cape Cod supporters, the action had an even greater impact. It "so terrified and amazed them," according to Winslow, "that they forsook their houses, running to and fro like men distracted, living in swamps and other desert places, and so brought manifold diseases amongst themselves, whereof very many are dead," including the "allied" sachems, Canacum of Manomet,

Aspinet of Nauset, and Iyanough of Cummaquid (modern Barnstable). The last of these, "in the midst of these distractions, said the God of the English was offended with them, and would destroy them in his anger" for sympathizing with the Massachusett.[43] Whether the Indians contracted some disease in the throes of their panic or suffered from a localized epidemic that coincided with the rout of the Massachusett is uncertain. What is clear is that Plymouth had again appeared, both to itself and to many natives, to be aligned with some powerful spiritual forces.

Alarm at Standish's action was not confined to Indians. Writing from Leyden, John Robinson, the Plymouth Separatists' former pastor there, denounced the militarization of Indian policy at the expense of missionary proselytizing. He deplored "the killing of those poor Indians," and lamented: "Oh, how happy a thing it had been, if you had converted some before you had killed any!" Indeed, he argued, "you being no magistrates over them were to consider not what they deserved but what you were by necessity constrained to inflict." As for Standish, Robinson suggested, he "may be wanting that tenderness of the life of man (made after God's image) which is meet." Moreover, his conduct could only have deleterious effects on the colonists themselves by attracting lesser men to violence and terror as psychic substitutes for piety.[44] Robinson had glimpsed further than most Europeans of his time into the psychology of Indian-hating, though its magnitude and origins were beyond his understanding.

Robinson's letter implies that emphasis on a missionary approach to Indians, rather than a military one, was the expectation of at least some of those who had helped give birth to the colony. And a letter to Bradford from one of the Separatists among the London Adventurers, written in January 1624, suggests that the group was badly divided on the issue: those favoring additional aid to the colony were those with an in-

terest in Indian conversion, while opposition to missionary
activity was part of a larger opposition to continued under-
writing of an investment that had yet to prove itself worth-
while.[45] Moreover, as the Leyden exiles' spiritual mentor,
Robinson can be assumed to have inspired many of the early
migrants. Yet aside from a tract published by Cushman in
1622—like Robinson's letter, written from abroad—there was
no official or quasi-official statement linking Indian missions
to the colony. Having left Holland and England, the colonists
left behind any notions of approaching the Indians on any but
a coercive basis. Beginning with the *Mayflower* Compact,
they passed over the subject of Indian conversion, even as
rhetorical flourish, in silence. The imperatives of the small
producer and the Puritan required that they assert mastery of
themselves and their political environment through rationalized discipline and aggressive action. To pursue loftier aims
was to invite masterlessness, anarchy, even death. As Edward
Winslow put it in his published response to Robinson and
other critics of the Wessagusset attack, "this business was no
less troublesome than grievous . . . especially for that we
knew no means to deliver our countrymen and preserve ourselves, than by returning their [the Indians'] malicious and
cruel purposes upon their heads."[46] By convincing themselves
that their own lives were at stake, the English found the mo-
tivation and justification for a policy of terror.

It could hardly have been accidental that Edward Winslow
was selected by the Plymouth leadership to respond to its
critics. Most likely he had been a strong supporter of Robinson's views before migrating. For he represented the single
exception, albeit a partial and timid one, to the colony's
aversion to preaching to Indians. Though undertaking no
formal program, Winslow sought opportunities to educate
Indians in the ways of Puritan Christianity when he could
move a conversation in that direction, and to report such con-

versations to his English readers. Thus a blessing at a meal in
an Indian wigwam was the occasion for a lesson on God's
sovereign powers and the Ten Commandments. (Winslow's
male hosts objected only to the seventh, with its prohibition
of polygamy.) And an Indian's theft of some English trifles
brought forth a lecture on God's wrath.[47]

Though Winslow was concerned primarily with imparting
notions of English and Puritan morality, he was not ignorant
of, or altogether hostile to, native religious beliefs. In fact in
his *Good Newes from New England* (1624), he recanted
statements he had published two years earlier in *Mourt's
Relation,* a promotional tract for the colony, suggesting that
the Indians had no religion and worshiped no God.[48] Instead
of denouncing the Indians as heathen or pagan, Winslow now
stressed the similarities between the Christian God and their
Kiehtan, a parallel which apparently struck him during the
discussion noted above of the Ten Commandments. Though
Kiehtan was not the only deity, he was, according to Winslow,
"the principal and maker of all the rest," as well as of "the
heavens, earth, sea, and all creatures contained therein," including humans.[49] In spite of an apparent polytheism, Winslow
implied, the Indians had developed the idea of divine sovereignty.

Winslow's discussion of native religion differs from Roger
Williams's far more penetrating account, published two decades later, in several significant respects. According to Williams, Kiehtan, or Cautantowwit, as the Narragansetts called
him, did not create the other deities; rather they were quite
independent of one another. In short, the Indians were pronounced polytheists, not crypto-monotheists. Moreover, Winslow's reference to Kiehtan's having created "one man and one
woman, of whom they and we and all mankind came" overlooked Williams's discovery that the creating deity had been
dissatisfied with his first human couple and had discarded them

and made a second, more perfect pair from which the human race was descended. In his eagerness for Indian-Calvinist parallels, Winslow bypassed an important difference in the psychologies of the two religions. Though both deities were dissatisfied with their initial human creations, Kiehtan made a more perfect one, while God blamed Adam and Eve for disobeying his command and sentenced them and most of the human race to damnation. Unlike Adam and Eve, moreover, Kiehtan's first man and woman were created independently of, and equal to, each other. And though Winslow noted that good Indians were thought to be rewarded after death and bad ones punished, he did not mention, as Williams later did, that the good were a majority and that their reward included eternal "carnal joyes."[50]

For Winslow, both the parallel between the two systems and the source of native religious deficiency lay in the Indians' worship of Hobbamock. "As far as we conceive," he wrote, this source of power who cured wounds and diseases through the medium of the pow-wow and protected and empowered those who obtained visions of him in one of his many shapes, "is the devil." To Winslow, who had cured Massasoit with some simple remedies, the pow-wows were at the root of this Satanism. Being called frequently to native sickbeds himself after his performance at Sowams, Winslow strove hard to convince the pow-wows and observing Indians that the devil would not appear and noted that the natives "have confessed they never saw him when any of us were present." This did not prove that the pow-wows were charlatans, but only that their devil had been bested by the God who accompanied the Puritans. Winslow believed that the pow-wows could cause the devil to appear and often successfully cured their patients. Likewise he did not suppress his admiration for the courage and moral integrity of the pnieses, men especially trained from boyhood to call upon and visualize Hobbamock for protection and power on the battlefield. And though doubting the efficacy of this protection (especially after the battle of Wessagusset, in which several Massachusett pnieses suffered casualties), he did not doubt that the devil, through their visions, "maketh covenant with them."[51]

Though he never addressed the subject directly, Winslow had suggested a missionary strategy by presenting the native belief system as possessing the same structural outline as Christianity. Kiehtan could be transformed into God merely by filling in some missing details, and Hobbamock already possessed many of the recognizable qualities of the devil. The principal task was to convince the Indians that a complete dependence on Kiehtan/God would allow the forces of good to overcome the forces of evil, led by Hobbamock/Satan. By no coincidence, the latter had his earthly minions, particularly among the pow-wows, who deluded and misled the Indians into worshiping him, becoming via illness or other misfortune, his victims. Thus, Winslow suggested, the pow-wows would be the principal earthly adversaries in any Puritan missionary effort. Though later missionaries often differed from Winslow's evaluation of native religion, all followed him in placing primary emphasis on Hobbamock and the pow-wows as the root of native "heathenism."[52]

For all his insights into native religion and his preaching and publicizing efforts, Winslow generated no visible enthusiasm for converting Indians among either the natives themselves or his fellow colonists. Although the mortality in their own ranks due to disease plus the technological prowess of the English repeatedly suggested to the Indians that they were spiritually deprived and that the English God had much to offer them, the colony's posture and policies not only precluded the reciprocity to which Indians were accustomed in their social relations but must have betrayed the English fear of Indians that lay behind it. As a result, most of Plymouth's "allies" turned out to be untrustworthy, offering tribute and loyalty when obliged to, yet supporting efforts to undercut the colony and, when sufficiently aroused, defying it directly. For Plymouth's leaders, on the other hand, the Indians had become a symbolic antithesis, threatening the material, political, and ideological foundations of the settler community. Not only did the natives defy cherished English notions of personal and social order, they welcomed, perhaps tempted, less wary and less disciplined colonists to do the same. As such, they constituted an anarchic potential that could only be contained through force. For the moment, then, Winslow's discovery of Satan in the Indians' camp was the signal not for evangelical activity but for ideological reinforcement of the boundaries separating the two peoples.

While suppression of the Massachusett "conspiracy" and Weston's plantation restored Plymouth's hegemony south of Massachusetts Bay and satisfied certain ideological imperatives, the action's political and economic effects were less comforting. The colonists' display of military prowess, coupled with the epidemic which followed, had, characteristically, at once frightened and alienated many of the very Indians on whom they depended. In a letter to the London Adventurers the following year, Bradford and Isaac Allerton apologized for sending but a "small parcell of furres," saying that since the Wessagusset incident, "we have been much endamaged in our trad." On Cape Cod, where Standish had successfully cowed the natives while trading the year before, "the Indeans are rune away from their habitations, and sett no corne, so as we can by no meanes as yet come to speake with them." The colonists faced a producer boycott which left them without a reliable supply of the corn they needed to eat as well as the furs they needed to help satisfy the Adventurers. Moreover, the availability of fish, furs, and land along the New England coast was attracting increasing interest in England.

By 1623, Gorges's Council of New England had granted two patents of several thousand acres each on the southern Maine coast and, in the fall of that year, sent over Sir Ferdinando's son, Robert, as governor-general.[53] Of even more immediate concern were the several hundred vessels which fished in coastal waters below Monhegan Island that year, often trading guns, among other items, it was feared, with the Indians.[54] As trade activity between these other Europeans and the coastal Indians increased, Plymouth's chances of attaining self-sufficiency diminished. New England was changing and, as the Adventurers in both Plymouth and London recognized, time was running out for the colony.

five

CLIENTS and TRADERS

PLYMOUTH SOON OVERCAME its twin crises by growing its own corn—a staple which the colonists could not only
eat but exchange for furs. This solution propelled Plymouth
into a new phase of Indian-European relations for, during the
middle 1620s, the political and economic geography of New
England was again transformed, this time by new trade patterns. Instead of disease, the major factor now was the rise to
predominance of settlement-based entrepreneurs, operating
out of New Netherland and Plymouth, who supplemented their
European wares with indigenous goods of value to Indian fur-
producers. The commercial production of corn by the Plymouth English and the mass circulation of wampum, begun by
the Dutch, brought not only a quantitative increase in the trade
but even greater specialization among the region's Indians as
they labored to service the encroaching market economy. The
new goods and resultant patterns also undermined the autonomy and reciprocity on which inter-band relationships had
traditionally been based, and had significant cultural effects.
And while the trade attracted even more European, particularly
English, attention to the region, leading eventually to its settlement on a massive scale, it made Plymouth and New Netherland, for a brief period, the dominant powers in New England.

The Pilgrims Transformed

Plymouth took its first step in dealing with the food crisis as
the ungrateful Wessagusset men were departing. It was in

order to increase corn production that Bradford, "with the advice of the chiefest among them," ordered an end to Plymouth's brief experiment in communal farming. In his history, Bradford implied that Plymouth's communism had been implemented for utopian reasons but that in so doing, the colony's leaders had overlooked the essential corruption of human nature. However, this explanation is suspect because it runs directly counter to the fear of anarchy underlying the *Mayflower* Compact. More likely, communal labor was initially undertaken as a means of exercising a closer watch over those who had threatened to strike out on their own. But once Wessagusset had been uprooted, it is unlikely that anyone at Plymouth still considered going it alone outside the village. At the same time, efforts to grow enough corn had been hampered by the complaints of settlers who felt that they worked more and/or received less than their due. According to Bradford, young, single men objected to providing "for other men's wives and children without any recompense," while those wives and their husbands found it "a kind of slavery" for the women to perform certain domestic services for the single men. Strong men resented receiving the same rewards as the weak, while the "aged and graver men" felt likewise about being treated on a par with "the meaner and younger sort." Though Bradford did not specify the actual distribution of labor and rewards, he made it clear that many Separatists as well as "strangers" now found interdependence to be burdensome.[1]

Bradford's immediate solution to the problems of underproduction and alienation was to allot separate parcels to families "according to the proportion of their number," for the 1623 growing season. Ironically, this system of land distribution resembled that of the Indians. Indeed, an outsider entering Plymouth within the next year might have thought that the colonists had "gone Indian." Not only had garden plots been parceled out to families but the principal crop was Indian corn and a good deal of the day-to-day field labor was performed by the women and children. But for the English, these arrangements represented a transitory move in a direction distinctly away from the Indian example. For them, the patriarchal household was replacing the covenanted community as the principal economic unit. It was also becoming the principal social unit, for the single young men who (though Bradford doesn't quite say it) appear to have been the major source of discord, were each "ranged . . . under some family" for purposes of the allotment. In the following year, the allotments were made permanent and private and within a decade of the Wessagusset incident, the remaining agricultural property of the colony—land, stock, tools—was divided among the founding families. According to Bradford, the results of even the first allotment resulted in happier, more productive workers. Characteristically referring to himself in the third person, he noted that "more corn was planted than otherwise would have been by any means the Governor or any other could use, and saved him a great deal of trouble, and gave far better content." By the middle of the decade, the colony was feeding itself. It was also moving away from both the Indians and its own communistic beginnings in other respects: the Indian method of planting corn was replaced by more familiar, less laborious English methods; and the large leading families who had gained most from the allotments abandoned corn altogether as they perfected the adaptation of English grains to New England soil.[2]

Plymouth's transformation from a collective community dependent on neighboring Indians for survival to a family-based economy and society providing for its own subsistence represented another major step in its becoming a completely self-sufficient society. The colony had yet to gain financial independence from the Adventurers, but in this case the latter were already taking the initiative. From 1623, the reports of discontented English migrants returning from Plymouth as well as Wessagusset, the growing antagonisms between Separatist and non-Separatist Adventurers and, most importantly, the failure of the colony to establish itself on a firm commercial footing, all led the majority of the London Adventurers to grow disillusioned with the enterprise. The prospect of de facto independence from their sponsors was almost certainly an additional impetus in the leaders' decision to divide the land as well as in their decision to press the search for a profitable product.[3]

Of the profit-making ventures open to the colony, fishing was initially the most attractive. But by 1625—after several ill-fated attempts—it was clear that Plymouth's tiny shallops and generally limited resources were no match for the growing number of well-outfitted vessels, now mostly English, that were visiting the New England coast annually.[4] The other possible venture for the colony was the trade in furs, an activity in which they had some experience. But as matters stood in 1623, the colony's supply of furs was sharply limited: its location provided no direct access to the larger quantity and thicker coats of the beavers inhabiting the inland and more northerly portions of New England; and its alienation of the Narragansett to the west and the Massachusett and Pawtucket to the north had made obtaining such access all the less likely. Moreover, the number of European traders working in New England was rapidly rising. The colony accordingly began to recognize that a successful fur trade beyond its immediate environs would require it to modify its approach to Indian relations, to appease rather than intimidate potential native trade partners. Thus when it finally made an effort to trade with the Narragansett in 1623, it dispatched a crew of newly arrived seamen who had no personal involvement in the earlier friction between the two groups. And the first Plymouth expedition to Abenaki country in 1625 was headed not by the bellicose Standish, who was conveniently sailing for England at the time, but by the shrewdly diplomatic, bilingual Winslow.[5]

The results of these two expeditions proved useful to Bradford, Winslow, and the other leaders as they sought to define precisely what kind of trade they wanted. The seamen who journeyed to Narragansett country "made," in Bradford's words, "but a poor voyage of it." Though obtaining some corn and beaver, they found the "few beads and knives" which they offered "were not . . . much esteemed" compared with the "cloth and better commodities" which the Narragansett regularly received from the Dutch. From this experience, Plymouth's would-be traders learned not only how ill-equipped they were to compete with the Dutch but how dependent fur traders were on European goods, which in their case could only be obtained from the increasingly skeptical Adventurers.[6]

It was in Abenaki country that Plymouth found a way out of this situation. Early in 1623, John Pory, an official of the Virginia Company making an extensive tour of the New England coast, had noted that among the Abenaki and other non-farming Algonquians, "Indian corn, pease and such like is the best truck for their skins—and then in winter especially, when hunger doth most pinch them, which is the season when the French . . . trade with them." Pory was indicating that the conditions which underlay the pattern of trade established by the French during the decade after Champlain's explorations, and described by John Smith on the eve of the plague epidemic, still held. As then, the Abenaki were so drastically altering their subsistence activities and movements in the quest for thick winter pelts that they required outside sources of food. If the Plymouth leaders did not appreciate the extent of Abenaki demand before Pory's visit, they almost certainly learned of it through him.[7] This demand may have been yet another factor in the decision to divide the land so as to increase corn productivity. For what the Abenaki sought that the Narragansett did not was a commodity that the colony could potentially produce on its own. In 1625, two harvests after producing its first visible surplus, Plymouth took Pory's cue and dispatched Winslow to the Kennebec in command of a small shallop loaded with corn. He returned, according to Bradford, with "700 pounds of beaver, besides some other furs," a respectable quantity given the size of the boat and the inexperience of Plymouth's traders in this region.[8]

Plymouth moved quickly to consolidate its success. In the fall of the following year, a second successful corn-for-furs expedition returned from the Kennebec. These successes were nothing if not timely. As Winslow was conducting the colony's first exchange on the Kennebec in 1625, the London Adventurers were splitting apart, with the majority refusing to extend any further support to the colony. In the fall of the following year, as the second expedition returned from there, the Adventurers proposed terms by which the colony could buy out the discontented among them. Now confident that they had established themselves in the trade, the colony's leaders offered to accept the Adventurers' terms by forming an enterprise of their own. A partnership of twelve men—Bradford, Standish, Winslow, five other leading settlers, and four Separatists among the London Adventurers—would assume responsibility for payments on the stock and other debts. To fulfill these obligations, the "Undertakers," as the new partnership was sometimes called, would monopolize the colony's fur trade. When the Adventurers received this offer in 1627, they accepted it without hesitation.[9]

By then, if not before, Plymouth was trading not only its own corn produce but that being collected, once again, from nearby Indian tributaries.[10] Now, however, such tribute meant additional profits rather than mere survival. But the colony's leaders recognized that the corn trade was only the first step toward realizing the full potential of the trade. Already they were expanding their activities to Narragansett Bay, cutting into a thriving commercial network which dwarfed their own and which had substantially altered the economic and political lives of its Indian participants.

Wampum Revolution

In contrast to the epidemic-stricken east coast, large native populations continued to flourish on Long Island Sound and Narragansett Bay and the rivers feeding them. Among these peoples, Dutch traders had enjoyed a free hand since Adriaen Block's voyage of 1614. As elsewhere in New England and North America, the regularization of trade relations provided certain bands with advantages over their neighbors. In order to trade, the disadvantaged bands paid tribute to Indian middlemen just as they would for hunting rights or protection against a powerful enemy. Thus the ceremonial exchange of goods which had once reinforced equality among bands became, under the impact of specialized hunting and the profit motive, a source of inequality.[11] The chief beneficiaries in this instance were the Narragansett, located on the west side of Narragansett Bay, and the Pequot, who lived just to the west on the Pawcatuck and Mystic rivers.

The heart of Narragansett strength was their close association with the Pawtuxet, Shawomet, and Coweeset on the west side of the bay. As we have seen, the Narragansett, after avoiding the epidemic of the late 1610s, became noted among coastal Indians for the intensity of their religious rituals. The close proximity to one another of these four large bands meant that ritual interaction among them was highly routinized, reinforcing the impression among Europeans that they constituted a single tribe. Under the uniquely arranged leadership of two sachems, Canonicus and his young nephew, Miantonomi, the Narragansett had risen from their home in the southwestern portion of the bay to dominate the alliance and to drive the depopulated, weakened Pokanoket from the mouth of the Seekonk. From there they extended their influence up the Blackstone and Seekonk rivers to the eastern Nipmuc, from whom they obtained furs. They also controlled the flow of pelts and trade goods between Massachusetts Bay and the interior. Finally, they oversaw Indian-Dutch trade relations for the Eastern Niantic, living near modern Charlestown, and the natives of Rhode Island and Block Island. Because of their geographic and demographic advantages, as well as the respect they enjoyed among other Indians as shrewd traders, devoted worshipers, and committed pacifists, the Narragansett obtained their hegemony through persuasion rather than violence.[12]

The Pequot, on the other hand, lacked the Narragansett's numbers and, confined as they were to the tiny Pawcatuck and Mystic rivers, ready access to an abundant supply of furs. But they drew upon kin ties, especially with the Mohegan on the Thames River, to carve out a sphere of influence west of the Narragansett's. Both the Pequot and the Narragansett, then, drew on familial connections and effective leadership, as well as a common linguistic and cultural base, to rise to positions of prominence on New England's southward-facing coast by the early 1620s. The same kinds of ties between the two groups themselves rendered them still stronger by disinclining them, at the outset, from competing with one another.[13]

The critical point in the rise of the Narragansett and the Pequot occurred as the result of a sudden turn of events during the trading season of 1622. A Dutch West India Company trader named Jacques Elekens seized the Pequot sachem, probably Tatobem, and threatened to behead him if he did not receive "a heavy ransom." The sachem promptly handed over 140 fathoms of what the Dutch called "sewan" and the English would soon call "wampum"—strings of purple and white shell beads. As a result of this incident, the West India Company discovered both the value to Indians of wampum and the power and prestige of the Pequot.[14]

Wampum strings were especially crafted sacred objects, worn by religious and political leaders on special occasions. The concentration of wampum shells on the beaches of Narragansett Bay and Long Island Sound gave the natives in these areas an item which they could exchange for other objects of utilitarian and non-utilitarian value as Indians in the northeast had done since Archaic times. The coming of the fur trade had already increased its flow, especially as the shells were most abundant at the seashores, precisely where furs were not. But Elekens's action transformed wampum from one among many items of exchange to a "currency" that flowed into the hands of prestigious and ordinary Indians alike.[15]

Though the Company indignantly denounced and withdrew Elekens, its traders were quick to recognize his contribution to their calling. By the end of the decade they were purchasing large quantities of wampum, which they exchanged for furs at Fort Orange, their post on the Hudson. By offering it among their trade items, they drew Indians from as far away as the St. Lawrence, whose French traders had no access to the treasured beads. The wampum revolution pervaded native culture to the extent that, by the late 1620s, Indians on both sides of Long Island Sound had made the manufacture of wampum their principal winter activity.[16] Like their fur-trading counterparts in the interior, they were modifying their seasonal cycle to engage in specialized production for a market whose needs were determined by non-natives and non-native values. The suddenly escalated pressure for wampum, and the fact that it was a natural resource unevenly distributed among native bands, undermined the traditional structure of inter-group reciprocity.

Elekens's unwitting discovery reinforced the dominant positions of the Narragansett and particularly the Pequot, both of

whom already had access to the prized shells. Soon after
Elekens's departure, the Company dispatched Pieter Barentsen,
a popular Algonquian-speaking trader, to the Pequot and acceded to the latter's demand that no other traders be allowed
in the area. This dramatic reversal of the Pequot's humiliation
at Elekens's hands only further enhanced their prestige among
natives. With both Barentsen and other natives acquiescing,
the Pequot soon dominated Indian-Dutch trade on Long Island. The Pequot consolidated their hold through the marriage
in 1626 of Tatobem's daughter (whose name is not preserved)
to Uncas, a son of Oweneco, sachem of the Mohegan. According to a later account by Uncas, this was done to "keep their
Lands entire from any violatio[n] either from neighboring or
forreign Indians." The result was a powerful, kin-based alliance that, by the end of the decade, dominated the region
from the Pawcatuck westward to the Connecticut, as well as
the east end of Long Island.[17]

As the leading Indian groups in Narragansett Bay and Long
Island Sound sought to expand their control of the wampum
trade, so did the region's two European colonies. In the same
year that the Pequot-Mohegan alliance was sealed, the widening New Netherland and Plymouth trade spheres were coming
into contact. Though the exact chronology is uncertain, it is
clear that by the time the two colonies began officially corre-
sponding in February 1627, Dutch traders were dealing with
some of Plymouth's Indian allies, including the Pokanoket, and
Plymouth had constructed a post at Manomet, enabling its
traders to reach Narragansett Bay without circumventing Cape
Cod.[18] When the stock at Manomet was specified in a document drawn up sometime before the following May, wampum
was among the items listed—its first mention in any Plymouth
document.[19] Nevertheless, Plymouth lacked direct access to
the beads, a deficiency which was undoubtedly a factor in

Bradford's demand of March 19 that the Dutch cease trading altogether in Narragansett Bay.[20] Despite Bradford's bellicose tone and an obvious conflict of interest between them, the two colonies' mutual desire to trade directly with one another eventually led them to reach an understanding. In October 1627, Isaack de Rasieres, second-ranking official in New Netherland, journeyed to Plymouth for this purpose. Among the items exchanged at their meeting were fifty fathoms of wampum which Rasieres sold the English in order to satisfy their desire for an ample supply. In return the English agreed to stay out of Narragansett Bay.[21]

Plymouth sought such a large amount in order to begin introducing wampum on a large scale among its Abenaki clients on the Kennebec. The superiority of wampum to corn was obvious: the latter could only be peddled following the fall harvest—when beaver pelts were at their thinnest and, hence, least valued on the European market. Wampum, on the other hand, could be sold at any time, enabling Plymouth's traders to obtain the coats of maximum thickness in late winter and early spring. Nevertheless, the new commodity moved slowly at first. As Bradford reported, ordinary Indians initially resisted the shell beads, which were customarily worn only by persons of rank. But after two years of trader persistence, wampum became an item of mass consumption, and Plymouth had effectively eliminated most of its small-scale competitors north of Massachusetts Bay. Bradford and his fellow colonists had fostered and witnessed the extension of what can truly be called the "wampum revolution" to Abenaki country. The beads that had formerly moved from south to north on an occasional basis now flowed in massive quantities from producers through various combinations of middlemen—Pequot, Narragansett, Dutch, and English—to consumers. Once a symbol of prestige, wampum had become a medium of exchange

and communication available to all, leading Indians throughout New England toward greater dependence on their ties
with Europeans.[22]

The Specter of Ma-re Mount

Plymouth's informal agreement with New Netherland
amounted to a division of New England into spheres of interest in which the Dutch West India Company kept Narragansett Bay and Long Island Sound while the Undertakers had
the coast from Cape Cod northward to themselves. Though its
lack of sources of wampum was not yet a serious deficiency,
Plymouth's sphere did pose a problem because of its ever increasing attractiveness to English settlers, traders, and fishermen, some of whom threatened the Undertakers' hoped-for
monopoly. Besides the uncertain number of fishermen who
visited the region annually, there were, by the middle of the
1620s, about a hundred English residents scattered along the
coast between the colony and its Kennebec outpost.[23]

Many of these residents had arrived as part of Ferdinando
Gorges's most serious attempt yet to establish the direct authority of the Council of New England in the region. It will be
recalled that in September 1623, six months after Plymouth
broke up Wessagusset, Gorges's son Robert arrived to assume
the governor-generalship of New England for the Council.
Though the grant for his headquarters lay on the north side
of Massachusetts Bay, the younger Gorges occupied the site
and buildings of Wessagusset from which Weston's men had
so recently been evicted. Ill-prepared and, after one winter,
ill-disposed to carrying out his mandate, Gorges returned
home. But while the Governor-General was disenchanted with
New England, a number of his companions were not and
settled on their own with the Council's blessing. The core of
this group remained at Wessagusset for the rest of the decade,

while others scattered to individual homes on the north side of Massachusetts Bay.[24]

William Morrell and Samuel Maverick left the only surviving mementoes of these settlers. Morrell, one of Gorges's two Anglican chaplains, lived at Wessagusset until returning to England in 1625. His Latin-English poem describes the region so as to encourage the building of "an English kingdome from this Indian dust." His Indians are possessed of tempers that lead, often unpredictably, to extreme violence. But this violence could be deflected if need be, he wrote, by destroying the Indians' crops, just as happened when the natives of Ireland resisted an earlier English invasion. Maverick, too, indicated that force was often necessary when dealing with Indians, but easily imposed. He fortified his house at Winnesimmet (now Chelsea) "with a Pillizado and fflankers and gunnes both below and above in them which awed the Indians who at that time," he claimed, "had a mind to cutt off the English."[25] Morrell and Maverick demonstrated how it was that they and other Englishmen could live outside of a covenanted community like Plymouth and retain that colony's distance from, and posture toward, the Indians around Massachusetts Bay. Such domination was easy to maintain, of course, because the depopulation resulting from the plague epidemic meant that there were probably no more able-bodied Indian males than English around the bay in the mid-1620s.[26] Just as important for Plymouth's purposes, these men were not engaged in high-volume trading with the Massachusett for purposes of exporting furs to England, and, therefore, not encouraging links between the Massachusett and inland tribes. In short, the presence and the attitudes of these scattered settlers were compatible with the colony's interests.

A second presence was that of a small settlement of English families at Naumkeag. The community had begun in 1623 as a fishing station at Cape Ann. Organized by John

White, an enterprising clergyman of Dorchester who never emigrated himself, Cape Ann evolved quickly to a tiny plantation. Its purpose was to absorb religious dissenters from England and impart the gospel to the Indians while bringing profits to its Dorchester backers through fishing and trading for furs. It was strengthened in 1624 by the arrival of several families which had left Plymouth out of disagreement with the latter colony's Separatism. In 1625 Cape Ann successfully defended itself, through the persuasiveness of Roger Conant, one of the newcomers, against Plymouth's efforts to reclaim a fishing stage it had built two years earlier but then abandoned. In spite of this victory, the Dorchester merchants found fishing as unprofitable a basis for settlement as had Plymouth's Merchant Adventurers, and in 1626 Cape Ann was abandoned. Though most of the employees returned to England, about thirty men, women, and children moved south to Naumkeag, where they hoped to find a more favorable location for trade and settlement. When the Massachusetts Bay colony was founded two years later, the settlement would be re-named "Salem" and these families would come to be designated the "Old Planters." But as of the middle of the decade, they were a struggling group whose inability to turn a profit for its Dorchester backers rendered it harmless from Plymouth's perspective.[27]

While the Naumkeag settlers and the former associates of Robert Gorges were no threat to Plymouth, there was one additional English settlement on Massachusetts Bay that differed from them in several important respects. In 1625, a Captain Woolaston, with three partners and about thirty indentured servants, established a settlement at a site just two miles from Wessagusset, which he modestly named "Mount Woolaston." Woolaston apparently held a patent from the Council of New England, and his arrival gave the English around the Bay a definite numerical advantage over the Massachusett. But while his enterprise had the appearance of legitimacy, its structure and the presence among its officers of Thomas Morton, avowed friend of both Weston and the Indians, vividly recalled the earlier plantation at Wessagusset and the alternative modes of Indian-European relations introduced there.[28]

It is in this context of a growing presence of non-Plymouth English, particularly at Mount Woolaston, that we should read Plymouth's complaints about its competitors during the late 1620s. These began to be recorded publicly after the second expedition to the Kennebec in 1626. Other traders, according to Bradford, now "envied" Plymouth's success and "went and filled the Indians with corn and beat down the price, giving them twice as much as [Plymouth], and undertraded [Plymouth] in other commodities also." Bradford's outrage was misplaced, if not feigned, for Plymouth had broken in on the thriving if disorganized trade of the Maine men, with almost certainly the same effect on prices. The colony displayed a similar attitude toward its competitors the following year when it accused them of trying to exclude the Undertakers from the Kennebec. This was the rationale it used in obtaining a patent from the Council of New England, giving it a monopoly on the Kennebec trade, and in establishing a permanent post there, near the site of modern Augusta, in 1628.[29]

While the Kennebec patent secured the Undertakers' trade where it was already established, it did not provide them with untrammeled access to other Indians along the New England coast. Accordingly, they tried to gain such access by appealing to Gorges's desires for orderly and profitable enterprises within his domain. Bradford wrote the Council in 1627 to complain of the "irregular living of many in this land," both some who lived there (almost certainly Mount Woolaston) and those "fishermen, who begin to leave fishing, and fall wholly to trading." Such men possessed no license or other permission from the Council, imported foodstuffs that were badly needed in

England instead of producing their own, and had no stake in
the region's future. Though Bradford implied that these men
often cheated the natives without regard for the retaliation
that might fall on those who were settled permanently, neither
he nor anyone else cited a specific instance of such a result.
Instead the substance of his objection concerned, apart from
the legal issues, a mode of trade that competed with Plymouth's locally based enterprise without offering it anything in
return. Permanent plantations, he suggested, would offer more
in the way of profits and security to both old and New
England.[30]

While filing this official objection, Bradford in his unofficial
and private writings focused on the more specific and more
serious charge that the fishermen were trading guns to the
Indians. Such a charge was not new: both the Virginia Company's John Pory and the Adventurers' trader Emmanuel
Altham had made the same accusation against some of the
Maine fishermen in 1623. The Abenaki, Pawtucket, and Massachusett were in the market for guns that year because the
French-armed Micmac were rumored to be on their way to
New England to launch yet another series of deadly raids.
Plymouth took little notice of this supposed threat to its security (and violation of a royal edict) for several years thereafter. In the wake of the Micmac's failure to appear, the Indians never used whatever guns, if any, they received. But as
competition among the traders stiffened, Bradford revived the
charge, complaining to Gorges in 1627 that the trade "will be
the overthrow of all, if it be not looked unto."[31] Bradford presumably lacked the evidence, as well as support from other
Englishmen on the scene, to press the issue more formally as
yet. But in implying that guns were the chief article of commerce between those of "irregular living" and "salvages," he
had created a forceful, symbolic antithesis to the orderly,
family-based, self-sufficient—militarily and economically—
plantation supposedly epitomized by Plymouth itself.

Behind his suggestion that the plantation as a New England institution was under attack, Bradford may well have had a specific perpetrator in mind. His letter to the Council indicates that someone living on the land, though not farming it, was causing even more trouble than the fishermen. He was almost certainly referring to Mount Woolaston. By 1627 that plantation's failure to realize a profit was leading its owners to change their plans. It was probably as Bradford was writing that Captain Woolaston took a number of his servants to Virginia to sell. Apparently successful, he summoned one of his partners, named Rasdall, to Virginia with another group of servants. Rasdall left Mount Woolaston under the command of a Lieutenant Fitcher. Besides Fitcher, the only remaining freeman was Thomas Morton. Soon afterward, according to Bradford, Morton invited the servants to join him as equal partners in the enterprise by ousting Fitcher, so as to avoid being "carried away and sold for slaves with the rest." Morton and his fellows renamed the post "Ma-re Mount," meaning mountain by the sea but also punning on "Mary" and "mare." (Bradford claims they called it "Merry-mount, as if this jollity would have lasted for ever," and his spelling, like his entire perspective, has prevailed among the partisans of both sides ever since.) They also erected a maypole, as had the fishermen at Damariscove, Maine, to celebrate a traditional English festival. This left a plantation that not only defied the most rudimentary English assumptions of social and political order but one that epitomized, with its maypole, Puritan notions of pagan idolatry. Moreover, it was led by a friend of Plymouth's Massachusett enemies, a friend whose intention was to establish trade relations with them.[32] It is hardly surprising, then, that Plymouth moved, in spring 1628, to deport Morton and the men he had gathered around him.

Yet Plymouth's accusations against Morton never mentioned the fur trade or the colony's own past relations with the Massachusett. They focused instead on his supposed trading of guns to the Indians and his social relationships with the Indians, emphasizing the former in explanations of his arrest to Gorges and the Council of New England and the latter in Bradford's history. Plymouth alleged that Morton had sold guns to the Indians, endangering all the stable plantations in the region. Underscoring this charge, they collected donations from those plantations, including Naumkeag, Wessagusset, and Winnesimmett, to defray the cost of arresting and deporting him. In their letter to Gorges (written by Bradford), the planters claimed that Morton, along with the fishermen-traders, had already placed more than sixty guns in Indian hands. Morton himself had supposedly traded some not only to the Massachusett but to the Narragansett and Pokanoket. Morton never responded to these charges, stressing instead the issues of trade competition and intolerance of his lifestyle as the causes of Plymouth's discontent.[33] His silence suggests that he may well have traded some guns and was loathe to admit the violation of a royal edict. But more to the point is the danger this action posed for the English settlers, and the evidence on this matter is telling. Shortly after Morton's arrest, Massachusetts Bay began to be settled by a new group of English colonists who were prepared enough for the possibility of Indian violence that they outlawed the selling of guns to the natives before leaving England. Yet none of those settlers who commented on the Indians mentioned their possessing guns. Instead of encountering Bradford's "savages, who are already abundantly furnished with pieces, powder, and shot, swords rapiers, and javelins," Francis Higginson found them armed only with "bows and arrows," and William Wood noted "that a hundred of them will run from two or three guns." Clearly, what few guns Morton and anyone else might have sold posed no danger to English settlers.[34]

The other charge, even more important than guns in Bradford's private account, centers on the social life at Ma-re

Mount, particularly its maypole. According to Bradford, "Morton became Lord of Misrule, and maintained (as it were) a School of Atheism." The men put on drunken celebrations, "inviting the Indian women for their consorts, dancing and frisking together like so many fairies, or furies, rather; and worse practices." He also saw the festivities as downright pagan and complained of the "sundry rhymes and verses" Morton composed for the occasions, "some tending to lasciviousness, others to the detraction and scandal of some persons."[35] Since Bradford penned his account, Morton's maypole and his two arrests and deportations, first by Plymouth in 1628 and, after he reappeared the following year, by the new Massachusetts Bay colony, have formed the centerpiece of both scholarly studies and works of imaginative literature. Among the authors attracted to it have been Nathaniel Hawthorne, William Carlos Williams, and Robert Lowell. The reasons are obvious: here was a classic encounter in the American "wilderness" between repressive Puritan and libertine Elizabethan lifestyles in which the victory of the former appeared to have set the course of New England's and America's history. Most of these writers followed Bradford more closely than Morton and lost sight of the question of how far Ma-re Mount actually went (as opposed to how far in Bradford's fantasies) in abandoning English notions of order for sexual and/or cultural anarchy.[36]

Morton says repeatedly in his *New English Canaan* that he found the Massachusett Indians more humane and hospitable than the Plymouth Puritans, and concludes that in New England, generally, "the more Salvages the better quarter, the more Christians the worser quarter." Yet he also notes that he never lost sight of the rule that "where two Nations meete, one must rule and the other be ruled," and points out that when he "had quarter" with the Massachusett, "I observed not their humors, but they mine." Moreover, in Morton's account of the maypole festivities, the only reference to the Indians' presence appears at the very beginning: they "came thether of purpose to see the manner of our Revels" and were enlisted to help erect the pine trunk that was to serve as a maypole. What followed, he claims, was innocent dancing and carousing by men "that lived in hope to have wifes brought over to them." This desire was apparent in the one bawdy song which Morton reproduced. Though the song contains a direct invitation to Indian women ("Lasses in beaver coats come away, / Yee shall be welcome to us night and day."), the lines appear at the very end of the last verse and what they express is more distant hope than realistic expectation. Morton's poems are full of classical allusions and tropes which, contrary to their author's assertion, were probably no more comprehensible to the natives and English servants than to "the precise Separatists." "Mine host of Ma-re Mount," as Morton styled himself, surely exaggerated the innocence of his followers' minds, but there is nothing in his account to suggest the "licentiousness and . . . profaneness" alleged by Bradford. Indeed such carryings on would have been entirely out of character for the Indians, as Morton himself recognized when he spoke elsewhere of the extreme modesty of native women.[37]

Morton's descriptions of Indian life and his projections for the future of Indian-English relations in New England are even more to the point in assessing his attitudes. Among the many examples of Indian humanity which he admired were their respect for age, their sense of justice, and their willingness to share whatever they had with strangers. And he noted in particular their "more happy and freer life, being voyde of care, which torments the mindes of so many Christians." In this discussion, which terminated his description of the native inhabitants, he pointed out that they sought no "superfluous commodities," but used, shared, and enjoyed whatever was available to them. These descriptions might have constituted a celebration of the "noble savage" were it not for Morton's conclusion that the Indians would have to make way for European colonization and the Christian religion. Morton devotes the second of *New English Canaan*'s three sections to a description of the New England landscape in terms not only of its beauty but also of its commercial potential. Indeed his admiration of the Indians' lifestyle was largely a shrewd recognition of their skills in efficiently extracting and utilizing the region's natural resources.[38]

Morton was even more explicit about the Indians' colonial future in his discussions of religion. Quite simply, he found no religion as such among the natives. He did note the beliefs about Kiehtan on which Winslow placed so much hope but classified them as mere traditions that had not inspired any form of worship. He likewise minimized the pow-wows' subversive potential, arguing that while they had "some correspondency . . . with the Devil," their witchcraft was generally weak. Morton saw a great need and future for Anglicanism in southern New England and, not unlike the Puritans, thought the epidemic made the region "so much the more fitt for the English Nation to inhabit it, and erect in it Temples to the glory of God." And before any Puritan had done so, he persuaded a native father to allow his son to be brought up in a colonial household. The boy would learn to read as a way of gaining access to the mysteries of the Anglican religion.[39] Whatever took place at Ma-re Mount on Mayday, 1628, did not mark a dissolution of the boundaries between English and Indian or "civilization" and "savagery." Morton was without doubt more tolerant in his dealings with Indians than were the Puritans or just about anyone else in his time, all of which is to his credit. But he sought colonization of their land, their resources, and their religion, a process that would have hastened the decline of that very autonomy he so much admired. Morton drew the same line as the Puritans, but less harshly.

Behind Morton's playful satire and Bradford's fears of sexual and cultural anarchy lay a conflict between two approaches to the colonization of the continent and its inhabitants. Plymouth's exclusive settlement was being successfully challenged by a tiny outpost of fur traders who approached the Indians (for the moment) as business partners. Stressing trade rather than coercion, Morton raised the possibility that the rest of New England might be colonized in a way different from Plymouth's. Moreover, by placing himself among the Massachusett, Morton was strengthening Plymouth's enemy on its northern flank as the Dutch were doing with the Narragansett to the west. To the Plymouth leaders, who had seen evidence of Massachusett-Narragansett collaboration in the past, such a prospect was terrifying. It is in the context of such fears that we should read Bradford's attempts to convince the outside world that Morton was selling guns to the Narragansett and even the Pokanoket. In Morton's own account, the Massachusett used subtlety to pit Morton and the Narragansett against each other in order to keep the latter *out* of their territory.[40] And as we have seen and will see again, the actual threat posed by the trading of guns to the Indians was virtually non-existent. But to the psychologically and ideologically rigid Plymouth leadership, the realities of band autonomy and competing colonial interests were overshadowed by the fear that all their enemies would combine to consume them. And the men of Ma-re Mount, with their celebrations of masterlessness and idolatry and their seeming descent into savagery, were the obvious source. Once again, Plymouth's leaders had portrayed an economic and ideological rival in symbolic terms in order to vanquish it and to remind the natives that terror, not friendship, underlay relations between the two peoples in New England.[41]

As the 1620s drew to a close, the vision of a Plymouth-dominated New England was fading rapidly as the colony's competitor found more subtle means of subversion. By 1629 Isaac Allerton had succumbed to the effects of his long exposure to colonial entrepreneurs in England on behalf of his fellow Undertakers. On his return from England that year he brought back not only Thomas Morton, whose efforts to re-establish Ma-re Mount he supported, but the offer of a trade partnership on the Penobscot with one Edward Ashley. Though Ashley clearly "had the wit and ability to manage the business," Bradford and his fellow entrepreneurs worried over the way in which he had acquired his expertise. Ashley, it seemed, "had for some time lived among the Indians as a savage and went naked amongst them and used their manners, in which time he got their language." What was perhaps even more galling than yet another flouting of Puritan moral boundaries was the fact that Ashley and the pious Allerton were prepared to form their own partnership if the colony declined to join them. Not wishing to be shut out, the Undertakers swallowed their moral pride and signed on "to prevent a worse mischief," as Bradford rationalized it. In the end, however, they did not prevent the "worse mischief"; Ashley and Allerton proceeded to dun the Undertakers by monopolizing the flow of trade goods to and from the Penobscot.[42]

Despite Bradford's rhetoric, Ashley, Allerton, and Morton could never be much more than thorns in Plymouth's side. The real blow to the colony's hopes for New England came from an enterprise whose intentions more closely resembled its own. John White, the Dorchester clergyman who had organized the Cape Ann fishing venture that evolved into the tiny settlement at Naumkeag, had not flagged in his efforts to make the enterprise productive from both an economic and a religious standpoint. By 1627, he had brought together some London merchants and a group of East Anglia Puritans with the intention of expanding Naumkeag to a scale far grander than anyone had ever dreamed of for Plymouth. Out of his efforts emerged the New England Company, a joint-stock enterprise which in 1628 obtained a patent from Gorges's Council of New England to settle the area roughly between the Merrimack and Charles rivers. That summer the Company dispatched John Endicott as commanding officer to supersede Conant, along with about forty other settlers. As a militant Puritan with Separatist leanings, Endicott alienated Conant and the other "Old Planters." He also had the offensive maypole at Ma-re Mount chopped down, symbolically completing, he supposed, Plymouth's expulsion of a few months earlier. (Morton was at that moment on his way back to New England with Allerton.) Meanwhile, Sir Ferdinando Gorges was protesting the Company's plans after belatedly discovering that the Council's patent included some of the land previously granted to his son, the long-departed "Governor-General." The Massachusetts Bay Company, as the New England Company was now called, responded to Gorges's claim by going over his head to the king. Through the offices of its respectable merchant and gentry partners, the Company obtained a charter directly from Charles I, empowering it not only to settle the territory designated in the Council's patent but to govern it. In the spring of 1629 a fleet of five ships carried about 200 planters, including family members and servants, to Salem. And in the year following, nearly a thousand more came to settle around Massachusetts Bay. Moreover, this group brought the Company's royal charter with them to keep it out of the hands of the non-Puritan merchants who had expected to exert ultimate control over the enterprise. Through a Trojan-horse maneuver, the respectable, London-based colonial enterprise had emerged as a colony dominated by Puritans who proclaimed their allegiance to King and Church but clearly expected to be free of both.[43] The passing of power from precarious Plymouth to the "instant city" of Boston was symbolized when, as one of its first acts, the new Massachusetts Bay colony arrested and expelled Morton. This time, it would be thirteen years before "mine host of Ma-re Mount" would return.[44]

By the end of the decade, then, New England had become a thriving commercial arena in which goods followed a variety of routes from their sources to their ultimate consumers and in which the division of labor had become highly specialized, involving as it did producers and suppliers of corn and wampum as well as of pelts and European goods. The one area where Indian-European trade relations had not been stabilized was around Massachusetts Bay. Here Plymouth's suppression of attempts by other Englishmen to trade with the Massachusetts in 1623 and 1628 had effectively precluded such stability. In this way, the colony had unwittingly facilitated the "Great Migration" and its own consequent decline. The Separatists' principal contribution to the making of "New England" proved to be not a conquest but a holding action.

six

SURVIVORS and SAINTS

THE EFFECT OF the "Great Migration" of the 1630s was to export to New England and its Indians many of the forces transforming English society. The commercialization of agriculture, combined with a population that had doubled during the preceding century, created upheaval in much of the English countryside, throwing small owners, tenants, and laborers off the land and rendering precarious the livelihoods of still more. In response, many of the "middling" or "industrious" sort embraced Puritanism as a means of orienting themselves and mastering the forces of a new order. From their ranks came most of those who sought in the lands of the once-populous Massachusett and Pawtucket the key to their search for economic and religious independence. The migrants arrived in such large numbers that, by 1633, commercial exchange around Massachusetts Bay had shifted from portable commodities, principally furs, to the land itself.

The Industrious Sort

Though nearly every county in England contributed to the Great Migration, those contributing the largest proportions of settlers were the agricultural counties of the south and east.[1] During the preceding century, the growth of the London market as well as increased international trade had transformed these regions of self-sufficient farmers into specialized, capital-intensive centers of grain, beef, and dairy production. In some areas the resulting rise in prices led to enclosures and bankruptcy. Many tenants and even smallholders were pushed into the ranks of the wage-earning poor and obliged to migrate to other areas of England in search of employment and sustenance. The circumstances of others permitted some degree of choice. In small family farming regions like Wiltshire, Suffolk, and the Kentish Weald the practice of partible inheritance led to ever-smaller landholdings that were, by the mid-sixteenth century, too small to support the growing population. When the resulting underemployed labor force co-existed with the rapid streams needed to power fulling mills, they attracted eager wool-producers. A pattern of by-employment emerged whereby many men worked part of each year on the family's farm and part in the local mill, while a few with capital were able to operate such enterprises simultaneously.[2] Operatives and owners alike were subject to new kinds of social and economic pressures that were not local in origin. The stable, predictable world of the self-contained village was a thing of the past in much of England by the late sixteenth century.

This pattern became more complex near the end of the century when the "Old Draperies," as the rural mills were termed, were on the decline—in part because of competition from the "New Draperies" located in cities like Norfolk and larger towns like Canterbury. Originally operated by Dutch and Walloon refugees who introduced new fabrics and techniques, the expanding urban mills turned increasingly for apprentices to young Englishmen who tended to come from immediately surrounding rural areas for the specific purpose of being apprenticed. They generally had contacts in the trade, usually kin, who assisted them in undertaking their new occupations. In general, the goal of these apprentices, as with their counterparts in the rural mills, was not to abandon their family farms but to help support them and, perhaps, eventually to return.

For the small producers of East Anglia, Kent, and other regions, then, the move back and forth between farming and skilled craft was neither difficult nor unusual at the turn of the century. Such moves were facilitated not only by geographic proximity but by the similarity of business conditions and ethics. Whether a man produced beef or woolen cloth, he sought independence from economic insecurity for himself and his family. And he found support for this quest among the merchants and fellow producers with whom he came increasingly into contact, especially the smaller ones often referred to as the "industrious sort."[3]

As these producers and entrepreneurs were rapidly learning, achieving independence in a market economy was ultimately a function of conditions over which they, as individuals, had little control. Many learned this lesson the hard way during the decade immediately preceding the Great Migration. A sequence of wildly gyrating harvests and price fluctuations in both food and clothing gave rise to a severe economic depression in Kent and East Anglia in the 1620s. Though Kent recovered partially in the 1630s, conditions remained unstable there throughout the decade. Worst hit by the economic instability were the unemployed poor, whose desperate condition aroused the anxiety of the respectable classes, middling as well as gentle, more than ever. Wage-earners fell into this group frequently when they went unpaid due to the inability of their farm- or mill-owning employers to market their products. Even lesser members of the gentry felt the pinch as income from rents proved insufficient for keeping pace with the rising living standards of their class. A further source of uncertainty and dread was the return of large-scale epidemic disease in the 1620s. The major epidemics of 1625-26 and 1636-37 cut off communication and trade, especially with the London market so vital to most southeastern producers, while striking particularly hard at the cramped streets and quarters of urban artisans and laborers. The customary solution to such conditions—migration—was even less effective than usual because the crisis was so uniformly widespread. For cloth-workers, however, this option remained—if they were willing to leave England. Thus in 1616 alone two thousand of them moved to the German Palatinate, reversing the Continent-to-England pattern of cloth workers of a generation earlier.[4] In this extension overseas of what had been a pattern of internal migration, an important precedent for overseas colonization was established, so that when the opportunity for migration to New England arose, thousands of small producers from these regions were prepared to move.

Though far too little is known about the backgrounds and motives of most of the migrants to New England, several significant patterns are apparent. Geographically, there was a preponderance of southeasterners, particularly from Kent and East Anglia, that is from the areas where large numbers of small producers already moved back and forth between town and countryside. For these people, the migration overseas appears to have represented an attempt to escape dependence on the fluctuating fortunes of an unstable market. Not only do surviving ship's lists show large numbers of husbandmen but a surprising number—on some ships, a majority—of urban tradesmen and artisans moving to New England to return to the land. Most of these were young men, still in the prime of life, and they brought households—nuclear families with an occasional servant or relative attached. Their goal, borne out subsequently in colonial landholding patterns, was to establish self-sufficient farms with enough land to bequeath to all their sons and, in so doing, maintain the continuity of the patriarchal, lineal families that had once flourished in their homelands but whose futures there were now so uncertain.[5]

It was among the small producers in the southeast and elsewhere that Puritanism enjoyed its greatest reception. Their experiences in adapting to long-range economic and social changes and their anxieties over the sequence of adverse circumstances from the late 1610s onward provided the foundations for Puritanism's popular appeal in the late sixteenth and seventeenth century. These converts recognized a relationship between what Michael Walzer terms the "unsettledness" in their own lives and the larger crisis in English society and culture. Like other Protestants since Luther, they experienced the crisis in terms of a profound sense of sin in the world which they sought to separate themselves from and to contain. As Walzer argues, this sin was portrayed politically as "masterlessness," a malaise that had supposedly come to pervade England with the decline of an older corporate order. Though the Puritan movement was led by more affluent merchants, professionals, and gentry, its broad support came from those whose independence was more tenuous. Puritanism provided such people with an ideology which enabled them to understand and act in a "masterless" world.[6]

In contrast (and in reaction) to the all-inclusive Anglican church, Puritan converts, or "saints," were distinguished by individual experiences of grace and conversion which they assumed God had reserved for a few elect persons who, among the depraved mass of humanity, were to be saved. The experience had the effect of legitimizing the individual pursuit of private ends, both spiritual and material. Puritan saints cultivated personal relationships with God through study, meditation, and prayer alone or in the exclusive company of other saints, rather than through priestly intermediaries in the communal, magical rituals of a parish church. They devoted much of their time and energy to self-conscious scrutiny of their spiritual states and oriented their conduct toward battling the Devil in themselves and in the world for the greater glory of God. In the fluid world of Tudor-Stuart England, their sainthood provided them with a radical new basis for personal identity that superseded, without necessarily negating, those of kinship and locality.[7]

In their secular lives, Puritans stressed that they had been "called" to their vocations in the course of being elected by God. This gave their economic activities and other worldly pursuits a spiritual underpinning. It was here that the psychological fortification provided by conversion became practically applicable. For market-oriented farmers, artisans, and tradesmen, survival in the rapidly changing, fiercely competitive world of late Tudor/early Stuart England required hard work, self-discipline, and withdrawal of communal loyalties. And as Christopher Hill has shown, constant labor marked a change from the seasonal work rhythms of pre-commercial, pre-industrial England. The practice of Puritan piety fostered what Max Weber termed the "worldly asceticism" needed to sustain such discipline, while the doctrine of the calling legitimized, even glorified, the pursuit of private, material interests.[8]

The experience of sainthood led Puritans to view the world primarily in terms of a distinction between themselves, the "regenerate," and the "unregenerate," for whom God held out no hope for salvation. Having made that distinction, however, Puritans differed widely among themselves as to its practical implications. For many, including the leaders of the Great Migration and of the Puritan cause in the Civil War, it implied that the saints had a collective calling to bring order and mastery to a chaotic world through rule by the elect. They would begin by reforming England and its national church. For Separatists such as those who settled Plymouth, however, the first priority was to remove themselves from all ties with spiritually polluted forms of worship, including the Church of England. And a few more radical separatists, such as Roger Williams, argued that congregations of elect saints must sever all institutional ties with the "world," including the state, even in a godly commonwealth. While the industrious sort was represented among the advocates of each of the approaches, most were probably less concerned, at least initially, with political and ecclesiastical doctrine than with the validation Puritanism, as both ideology and movement, gave their personal quests for independence and security.[9]

On top of an economic situation that offered little promise to would-be independents, religious persecutions of nonconformists reached massive proportions in the 1630s. The story of these persecutions and of their impact on the migration to New England is too familiar to bear repeating here.[10] What is significant is that the efforts of the Archbishop of Canterbury, William Laud, to enforce religious conformity reinforced and intensified the sense of uncertainty and alienation among marginally independent Puritans. But repression also heightened solidarity within the ranks of the saints and enabled them to develop a powerful, widely appealing interpretation of their collective experience. This interpretation provided the ideological underpinning for the Great Migration and helped submerge, for the first three years, the movement's more atomistic tendencies.

New England III

In their own accounts of the causes of the migration, the Puritan authors of promotion literature and of the earliest letters from New England confirmed the pattern of economic and spiritual alienation sketched here. The theme of England's overpopulation and land shortage was consistently sounded. "So many honest men and their families in old England," wrote Francis Higginson from Salem in 1629, "through the populousness thereof do make very hard shift to live one by the other." Compared with New England, Edward Winslow had written from Plymouth a few years earlier, "those parts of the world wherein you live [are] greatly burdened with abundance of

people." The result, as John White saw it in yet another promotional effort, was as in an overcrowded nursery "where a
few men flourish that are best grounded in their estates, or best
furnished with abilities, or best fitted with opportunities, and
the rest waxe weake and languish, as wanting roome and
meanes to nourish them." The result was not only the stifling
of talent and ambition but the corruption of human relationships growing out of competition for limited resources. "The
straitness of the place is such," wrote Robert Cushman in a
promotional pamphlet for Plymouth, "as each man is fain to
pluck his means, as it were, out of his neighbor's throat."[11] For
the migrants, or at least for those who spoke to them and for
them in print, economic and demographic conditions were the
cause of spiritual alienation.

By the same token, New England promised the godly an
escape from corruption and an opportunity to practice their
callings in a benevolent setting. "If the Lord seeth it wilbe
good for us," John Winthrop, the future governor of Massachusetts Bay, assured his wife, Margaret, a year before his departure, "he will provide a shelter and a hidinge place for us
and ours." Robert Cushman drew the conclusion more bluntly:
"Let us not thus oppress, straiten, and afflict one another," he
counseled, "but seeing there is a spacious land, the way to
which is through the sea, we will end this difference in a day."
Colonization provided the cure for both material and spiritual
ills. "The husbanding of unmanured grounds, and shifting into
empty Lands, enforceth men to frugalitie, and quickeneth in-
vention," wrote John White, ". . . and the taking of large
Countreys presents a naturall remedy against covetousnesse,
fraud, and violence; when every man may enjoy enough without wrong or injury to his neighbour."[12] The new lands promised not only personal redemption for every Puritan migrant
but collective redemption through an end to the conditions
which set saints against one another.

In order to succeed, however, colonies would have to discourage the migration of those who contributed to disorder
and anarchy at home. Referring to the kind of settlers who presumably brought about early Jamestown's repeated break-
downs, the promoters of Plymouth and Massachusetts Bay
made it clear that their colonies were not fit for the poor, the
lazy, the unskilled, and the seekers of strictly worldly riches—
by which they meant those who did not share their religious
and communal goals. Indeed Thomas Dudley felt compelled
in 1631 to counter Francis Higginson's lavish praise of the
Massachusetts Bay soil two years earlier out of concern that
Higginson was raising unwarranted expectations and attracting the wrong kind of people. Other writers, contemporary
with Higginson and earlier in Plymouth, had warned the pur-
suers of purely material comforts that New England would not
prove hospitable. These writers implied that such individuals
would find the political as well as the physical climate incompatible. It was Edward Winslow who put Puritan goals most
succinctly when he stated that New England was for those in
whom "religion and profit jump together."[13] The ideal settler
was one who entertained altruistic and self-serving motives
simultaneously, one for whom public and private interests
were indistinguishable.

Colonial recruiters recognized that the kind of settler they
sought would have a direct impact on English relations with
the natives. In articulating that impact they followed the precedent established in the design of the first "New England" by
the non-Puritan John Smith. Virginia had taught Smith that
a colony would not succeed when peopled with immigrants
whose selfishness was not tempered by virtue, courage, hard
work, and piety. He thus made his pitch to the ambitious but
constricted farmers and artisans of England and appealed to
their highest ideals. Such men would establish a new foundation not only for their descendants but for humanity. They

would advance the cause of their country, provide honorable relief for the poor, and help to end ignorance and injustice. Smith also appealed to the independent smallholder's characteristic combination of piety and rational calculation in urging the natives' conversion to Christianity. If a colonist possessed any "graine of faith or zeale in Religion," Smith noted, he would find his missionary "labors with discretion will triple requite [his] charge and paines." But Smith made no mention of an organized program manned by clergymen; rather he suggested that the mere example of virtuous colonists (within a context of military domination) would suffice to awaken the Indians' desire for the Word and for assurance regarding their salvation.[14]

The second and third "New England," as imagined by the early Puritan promoters and leaders, were in many respects like that of Smith. These designs too stressed the need for hardworking, self-sufficient individuals as opposed to the idle rich and idle poor. Like Smith's proposals (and like those of colonial advocates dating back a half-century), the Puritan colonies—especially Massachusetts Bay—were expected to solve the problems of overpopulation, underemployment, and land shortage in England and the alienation of the "industrious sort" that resulted. There were two conspicuous differences between these later visions of New England and Smith's. One was the Puritans' emphasis on the covenants as the basis for social and political organization and for the collective identity and purpose of the saints. The other was the relative absence of Indians in the Puritans' utopia due to the depopulation that had occurred since Smith's time.

The epidemic of 1616-18 had, in a literal way, prepared the coastal region for settlement. It had wiped out the entire village of Patuxet so that the Plymouth colonists found, in one leader's words, "none to hinder our possession, or to lay claim unto it." Moreover the Indians positively welcomed the En-

glish, not only because there was more land than they needed
but because, in the future missionary John Eliot's words, "we
are as walls to them from their bloody [Micmac] enemies, and
. . . also they have many more comforts by us." It is not surprising that the Puritan penchant for discovering God's hidden
purposes in anything remarkable was exercised extensively to
explain the epidemic and the amicable relations that prevailed
in most (though not all) of the earliest native-settler contacts.
Colonial spokesmen maintained that only Divine Providence
preserved the earliest settlers from attacks by the weak but
fearsome natives. "If God had let them loose," wrote Edward
Winslow of the surviving remnants near Plymouth, "they might
easily have swallowed us up." Instead he possessed their "hearts
. . . with astonishment and fear of us." The first settlers at
Dorchester in 1630 had the same experience. Numbering "not
above ten," according to the account of one of them, they were
approached by "some hundreds" of Indians (a doubtful figure
in post-epidemic Massachusetts Bay). But instead of permitting
an attack, "God caused the Indians to help us with fish at very
cheap rates."[15]

The depopulation and generally weakened condition of the
Indians provided powerful reinforcement for the legal justifi-
cations which colonial leaders employed to support their claims
to, and occupation of, Indian land. They argued, to begin with,
that they were obeying the Biblical injunction to "be fruitful,
and multiply, and replenish the earth, and subdue it," and the
pronouncement that while the heavens are God's, "the earth
hath he given to the children of men." Beyond that, and more
specifically, they cited the doctrine, recently emergent in international law, of *vacuum domicilium*. As spelled out by Winthrop in 1629, this doctrine distinguished between two cate-
gories of right to the earth, natural and civil: "The first right
was naturall when men held the earth in common, every man
sowing and feeding where he pleased: Then, as men and

cattell increased, they appropriated some parcells of ground by enclosing and peculiar [particular] manurance, and this in tyme got them a civil right." While the second, civil stage of this evolutionary process might seem to apply equally to Indian and English agriculture, such was not the interpretation of the colonial spokesmen. "The Indians," declared Francis Higginson, "are not able to make use of the one-fourth part of the land, neither have they any settled places, as towns to dwell in, nor any ground as they challenge for their own possession but change their habitation from place to place." And Robert Cushman noted that "their land is spacious and void, and there are few and [they] do but run over the grass, as do also the foxes and wild beasts. They are not industrious, neither have [they] art, science, skill or faculty to use either the land or the commodities of it, but all spoils, rots, and is marred for want of manuring, gathering, ordering, etc." According to both Biblical and legal authority, those not "using" the land were to make way for those who would: "As the ancient patriarchs therefore removed from straiter places into more roomy, where the land lay idle, and none used it, though there dwelt inhabitants by them . . . so it is lawful now to take a land which none useth, and make use of it." New England was full of idle land and idle people. As other Puritans would later argue with respect to wealthy English landholders during the Civil War, those who did not work the land had no right to withhold it from those who would.[16]

In this rhetoric of justification, we can detect the several themes which attracted individuals to Puritanism and the New England colonies. The hunger for land, for social and cultural order through control of the environment and its non-covenanted inhabitants, and for legitimacy for their own radical undertakings was hereby rationalized and extended to the New World. Yet there was another side to Puritanism and to the ostensible purposes of colonization—namely, the fulfillment of God's will and extension of his glory. A principal component of this side was conversion of the natives to Christianity. In the ways that Puritan colonial planners—particularly in Massachusetts Bay—sought to reconcile this evangelical thrust with an otherwise exclusivist, domineering approach to Indians lay much of the uniqueness of their "errand into the wilderness."

In keeping with the utopian and voluntaristic dimensions of Puritan colonization, the promoters followed Smith in stressing the exemplary conduct of settlers rather than preaching by ministers as the principal means of conveying the message to the Indians. The Massachusetts Bay charter expressed the hope that the settlers' "good life and orderlie conversation maie wynn and incite the natives of [the] country to" Christianity. To John White, "commerce and example of our course of living, cannot but in time breed civility among them."[17] Though colonial planners fully expected education and preaching to play a role in conversion, it is clear that lay persons by their very carriage were expected to provide the impetus. This expectation underlay the illustration in the colony's earliest seals, which depicted an Indian pleading, "come over and help us" (fig. 6).

To Puritan leaders there was no conflict between their claims to Indian land and their expectations of converting Indians, any more than there was conflict between the settlers' desires for economic independence and for piety. Each was integral to the other. The leaders did, however, acknowledge that land hunger, especially when combined with Indian vulnerability, threatened to drive a wedge between material and spiritual goals to the detriment of the latter. They said as much in their remarks about the land shortage in England and repeated it with respect to New England. Indeed they sometimes implied that the godly example sought in the settlers' behavior was as much a means of restraining the English as of converting the

Figure 6. Representation of the early Massachusetts Bay colony seal, depicting an Indian pleading, "Come over and help us." Some early colonial writers and leaders confidently anticipated an Indian population waiting to receive Christianity and English domination and a settler population ready to impart these by godly example. *Courtesy of Massachusetts Archives, Office of the Secretary of State, Commonwealth of Massachusetts.*

Indians. This was suggested, for example, by the Bay Company directors in 1629 when they instructed John Endicott, as leader of their vanguard expedition, to "have a diligent & watchful eye over our owne people, that they . . . demeane themselves justlye & curteous towards" the Indians. It was made more explicit by Edward Winslow who, reflecting on Virginia and Wessagusset, noted "what great offense hath been given by many profane men, who being but seeming Christians, have made Christ and Christianity stink in the nostrils of the poor infidels."[18]

The need to restrain the settlers' more selfish proclivities sprang from a recognition of the potential repercussions, both in England and among the natives, of a policy of indulgence. Massachusetts Bay's claims to represent the realm were undermined by its tendencies toward religious and political separatism, symbolized by the leaders' decision to take the colony charter with them to Boston. The charter's validity was challenged by Sir Ferdinando Gorges, who revived his claims to all of New England during the 1630s. In this delicate situation, the colonists could not afford to draw additional attention to themselves by arousing discontent among the Indians and/or by demonstrating an inability to master them easily. Though the Massachusett and Pawtucket posed little direct threat themselves, they were on good terms with the powerful Narragansett, who were in turn allied for purposes of trade with the Dutch. The lack of a carefully rationalized policy toward Indians and Indian land could conceivably lead to a diplomatic crisis or, if the Dutch were not involved, to an Indian uprising such as that in Virginia which resulted in more than three hundred English deaths in 1622. Either outcome would not only weaken the colony internally but strengthen the arguments of its enemies in England. For these reasons, the Massachusetts Bay Company was willing to overlook its legal principles for the sake of expediency and purchase land from any Indians who "pretend" to have title so as to "avoyde the least scruple of intrusion." At the same time, with a direct reference to Virginia, the Directors cautioned Endicott "not to bee too confident of the fidellitie of the salvages. . . . And as wee are commanded to be innocent as doves, soe withall wee [are enjoined to be] wise as serpents."[19] Legal nicety backed by military force constituted the colony's approach to establishing its legitimacy in the face of potentially destructive forces within and without.

But even if the colony averted a crisis severe enough to threaten its existence or its autonomy, Massachusetts Bay's self-proclaimed role as a revolutionary commonwealth with a divine mission placed a high premium on the suppression or sublimation of private interests within its own ranks. As Winthrop reminded his fellow *Arbella* passengers during the 1630 migration, "wee must Consider that wee shall be as a Citty upon a Hill, the eies of all people are uppon us."[20] For this reason, the competitiveness that had prevailed in England had now to be subordinated to a covenant among saints founded on Christian love. Here was the keystone in the design of the third New England. Winthrop did not suggest that self-interest would disappear in this New England: on the contrary, his address evinced an acute awareness of the difficulties of reconciling private ends with those of the community and with New England's cosmic mission. But he assumed at bottom that the migrants shared his vision of the "Citty upon a hill" in which their role would be to subordinate personal rewards and gratification to the fulfillment of God's will as interpreted by himself and a few others who had been especially called for that purpose. Aboard the *Arbella*, Winthrop—ever the country gentleman and lawyer—remained unable or unwilling to acknowledge the motives propelling the "industrious sort" toward Puritanism and New England. All this changed once he disembarked and assumed the duties of magistrate.

The South part of New-England, as it is Planted this yeare, 1634.

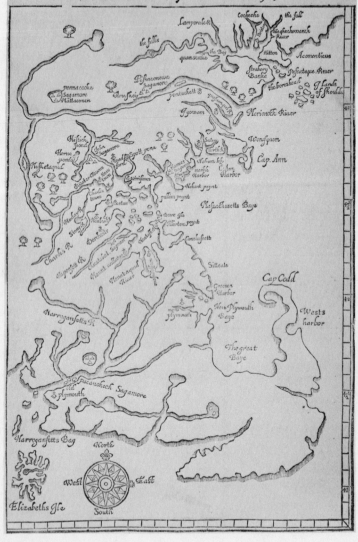

Indians in the "Citty"

Between 1630 and 1633, approximately 3000 settlers poured into Massachusetts Bay to establish their farms, churches, and towns. Already outnumbered by English settlers, the 200 Massachusett and Pawtucket who had survived a decade and a half of epidemics and of Micmac and Plymouth raids were now overwhelmed (see fig. 7).[21] As John Winthrop rightly foresaw before leaving England, the Indians would represent little threat to the colonists for "there are not so many of them in 20: miles compasse as wilbe of us." The terrorizing effects of the raids, plus the overwhelming numbers and close proximity of the English, left the surviving bands of Pawtucket (often called "Aberginians" by contemporaries) and Massachusett with even less room to maneuver or resist than their Plymouth area counterparts had enjoyed a decade earlier. As early Massachusetts Bay writers frequently pointed out, the natives welcomed the colonists as protectors.[22] At Salem, only two or three Pawtucket families remained where the large village noted by John Smith had formerly stood. Mascononomo of Agawam (later Ipswich) personally welcomed the colony's new governor, John Winthrop, upon his arrival in 1630. The Pawtucket followers of Nanepashemet and his widow, the "Squaw Sachem," were concentrated in two villages, each headed by one of their sons: Wonohaquaham (soon renamed Sagamore

Figure 7. A map of "New England's Prospect." By identifying the 13 English towns and the remaining three Indian villages (the latter each represented by a trio of triangles) around Massachusetts Bay, William Wood's map graphically points up the demographic dimension of colonization there. William Wood, *New Englands Prospect* (London, 1634). *Courtesy of Chapin Library, Williams College, Williamstown, Mass.*

John) resided on the Mystic River while Monowampate (later Sagamore James) lived on the Saugus. John in particular became a close and important friend of the English. According to Thomas Dudley, the brothers commanded thirty to forty men between them. On the south side of Massachusetts Bay, Chickataubut and his fifty to sixty Massachuset followers, despite their continued enmity toward Plymouth, paid tribute to the new colony soon after the 1630 contingent had settled.[23]

The demographic disparity enabled the colony to acquire its dominant role without exercising any real initiative. In August 1631 the Micmac attacked Agawam while Mascononomo was entertaining his Pawtucket allies. The raiders killed seven, wounded many more, including Mascononomo and Sagamores John and James, and captured James's wife. Those who could escaped to the nearby English settlement, where the Micmac forbore chasing them. Though the English remained strictly passive, their mere presence proved sufficient to deter the invaders then and thereafter. The Micmac never again attacked below the Merrimack.[24]

Though the colony's magistrates were under instructions to purchase title to any land that was claimed by the natives before granting it to towns or directly to individuals, no such claims appear to have been advanced before 1633. On the contrary, the earliest towns appear to have been occupied with native consent. The natives presumably granted these rights of occupancy in order to secure the protection they so badly needed. Having learned nothing yet of English concepts of title and sovereignty, they were in no position to raise the objections anticipated in the Company's instructions or to foresee the interpretation the colonists would place on the absence of such objections. As a result, the English of Massachusetts Bay were able to establish their first settlements without acknowledging the existence of native sovereignty or title.[25]

The Indians' trade-off between land and protection illustrates, far more effectively than the verbal testimony, the relative balance of power and wealth between themselves and the newcomers. The same balance is apparent in other early exchanges of goods and services. As before the Puritans arrived, the most important trade items were corn and furs. When he arrived in 1629, Francis Higginson found one English trader who had recently paid six shillings and eight pence for some seed corn, the yield of which he traded to some Indians for a quantity of beaver skins that netted him a clear profit of £327 on the London market. Though obliged to purchase corn from the Indians on Cape Cod that winter, the new colony had to restrain some of its profit-minded members who sought to trade their corn rations to other Indians in exchange for beaver pelts. While making inroads, items of European manufacture do not appear to have become objects of irreversible dependence among the natives before or during the early years of the Great Migration. As seen in the previous chapter, Bradford's hysteria about Morton's supplying the Indians around Massachusetts Bay with guns was an exaggeration; indeed, the earliest settlers there reported no weapons more potent than bows with brass-tipped arrows. That other staple of the North American trade, alcohol, had made its appearance during the 1620s and remained despite colonial laws against it. However, none of the evidence suggests that its consumption by Indians had become extensive or raised dangers for the English. The Massachusett and Pawtucket primarily sought the usual metal tools, and many of them expressed preferences for English cloth. Some also furnished labor to the English. As early as 1631, the colony's Court of Assistants, as the body of magistrates was now called, expressed alarm at the proliferation of Indian servants among the settlers, and ordered that all such arrangements must have the Court's approval. Indians also helped kill wolves near the settlements before bounties were suspended in 1632.[26] Though the Indians could hardly be said to have become dependent on the supply of English goods by 1633, two important patterns can be discerned in these earliest exchanges that pointed in that direction. One is the appearance of Indian land and labor as commodities of exchange, sure signs that other native resources were diminishing. The other is the colony's difficulty in regulating the economic activities of its own members, a difficulty that was rooted in the composition and motives of the settler population.

The imbalance of power and resources was also apparent in the early legal relationships established between the colony and local Indians. Beginning with the Company's instructions of 1629, the colony took its sovereignty and legal-judicial authority over the Massachusett and Pawtucket for granted. But rather than announce to the Indians through proclamation or treaty that it was assuming such sovereignty, the colony allowed its position to emerge implicitly from the laws and judicial decisions that it made. Thus the General Court, consisting of Deputies elected by the "freemen" (adult male church members), and Court of Assistants resolved disputes and administered justice in cases involving both Indians and English, as they did for cases in which no Indians were involved. The thrust of these actions was to keep the two peoples apart as much as possible. Following Plymouth's lead, the Company's original instructions advised Endicott that "for the avoyding of the hurt that may follow through over much familiaritie with the Indians, wee conceive it fitt that they bee not permitted to come to your plantation but at certain tymes and places to be appointed them." But the two colonies' approaches differed because of both numbers and geographic distance. Plymouth was dealing with a series of native communities which together outnumbered it, while the Bay Colony held an easy numerical preponderance over the local Indians. On the other hand Plymouth's nearest neighbor was fourteen miles away, while several Bay Colony towns were immediately adjacent to those of Indians. Thus Plymouth dealt diplomatically and militarily with tributary "allies," while Massachusetts Bay administered justice to domesticated subjects. The latter colony, therefore, not only took steps to regulate economic and social contacts between the two peoples, it also protected Indians from, and compensated them for, various kinds of depredations by settlers, including theft and arson.[27]

The natives quickly learned that they would have to modify some of their ways in order to live near the English, even on a segregated basis. In particular, the incursions of free-roaming English livestock into Indian cornfields provided an ironic comment on the rationalizations of the English that they were stable horticulturalists while the Indians primarily roamed and hunted oblivious to notions of territoriality. In one long-running case, Chickataubut and Sagamore John were repeatedly haled into court for the revenge their followers took against invading livestock. In the end, Sagamore John and his band were ordered to fence their gardens, though this did not prevent further incursions.[28]

As the livestock cases illustrate, Massachusetts Bay, like Plymouth, placed responsibility for native "offenses" on the sachems. Sachems were required to bring their offending followers to court to make restitutions for any property damage the latter inflicted and to administer punishments in the form of beatings.[29] Though sachems traditionally administered justice in extreme cases by beating, they did so to satisfy the wronged members of other families or bands. In this way, they restored peace and equilibrium between the parties. Justice, or the revenge that followed in its absence, was part of the system of reciprocities that held the world of autonomous bands together. In administering their justice through the sachems, the colonies helped preserve the band structure but with results that were anything but traditional. For in performing their assigned roles, the sachems did not restore a balance

between the parties but reinforced their bands' subordination
to the English.

In the opinion of one Englishman, the Indians' various ad-
justments to the English presence were working in their favor.
Indeed for William Wood, who lived in the Bay Colony from
1629 to 1633, the Pawtucket "Aberginians" were the more noble
for being weaker and more accommodating to the English than
other natives. Among Indians in and around New England,
Wood reported, the Mohawk exceeded all in savagery because
of their reputed cannibalism. Only slightly less depraved were
the Micmac "Tarrenteens," who were not cannibals but whose
excessive cruelty toward the "Aberginians" Wood attributed to
French corruption. Then came the Bay Colony's nearer neighbors, the "stately, warlike" Pequot and the enterprising, peaceful Narragansett—both powerful yet (contrary to most English accounts, earlier and later) both friendly toward the
colonists. But highest in Wood's estimation were the "lusty,"
"affable" Indians around Massachusetts Bay. Wood dwelt at
length on the physical and emotional health of these natives
(despite the earlier epidemics), on the lack of crime and violence within their ranks, and on their unswerving loyalty to
the English. Moreover, he implied, the Company's injunction
to win and incite the natives to Christianity by example was
being followed successfully. The Indians had accepted the
superiority of English technology and had already "a little de-
generated from some of their lazy customs and show[n] themselves more industrious." By the same token, the customary
habit of beseeching Hobbamock (termed "Abbamacho" by
Wood) when Kiehtan was inaccessible was giving way to an
active interest in Christianity.[30] For Wood, "New England's
prospect" was one of native-settler cooperation based on mutual trust and a benevolent English hegemony.

In what would prove to be a characteristic tendency in the
thinking of those who foresaw such cooperation, Wood's opti-

mism was rooted in an obliviousness to the anxieties and concerns of his fellow English. More typical was the reaction of
John Pond, a servant of Winthrop's, who wrote home to his father a few months after arriving: "They are a crafty people and
they will cozen and cheat, and they are a subtle people." Crafty,
subtle personalities and the culture that nourished them were
sources of fear from which the settlers sought to distance themselves even when enjoying every material advantage. Though
lacking a William Bradford to articulate its fears of cultural
amalgamation, the Bay Colony's own most prominent early
governor, John Winthrop, betrayed similar anxieties when he
prevented an Indian woman from entering what was probably
her menstrual hut, which he had occupied after getting lost
in the woods. Though written with his characteristic detach-
ment, Winthrop's action suggests an irrational fear at sharp
variance from the cool, rational temperament generally encountered in descriptions of him.[31] The first few years also witnessed the colonists' haste in ridding themselves of any suggestion of dependence upon, and acculturation to, native ways.
We have seen how Plymouth abandoned Indian corn and cultivation techniques as soon as more familiar grains and plows
became available. Tobacco growing and consumption by settlers were outlawed from the beginning in Massachusetts Bay.
After English attempts to fashion wigwams in advance of the
arrival of building materials resulted in repeated fires, wigwams were officially outlawed there too.[32] From the very beginning of contact, the colony sought to maintain cultural distinctions between its settlers and the natives.

As in Plymouth, the relationship between the two peoples
was defined primarily by the colony's military superiority.
Though Massachusetts Bay had other enemies to worry about,
it was the Indians who directly inspired the formation of the
colony's militia. In their instructions, the Bay Company had
reminded Endicott of the duplicity displayed by the Indians in

Virginia when they arose and attacked their English "friends" in 1622. For the next several years the colony oscillated between a sense of security engendered by the Indians' obviously weak position and lack of hostility, and occasional periods of panic arising from rumors of an Indian "conspiracy" against the English. Charlestown erected a fortress in 1630 on the strength of such a rumor. Yet the town's own records indicated that the design was directed exclusively at Plymouth, suggesting the resurgence of Chickataubut's grievance against that colony. There were echoes of Wessagusset in the town's fear that Indian hostility toward any English represented a conspiracy against all. Though mandated in the 1629 instructions, the Massachusetts Bay militia was only formed two years later, after a settler's shot at some wolves one night sent the entire colony into a panic. Yet the training of militia units discouraged neither English oscillation between apathy and panic nor the Indian gatherings that fed the panic, so that in the minds of the colony's watchful leaders, Massachusetts remained unprepared for a possible attack in late 1632.[33] Three and a half years of domination had not brought stability or ease to the colony's relationship with the Indians.

A Question of Title

These tensions suggested that Wood's optimism about the future of Indian-English relations was unfounded even as he set sail for England in 1633 to publish his book. A series of events later that year destroyed whatever basis remained for such hopes. First a drought brought severe food shortages to both Indian and English and ended—as it appeared to both parties—only when the God of the English responded to their prayers by sending rain.[34] Then came New England's second major virgin soil epidemic, this time of smallpox but as deadly as the plague of a decade and a half earlier. Like the earlier epidemic it spared the immune English while wreaking havoc among the natives. Beginning around Massachusetts Bay, the smallpox epidemic spread over all New England, striking both the Abenaki to the north and east and the Narragansett and other groups south and west. Eventually it spread up the Connecticut River and into the St. Lawrence Valley.[35] Though no reliable figures on casualties are available, except the general impression that "most" of the Indians around Massachusetts Bay died, three significant deaths were those of the leading sachems, Chickataubut and Sagamores John and James. On their deathbeds the Pawtucket brothers converted to Christianity, and John left his two sons in the care of the leading Puritan minister and magistrate respectively. How many additional conversions were effected by the outbreak is uncertain, but a number of Indians followed the sachems' lead and left their children with English families in hopes of saving them. Only three of these children survived. Once again, an epidemic was fraught with supernatural implications for all concerned. The natives saw an additional proof of the English God's power, while the English again assumed that Divine Providence was working in their favor.[36]

Given the proclivity of both peoples to understand patterns of fortune and misfortune—including virgin soil epidemics—in supernatural terms, these interpretations were characteristic. Besides the plague epidemic of 1616-18, the survivors must have recalled the less extensive epidemic of 1622 which struck some of their Cape Cod neighbors after they had defied Plymouth. For the Massachusett and Pawtucket, too, had recently begun acting as if they considered themselves independent. Without the epidemic, according to the Charlestown records, the hundreds of English settlers who poured in annually "would with much more difficulty have found room, and at far greater charge have obtained and purchased land." The suggestion that settlers might have had to purchase land from

the natives marks a break from the latter's previous acquies-
cence in the English presence. According to Edward Johnson,
the Indians had actually begun to "quarrell with them about
their bounds of Land" until the epidemic put an end to the
issue. And Winthrop wrote Sir Simonds D'Ewes in the following year that by this epidemic "God hath hereby cleared our
title to this place."[37] As these glimpses suggest, whatever land
had been, from a native perspective, rendered surplus by the
epidemic of 1616-18 was gone by 1633 and, for the first time,
the issues of boundaries and the purchase of title were being
raised.

The precise manner and sequence in which the land issue
arose are obscured by the same absence of documentation
that clouds most aspects of the Bay Colony's first half-decade.
There is, however, fragmentary evidence to suggest that some
colonists were purchasing land directly from Indians, a proce-
dure that undermined the land-granting authority claimed by
the colony on the basis of its royal patent, and the colony's
subordinate land-granting units, the towns. The most prominent figure in the surviving evidence is Poquanum, a minor sachem of the Pawtucket residing on Nahant Neck and known
to the English as "Black William" or "Duke William." Soon
after settlers began moving onto the Neck in 1629, he made
separate agreements with two (and perhaps more) of them in
which each Englishman thought he had acquired rights to the
peninsula as a whole, one for a suit of clothes, the second for
two pestle stones. Yet William Wood, a Saugus resident and
close acquaintance of the first purchaser, Thomas Dexter,
touted "Black William" in his *New Englands Prospect* as having given the Neck "in general to this plantation of Saugus so
that no other can appropriate it to himself." The motives and
intentions of the parties to these transactions are not spelled
out in the records that survive. Presumably the town intervened to obtain its own grant from the sachem as a means of

reasserting its land-granting authority in the face of eager Indian sellers and English buyers. The General Court took the same step at the colony level in March 1634 when it outlawed private purchases of Indian land without its prior approval. Just how unique Poquanum was in this period is unclear. The only other definite reference to a pre-epidemic private transaction appears in 1635, when the Court of Assistants was trying to determine the boundaries of a tract that Chickataubut had sold to William Pynchon of Roxbury. Even this fragmentary evidence suggests the existence of an effort by Indians, the content and dimensions of which are now obscure, to establish some kind of title to lands for which settlers would have to pay. By eliminating the three leading political figures, as well as a substantial portion of the population, the 1633 epidemic effectively weakened this movement.[38]

Meanwhile the cause of Indian title was acquiring a powerful, articulate ally. It was the same year—1633—that the radical separatist Roger Williams first confronted the colony on the validity of its occupation of Indian lands. Arriving in Boston in February 1631, Williams almost immediately caused the first of many stirs by refusing the Boston church's call to its ministry because its members refused to repent for having worshiped in the Church of England before migrating. Within two months he accepted instead a call from Salem, where Separatist tendencies were strong. Here he expanded his criticism of the nascent "New England Way" to argue that a true separation of church and state would preclude secular magistrates from punishing the spiritual offenses of the First Table of the Decalogue. For this he drew his first official notice, a letter from Governor Winthrop and the Court of Assistants to Salem magistrate John Endicott, advising that the congregation consult with the Court (another intrusion of state upon church) before proceeding with Williams's appointment.[39]

Winthrop and the Assistants were apparently successful for

the time being. In any event, Williams had moved by late 1631
to Plymouth, where, as a layman, he assisted another former
Salem minister, Ralph Smith, by prophesying. But preaching
to English Puritans was rapidly losing its appeal for Williams.
His disgust with the compromising of the spirit, even in ostensibly Separatist Plymouth Colony, was alienating him from the
worldly religion emerging in Puritan New England. In his relentless exploration of personal and intellectual alternatives to
compromise, he encountered the natives of the Narragansett
Bay region, both the Pokanoket allies of Plymouth and their
Narragansett enemies. With these encounters began Williams's
immersion in Indian culture. He initially approached the natives as a missionary. "I am no Elder in any church," he wrote
Winthrop in mid-1632, ". . . nor ever shall be, if the Lord
please to grant my desires that I may intend what I long after,
the Natives Soules." And recalling his experiences forty years
later, Williams noted that he had possessed not only "a constant zealous desire to dive into the Indian language" but "a
painful Patient spirit to lodge with them, in their filthy smoke
holes (even while I lived at Plymouth and Salem) to gain
their tongue." By his own account, he "could debate with them
in a great measure in their own Language." Discreetly omitting
the name of the controversial Williams, Wood optimistically
noted in his 1634 tract that "one of the English Preachers . . .
hath spent much time in attaining to their language, wherein
he is so good a proficient that he can speak to their understanding, and they to his, much loving him and respecting him
for his love and counsel."[40] In short, Williams had undertaken
what Massachusetts Bay, Plymouth, and even Ma-re Mount
had all professed as a goal but never put into practice: the conversion of the native population to Christianity.

In August 1633, Williams left Plymouth to return to Salem.
His reasons for departing are not spelled out in the surviving
evidence. We have only Bradford's comment that "he this year

began to fall into some strange opinions, and from opinions to practice, which caused some controversy between the church and him." After "some discontent on his part," Bradford continued, Williams "left them something abruptly." Bradford also wrote that the Plymouth brethren advised their Salem counterparts "concerning him and what care they ought to have of him." These remarks might suggest that Williams's quarrel with Plymouth was strictly a church affair. Yet Williams had hardly re-established himself at Salem when he received a request from Winthrop for a tract he had written "for the private satisfaction" of the Governor and Council at Plymouth. The tract's principal argument was that the royal patent did not entitle English colonists to Indian land and that such land had to be purchased from the natives themselves. Though seemingly a secular issue, the patent argument, as Williams soon developed it at Salem, was not divorced from church practices. For while there, Williams hammered frequently in his sermons on the sinfulness of the patent and conducted days of public humiliation among his parishioners for their having used it to usurp land from the natives.[41] Thus it would appear that the patent issue was what divided Williams from the Plymouth church.

There was, of course, a difference between merely purchasing Indian title and acknowledging that title as having equal weight with the king's sovereignty. As we have seen, the Massachusetts Bay Company intended from the beginning to purchase title from any Indians who "pretend right of inheritance . . . that wee may avoyde the least scruple of intrusion." The distinction between an expedient purchase and a principled one may have been on Bradford's mind when he noted that although he had had to warn Salem about Williams's excesses, "I still bless God and am thankful to him even for his sharpest admonitions and reproofs so far as they agreed with truth." For at about the time that Williams penned his treatise, Plym-

outh entered the trade sweepstakes in the Connecticut River
Valley by purchasing title to a tract there from a sachem
named Natawanute. This sachem claimed that he and his
band had recently been driven from their village on the river
by the Pequot, who then "sold" title to a plot there to the
Dutch West India Company. As will be explained more fully
in the next chapter, Plymouth made its move to counter this
and another recent purchase of Indian land by which the
Dutch might have laid claim to sovereignty over the entire
Connecticut River Valley. Though none of the extant sources
credit Williams with a direct role, his hand is evident not only
in the timing but in the knowledge (afforded by his relationship with the Narragansett) of native politics and of Indian-
Dutch relations reflected in the purchase. Also telling is Plymouth's shrewd dismissal of the Dutch claim on the grounds that
it was obtained from an unjust conqueror.[42] Indeed it is not too
much to suggest that Williams penned his tract to assist the
magistrates in dealing with this complicated theoretical problem. They drew from it what they needed but shrank from
Williams's suggestions that the land they already presided over
had been illegally and sinfully seized and occupied.

Because Williams's tract was condemned by the Massachusetts magistrates and righteously burned, we know its contents
only from the discussions of them that survive. For Winthrop,
the tract was offensive principally because it repudiated the
royal patent as the basis for Massachusetts Bay's claimed title
and jurisdiction. Williams wrote at a time when the Crown was
acutely concerned with the colony's *de facto* separation from
the realm, a reality that the magistrates and clergy were trying
to paper over by emphasizing the colony's *de jure* nonseparation
from both church and state in England; thus the magistrates'
sensitivity when Williams accused the king of blasphemy and
identified him with the cause of Babylon for claiming to act in
the name of Christendom. In urging Endicott to lead his fellow

Salem residents in a repudiation of Williams, Winthrop noted that "all Israelites (good and bad)" had been called the people of God "to distinguish them from the Heathen." And "because Baptisme was the first pub[lic]k badge whereby a Christian was distinguished from a Pagan," it followed that nations practicing baptism had inherited Israel's mantle. Thus Winthrop was led to a remarkable conclusion for a Calvinist to come to while the Thirty Years War was raging in Europe—that a nation was Christian when it did no more than "professeth the Faith of Jesus Christ (be it in trueth or not)."[43] What Winthrop was desperately trying to stave off was Williams's relentless pursuit of separatist logic, which demanded that true Christians renounce any exercise of political authority or aggression in the name of God or of things spiritual. Williams's argument not only struck at the ideological heart of the colony's purpose and existence but implied that Christians and heathen were alike in all matters non-spiritual, including politics, economics, and culture. While Puritans in England (and Williams) increasingly saw the world as divided between the forces of Christ and Antichrist, Winthrop minimized this division in favor of that between Christian and heathen.

Winthrop avoided confronting Williams's implication of Indian-European equality, in part because his temperamental devotion to hierarchy could not abide it (he was as shocked by Williams's boldness in making his charges as by their content) and also because the patent issue required the most immediate attention in view of Charles I's concerns for the colony's status. But the Boston clergyman John Cotton noted that Williams's argument for the purchase of title ranged beyond the patent to include a second line of attack on the doctrine of *vacuum domicilium,* one that arose from first-hand experience with Indians. Williams pointed out that while the natives cultivated only a small portion of their land, they used virtually all of it for hunting. And, "for the expedition of their hunting voyages,"

they burned the underbrush annually or semiannually. If the
English were entitled to these hunting lands, then the Indians
were equally entitled to the great hunting parks of the English
Crown and nobility. Here was an argument based not, like that
of the Massachusetts Bay elite, upon the abstractions of international law but upon direct ethnographic observation. Williams recognized that Indian hunting and burning were not
the random activities assumed in the law of *vacuum domicilium*
but systematic, rational uses of land in the same sense that
cultivation was for Europeans. Moreover, the natives of southern New England were partially dependent on hunting for
their livelihoods. Because they used their land as fully as English farmers did theirs, "no man might lawfully invade their
Propriety."[44] In dealing with Indians, then, colonists had to
shed those prerogatives claimed on the basis of links not only
with Christendom but with England. As a secular political
principle, sovereignty was common to all peoples who exercised territoriality and was inviolate. For this reason, Williams
could advise Plymouth that title purchased from Natawanute
would be superior to that of the Dutch, purchased as theirs
was from the Pequot. But the same logic that made the Pequot
and Dutch usurpers on the Connecticut made the English
usurpers in Massachusetts Bay.

For the moment, Williams deferred to the magistrates' wishes
that he cease speaking out on the patent and even consented
to having his tract burned. But the General Court was not taking any chances. Sensing that Indian title purchase was an idea
whose time had come, it moved at its next session to halt the
most subversive aspect of such purchases by requiring that
they have the Court's prior approval. Meanwhile, Williams
expanded his contacts and familiarity with Indians. At Salem
(as probably earlier at Plymouth), he established himself as a
trader and did extensive business with the natives, an occupation that undoubtedly heightened his appreciation of the im-

portance of Indian hunting. This activity extended to his Pokanoket and Narragansett friends, from whom he obtained several tracts of land in 1634 and 1635. A mark of Williams's further "Indianization" is that he never viewed these transactions as purchases on his part but as the exchange of "gifts" in accordance with traditional native practice.[45]

In November 1634 the Massachusetts Bay magistrates learned that Williams "had broken his promise to us" in resuming his speaking out against the patent, this time in the form of a letter addressed directly to Charles I. Now the magistrates began a concerted effort to root out Salem's separatist tendencies once and for all, the end result of which was the banishment of Williams from the colony on pain of death in January 1636. Though dissuaded from sending his letter to the king and though punished obtensibly for his views on church governance rather than on the patent, Williams never doubted that it was the latter issue that had led to his expulsion.[46] Before he could be shipped off to England, he made his way to Narragansett Bay and the lands he had obtained from his friends there.

Throughout the period during which the Williams controversy waned and waxed, Massachusetts Bay moved toward greater regulation of its Indian population. As we have seen, the General Court outlawed the kind of private transactions that had led to the pre-epidemic agitation and to which Williams had lent his implicit, if not explicit, support. But at the same time it encouraged towns and prominent individuals to purchase what amounted to Indian quit-claims. During the decade following the act's passage (and beginning while Williams was still at Salem), payments were made to the Squaw Sachem and her Pawtucket followers by the towns of Cambridge, Charlestown, and Concord; to Mascononomo and the Agawam Pawtucket by Ipswich; and to the Massachusett under Cutshamekin, brother and successor to Chickataubut, by

Boston and Charlestown. These payments were for tracts *previously* granted to the towns by the General Court and, in most cases, already occupied and cultivated by English settlers. In a 1637 deed, for example, Mascononomo agreed to give up his claim to "the whole towne of Ipswich as far as the bounds thereof shall goe—all the woods, meadows, pastures and broken up grounds unto . . . the English there planted."[47] These deeds make clear that Massachusetts Bay's reputation for having purchased titles from Indians in the same manner as it would have done from Europeans is unjustified. Contrary to assertions by Alden T. Vaughan that the colony's purchases marked a pragmatic departure from the principles of *vacuum domilicium* and an effort to be fair to the Indians, the purchases were pragmatic adaptations of those principles to a situation in which justice was not a consideration. They were employed, as the Company's directors had anticipated in 1629, when "any of the salvages *pretend* right of inheritance to all or any part of the lands graunted in our pattent. . . ."[48]

Though the prices paid by the English for all of these purchases cannot be ascertained from surviving references, it is clear that some combination of wampum, tools, and cloth was typical. In some instances, the natives retained limited rights to use portions not contemplated for immediate occupation. For formally quitting Charlestown in 1639, the Squaw Sachem received 21 coats, 19 fathom of wampum, and three bushels of corn. In addition, her people would retain the small tract she still occupied complete with hunting, fishing, and even planting rights so long as she lived. Thereafter her survivors would be obliged to depart.[49] When this sale is placed alongside the others made by the Squaw Sachem during the late 1630s it is clear that she had sacrificed virtually the entire land base of her people. English coercion, Indian inability to conceive of populations on the English scale, and the wholesale shock of the epidemics and invasion are probably sufficient to account for the Pawtucket's and Massachusett's acceptance of such paltry returns for land which their ancestors had occupied for centuries. In addition, we must remember that the Indians involved had been brought up to think of exchanges of goods as the sealing of friendships and alliances, not as means of gaining exclusive possession and profits. Still, questions remain as to how the natives viewed these purchases. What is most obvious is that they were receiving for their land precisely the same kinds of goods that they had been receiving for furs and corn. Scholars have often gone wrong in discussing land cessions by isolating them from the larger pattern of economic relations, when in fact land and furs were alike commodities desired by Europeans. And if we look closely at the pattern of trade in Massachusetts Bay in the early 1630s, we find that the Pawtucket and Massachusett had run out of furs to trade.

Though of peripheral interest to most settlers, the fur trade was integral to the colony's purposes. The English merchant backers of the Massachusetts Bay Company, like their Plymouth counterparts, looked to the trade as the principal source of returns on their investment. Yet within two or three years they discovered that the fur-bearing animal population near the coast had been depleted and that the rivers and streams flowing into Massachusetts Bay did not yield adequate access to the New England interior. Beginning in 1633, the colony not only expressed interest in trading on the Connecticut River and Long Island Sound (to be discussed in the next chapter) but initiated activity on the Merrimack. Winthrop understood from his Indian informants that this river, like all the major ones from the St. Lawrence to the Potomac, originated in a single "Great Lake" to the northwest. By ascending the Merrimack, he thought, Massachusetts Bay traders could intercept some of the 10,000 skins that were reaching the Dutch each year. Accordingly, Ipswich was founded in 1633 and, more critically for the future, Concord in 1635. The latter post facilitated the easy transfer of Merrimack furs to the Charles River, bypassing the longer route out the Merrimack via Ipswich and ensuring Boston's continued economic predominance. Concord also cut out a host of middleman networks in the Bay region, including not only English traders like Roger Williams in Salem but the Pawtucket as well.[50] Having been dependent on European trade for two decades, and now deprived of access to their most important ware, the Pawtucket turned increasingly to their own land, the commodity which the English coveted most. A similar pattern emerged on the south side of Massachusetts Bay. The decline of their own population and that of the animals was devastating to the Massachusett. Though they would have a political role to play in the colony's diplomacy with the Narragansett, they too had lost their economic usefulness. Around Massachusetts Bay trade had given way completely to settlement, and with it went the remaining vestiges of the natives' political and economic autonomy.

seven

LOSERS and WINNERS

As IMMIGRANTS CONTINUED to flood Massachusetts Bay after 1633, pressures for land outside the immediate environs of the Bay mounted. The attention of the most militantly discontented settlers was drawn to the west and south. As we have seen, the Dutch West India Company had monopolized trade in this region since the early 1620s. The Narragansett and Pequot, in turn, dominated the tributary systems through which commodities passed back and forth between fur- and wampum-producing Indians and floating Dutch traders. These networks now became the focus of English expansionist activity. Introducing new modes of conquest and domination to the south coast, within a decade the English utterly displaced the Pequot and effectively contained the Narragansett, in a sequence of events which marked not only the transition from trade to settlement as the shaping force in Indian-European relations in southern New England but also the resolution of economic and ideological conflicts within the English community. In the course of overriding the Pequot and Narragansett, Puritan leaders fashioned yet another model of "New England" in which they sought to reconcile Winthrop's "Citty" with the realities of geographic, political, and social atomization.

Convergence on the Connecticut

The early trade on Narragansett Bay and Long Island Sound was prosperous, but only because it existed in a political vacuum. The Dutch had no substantial military force in their colony and were thus dependent on the ability of the Narragansett and Pequot to obtain the cooperation of other native groups and, generally, to ensure stability in the trade. Though evidence on the 1620s is virtually non-existent, it is clear from what was happening during the early 1630s that the Pequot were alienating many of their tributaries as well as their Narragansett partners. But so long as the Dutch were the sole source of trade goods and so long as they supplied those goods exclusively to the Pequot, as they had since Barentsen's agreement of 1622, there was no alternative to Pequot hegemony. A large measure of the system's success, then, lay in the absence of a European rival to the Dutch with whom disaffected Indians could trade.

There was, of course, one potential rival which was well positioned to play just such a role—the Plymouth colony. But Plymouth's myopic perceptions of its interests led it to alienate the Narragansett from the start by depriving them of their Pokanoket tributary. The Narragansett's hostility toward Plymouth reinforced their ties not only to the Dutch but to Plymouth's Massachusett and Pawtucket enemies around Massachusetts Bay. When the first Puritan settlers arrived at the Bay, they feared that they would inherit this hostility. But they succeeded in establishing relationships independent of Plymouth's, not only with the local Indians but with the Narragansett. Some of the newcomers found the Narragansett-controlled trade links between Massachusetts Bay and the interior compatible with their own interests, and almost immediately began shipping goods and receiving furs through them. According to William Wood, this arrangement further enhanced the wealth of the Narragansett and their prestige among the Indians of southeastern New England.[1]

The first hint that this new relationship might affect the balance of power in the lower Connecticut River Valley came as early as April 1631, when a sachem there named Wahginnicut invited the leaders of both Massachusetts Bay and Plymouth to send settlers and traders to his territory near modern Windsor. Wahginnicut and his band would guarantee them an annual tribute of eighty beaver skins, besides what they produced and procured on their own. Pleading preoccupation with other affairs for the moment, the colonies did not accept the offer. Governors Winthrop and Bradford later learned that the band had been driven from the territory in question by the Pequot and hoped to return there with English protection. The fact that Wahginnicut appealed to the English indicates that he had fallen out with the Dutch too and that Dutch-Pequot hegemony on the Connecticut was still formally intact. But the fact that he was accompanied to Boston by Sagamore John, a friend of the Narragansett, suggests that the latter were, if not the invisible architects of the plan, by no means oblivious to its existence. More definite evidence that the Narragansett considered their interests separate from those of their Dutch and Pequot allies came three months later when their sachem Miantonomi paid a formal visit to Boston and was roundly feted by the magistrates.[2]

By spring 1632, the Narragansett had not only established cordial relations with Massachusetts Bay but had moved from a state of near war toward a rapprochement with Plymouth and their Pokanoket enemies. The occasion for war was Plymouth's placing of a trading post near the Pokanoket village on Narragansett Bay. The Narragansett responded to this incursion by chasing Massasoit and his followers into the compound and besieging them there along with Plymouth's three resident traders. Before a relief force headed by Miles Standish arrived, however, the Narragansett were diverted by the outbreak of a more serious conflict with the Pequot. The diversion was timely because it finally enabled Plymouth to achieve a truce with their powerful Narragansett neighbors. Though the sequence of events leading to the truce is not clear, it is noteworthy that it was achieved when Roger Williams was preaching to the Pokanoket, Narragansett, and Plymouth and advising the latter two.[3]

The Narragansett made peace with their neighbors to the east, therefore, as they went to war with their Pequot confederates to the west. Though contemporary European sources give no indication of the causes of the split, a significant hint is contained in testimony given by some Pequots and Narragansetts thirty years later regarding Mohegan land claims. According to the witnesses, the Mohegan were, during the early 1630s, in the process of expanding their bounds eastward to the Pequot's own and westward "almost to [the] Connecticut [River]." In so doing, they "grew so great and so proud that upon hunting they quarrelled with the Pequots." As a result, Tatobem "made war upon them" and drove their five leading sachems and the minor sachem Uncas (all of whom were sons of Tatobem's sister) into Narragansett country.[4] Though hardly a complete summary of the causes of the conflict, the testimony does indicate that in growing "proud . . . upon hunting," the Mohegan, like Wahginnicut the year before, had openly contested Pequot authority and that, in so doing, they enjoyed support from the Narragansett. This second, and even more serious, sign of a smoldering resentment against Pequot domination, along with the presence of a powerful European rival who enjoyed amicable relations with the Narragansett, threatened the Dutch West India Company's monopoly on the trade in furs and wampum. The continuation of the Pequot's special status could only bring that resentment to bear upon the Company itself, while the prospect of European rivals doomed the system whereby floating traders from Fort Orange made regular visits to their Indian customers. To ensure both their territorial claims and the steady flow of pelts, the Dutch would have to occupy the Connecticut themselves and trade directly with the local bands.

A shift in Dutch policy became apparent soon after the out-break of violence between the Pequot and the Narragansett and Mohegan in 1632. The West India Company purchased a small tract at the mouth of the Connecticut, probably from the Western Niantic, thus establishing title and occupancy in ad-vance of any English claims that might be put forward. In June 1633 it purchased a second tract near modern Hartford for a trading post, to be called—inappropriately, as it turned out—The Hope. Though the deed for this second transaction recognized the Pequot sachem Tatobem as the "owner" of the Connecticut River Valley, its effect was to annul that owner-ship around The Hope, creating a free trade zone where "all tribes of Indians shall be permitted to come freely . . . to trade with us; and [where] the enemies of the one or the other nation shall not molest each another." In other words, the Pe-quot had lost their monopoly. In exchange, they received a spool of cloth, an assortment of metal tools, and "some toys." As the description of the signing ceremony in the deed itself makes clear, this was no mere real estate sale. It was rather a treaty that established a new political arrangement among the Com-pany's Connecticut River clients. A major beneficiary was the local Sequin band. Not only were the Sequin said to be "espe-cially" satisfied with the Dutch purchase, but "at the request, and to the great joy" of themselves "and all interested tribes," they would actually reside at The Hope. The deed singled out the Narragansett from the "interested tribes" for special men-tion.[5] Thus the Dutch, with the approval of the Narragansett, the Sequin, and other local Indians, moved to establish direct control of the Connecticut River trade and to displace the Pe-quot from their favored position.

The significance of these events needs to be emphasized be-cause of the very different picture of the Pequot that appears in virtually every history written since the colonial period. Overlooking the early Dutch trade and the essentially autono-mous character of native bands in southern New England, these histories first notice the Pequot entering the Connecticut Valley (usually from the west rather than the east) and beginning their ascent there during the early 1630s. According to this interpretation, their upward trajectory was only halted by the Mohegan "secession," usually placed shortly before the English conquest of the Pequot in 1637.[6] If we examine their history more carefully, however, it becomes clear that, far from being on the rise in 1633, the Pequot had already passed their zenith.

The collapse of the Pequot-Narragansett alliance, upon which Dutch hegemony had depended, stimulated more overt interest in the Connecticut Valley on the part of the two English colonies. For Plymouth, the establishment of the Massachusetts Bay Colony had created both a rival and a barrier between itself and its Abenaki trade partners. Thus it turned westward as early as 1631, when it erected its post on Narragansett Bay, effectively nullifying its agreement of 1627 with New Netherland. The Pequot-Narragansett conflict not only ensured Plymouth's access to Narragansett Bay but emboldened the colony—as we noted in the preceding chapter, with the guidance of Roger Williams—to look directly to the Connecticut River valley. In the summer of 1633, soon after the Dutch purchased the site for The Hope, Plymouth belatedly accepted Wahginnicut's invitation, since renewed by his successor, Natawanute. Massachusetts Bay again declined because, in Winthrop's words, "the place was not fit for plantation, there being three or four thousand warlike Indians, and the river not to be gone into but by small pinnaces." So Plymouth, whose aim was trade rather than settlement, received the Bay Colony's blessing and established a post of its own. In so doing, wrote Bradford, "they brought home and restored the right sachem of the place. . . ." Bradford's words were, as usual, carefully chosen. For the Plymouth colonists maintained that the Dutch purchase was invalid because the seller had been the Pequot, an unjust conqueror. But it should be clear by now that this was an ironic twisting of what the Dutch had actually done to the Pequot. The rhetoric of justice and legitimacy was even more obviously belied by the convenient location of Natawanute's home, which was a mile and a half above The Hope at a site that would enable Plymouth's traders to intercept the rich stores of furs from the interior as they were brought downriver.[7]

In declining to join Plymouth on the Connecticut, Massachusetts Bay was indicating only that it had no intention of tying its fate to a trading post, not that it was uninterested in current developments there. Though its relations with the Narragansett had soured temporarily, the two powers maintained contact via trade and their mutual Massachusett and Pawtucket friends. At the same time, the powerful colony sent a series of trading expeditions to the Connecticut area, initiating contact with, among others, the Pequot and their remaining tributaries on Long Island.[8]

As on the Massachusetts coast a decade and a half earlier, the transition from trade to settlement as the dominant mode of European activity was facilitated by an epidemic. Though the effects cannot be traced with precision, it is clear that the smallpox epidemic which devastated the Massachusett and Pawtucket also halted all Indian trading activity between Massachusetts Bay and the Connecticut River for a year following its outbreak in the fall of 1633. According to Plymouth's resident traders, Natawanute and nearly all his followers perished. A party of Dutch traders, wintering in a village north of Plymouth's post, reported that about 950 of the 1000 residents there died, although, according to an informant of Winthrop's, only 700 of the Narragansett and their allies perished. Though not completely spared this time, the Narragansett appear to have avoided the epidemic's worst effects. The lack of additional figures, especially for the Pequot, precludes a more thorough assessment. But the abrupt loss of the "three or four

thousand warlike Indians" whose presence had discouraged
Massachusetts Bay a few months earlier, and the certain psychological and cultural aftershocks (further stimulated by English and Dutch immunity), could only have rendered the natives the more vulnerable at a moment when political stability
in the region was evaporating.[9]

The epidemic was followed by a new round of violence, occasioned by a desperate effort by the Pequot to regain their
monopoly. In 1634, a group of them attacked and killed some
Indians attempting to trade at The Hope. As protectors whose
own position was in jeopardy, the Dutch retaliated. In one of
the skirmishes that followed, they killed Tatobem and some of
his followers. The loss of their powerful, charismatic leader at
this critical juncture dealt the Pequot their most fatal blow
yet. For while Tatobem had alienated many of the Pequot allies, his son and successor, Sassacus, was unable to hold together even those who were nominally Pequot. He succeeded
in retaining only his own village at Weinshauks, between the
Thames and the Mystic, and Pequot itself, plus the Niantic
band at the mouth of the Connecticut. The rest defected to the
Narragansett. Among the most prominent were those who later
contributed to the Pequot demise—Wequash, passed over for
the sachemship at Pequot, and Soso, or Sassawaw, who led the
Pequot's easternmost village, near Weekapaug, Rhode Island,
into the Narragansett camp.[10] Also defecting after initially pay-
ing homage to Sassacus was Uncas of the Mohegan. This husband of the new sachem's sister would move back and forth
between the Pequot and Narragansett four more times, ritually
humiliating himself before Sassacus at each return to the Pequot, before finally joining with the English against the Pequot
in 1636.[11]

Repudiated by the Plymouth traders and at war with the
Dutch, Narragansett, Mohegan, and many of their own followers, the Pequot could not, in Winthrop's understated assess-

ment, "trade safely any where." It was now their turn to invite Massachusetts Bay to the Connecticut. When they did so, in November 1634, they begged the colony not only to send its traders and settlers but to obtain a truce with the Narragansett for them. Though again declining—at least for the moment—to send settlers, erect a post, or defend the Pequot, the colony was willing to "be at peace," send a pinnace, and arrange the truce. In return, it received 400 fathom of wampum, thirty otter skins, and title to the Connecticut River. The last, and the alliance itself, were in preparation for eventual settlement. Though the stakes were larger and the proceedings more civil, Massachusetts Bay's magnaminity in this instance hardly exceeded that shown by Jacques Elekens in 1622. As Francis Jennings has shown, the Pequot discovered what the bands near Plymouth and Massachusetts Bay had known for some time—that an alliance with a colony of settlers was quite different from an alliance among Indians or even with European traders. It required complete subjugation and humiliation in the form of an exorbitant tribute. In the Pequot case, the demands for tribute were supplemented by accusations, on the flimsiest of pretexts, of Pequot responsibility for the death of an English trader, John Stone, and demands that they turn the suspected murderers over for punishment by the colony.[12]

Thus the Pequot of the mid-1630s were anything but the ruthless conquerors of the Puritan-inspired legend that continues to enjoy historical currency. By the summer of 1636, the tide of English settlement was rising on the Connecticut, and Massachusetts Bay was blaming them for the death of another trader, John Oldham.[13] In their desperation the Pequot now groped toward an interpretation of, and solution to, their situation that would have been unthinkable at an earlier time. They humiliated themselves by turning directly to the Narragansett and addressing to them what amounted to a pan-Indian appeal for unity against the English.[14] According to

William Bradford, the Pequot pointed out that "the English
were strangers and began to overspread their country, and
would deprive them thereof in time, if they were suffered to
grow and increase." Under these conditions, the Pequot al-
legedly argued, only a concerted policy of guerilla attacks on
settlers and their farms would force the intruders out.[15]

Received historical wisdom has it that the Narragansett
were ready to join with the Pequot against the English at this
point, and were only prevented from doing so by the timely
and effective diplomacy of Roger Williams. This account,
based entirely on Williams's later recollections, has particular
force because of the possibility that a combined Pequot-
Narragansett effort could have prevented English colonization
of the New England interior. But a close look at the negotiations that preceded the outbreak of war in 1637 suggests that
Williams and subsequent authors have exaggerated the possibilities of a Narragansett-Pequot combination and, thereby,
the actual danger to the English in 1636. For the Narragansett-Pequot truce was strictly one of mutual convenience that
hardly obscured the deep-seated antipathy between the two
groups. Moreover, the Narragansett, recognizing the rapid ascent of English power, had strengthened their ties with the
English over the previous two years, in part through Williams's own mediation. In 1634, while the Pequot were inviting
Massachusetts Bay to settle on the Connecticut, the Narragansett sought to interest both Williams and John Oldham in establishing a trading post in their territory. In the following
year, soon after renewing his attack on the patent, Williams
acquired his first piece of real estate on Narragansett Bay, a
tract that included the future site of Providence. His pronounced intention was to establish a dissenting colony there,
"from whence," some of the Massachusetts Bay leaders feared,
"the infection would easily spread into these churches." Thus
when Williams was banished from Massachusetts Bay in the

winter of 1636, and allowed by Winthrop to escape so as to avoid being shipped to England, he had a very specific destination in mind. (Winthrop saw, as many clergymen and magistrates did not, that having a colony under Williams's leadership on Narragansett Bay was far more valuable than sending Williams to England, where he could only draw unwanted attention to New England.) As Williams himself later recounted, Winthrop had "many high and heavenly and public ends" in directing him to Narragansett Bay, particularly "the freeness of the place from any English claims or patents." And when Williams first sought to build on a portion of his tract east of the Seekonk River, Plymouth's Governor Edward Winslow "lovingly" advised him to cross the river to avoid Plymouth's counter-claim (by virtue of the tract's having previously been occupied, and still claimed, by the Pokanoket).[16] Williams's establishment of "Providence" colony at the head of Narragansett Bay was, of course, a critical event in the religious history of New England. But its primary significance in 1636 lay in its impact on the rapidly shifting balance of power in the region. For Massachusetts Bay and Plymouth, it simultaneously rid them of an ideological thorn while establishing a reliable, knowledgeable countryman among the Narragansett. Now that an English claimant occupied Narragansett Bay, the overland connection between the two colonies and the Connecticut had been made more secure. For the Narragansett, Williams' arrival appeared to ensure their continued hegemony on Narragansett Bay as the English supplanted the Dutch there. When the Pequot approached them six months later, the Narragansett could find little to be gained from abandoning the expanding English in favor of their declining, detested enemies.

Yet they listened to the Pequot's appeal, not because they seriously entertained the notion of joining their old rivals but rather to dissuade them from fighting the English. The Narragansett had been approached only recently by Massachusetts

Bay about withdrawing from their truce with the Pequot so as
to join in a war against them. Acknowledging the superiority
of English weaponry and (potentially) numbers, Canonicus
had expressed support for the English in the upcoming conflict without committing his followers to direct involvement.
He made the same acknowledgment to the Pequot, asserting
that even the two groups together could not turn back the
English tide. According to Edward Johnson, the Pequot dele-
gates were impressed but were unable to convince their fellows
at home to follow the Narragansett's course.[17]

Though Williams deserves credit for strengthening the Massachusetts Bay-Narragansett connection, the most effective single agent in dissuading the Narragansett from neutrality was
Cutshamekin, brother and successor to Chickataubut, late sachem of the Massachusett. Throughout this period Cutshamekin
appears in the records in one or another capacity, helping to
forge the link between the two powers. He had accompanied
two or three Bay Colony men as interpreter and general go-
between on the mission to the Narragansett that had preceded
the Pequot's appeal. In September 1636, he accompanied a
Massachusetts Bay expedition under Endicott to search Block
Island and the lower Connecticut for the elusive murderers of
Stone and Oldham. Along the way, he killed a Pequot and
sent his scalp to Canonicus. According to custom, Canonicus
circulated the scalp among his tributaries and collected a gift
of wampum for Cutshamekin. By this action, he symbolically
reaffirmed the alliance of the Narragansett and Massachusett,
but the latter, acting for Massachusetts Bay, were now calling
the shots. Though Cutshamekin's action made their continued
neutrality even more difficult, the Narragansett continued to
refrain from actively siding with the English in their quarrel
with the Pequot. Winthrop's account suggests that Williams
now tried but failed to convince them to break their non-
combative stance. Massachusetts Bay then turned again to

Cutshamekin, who brought Miantonomi, nephew and designated heir to Canonicus, and several tributary sachems to Boston on September 21. After the colonists unceremoniously
obliged the Narragansett to choose sides in the now-inevitable
war, the two parties signed a treaty in which the Narragansett
agreed to cut all ties with the Pequot and to cooperate in pros-
ecuting the effort against them.[18] A comfortable economic and
political position, as well as a traditional aversion to fighting,
made the Narragansett an unlikely ally of the Pequot from the
beginning. Yet they were forced to enter the conflict on the
English side against their better judgment; their reluctance
and ambivalence would be reflected in their subsequent conduct. They were as trapped as the Pequot in mid-1636.

It was the remnant Mohegan, following the mercurial Uncas,
who had the least to lose among the various native groups in
south-central New England in 1636. Having apparently vacil-
lated between the Pequot and Narragansett and humiliated
himself five times before his rival Sassacus, and then seen the
Narragansett waver, it is no surprise that Uncas sought his
own accommodation with the rapidly growing English community on the Connecticut. In his first appearance in the English records he is providing intelligence about the Pequot to
Plymouth's Connecticut River traders in spring 1636.[19] Finding
ready ears for his tales, Uncas began the role that he was to
play for the next four decades—that of advancing his own ends
by manipulating the English fear of Indian "conspiracies."

Leviathan and the Pequot

While English and Indian political units were jockeying for positions in the Connecticut Valley, groups of Massachusetts Bay
settlers were acting on their own there. The ever-burgeoning
population's hunger for land was hardly abated by the paltry
gains around Massachusetts Bay that followed the smallpox

epidemic of 1633. From about 4000 persons at the end of 1634, the Bay Colony grew to 6000 a year later and to 11,000 by the end of 1638. Though their numbers were still well below the probable Indian density of a quarter-century earlier, the settlers' definitions of their requirements made the area around Boston, like their home counties in old England, overcrowded. This posed a problem for the colony's Puritan ideologues in that the influx of saints was rendering the vision of a "Citty upon a hill" more, rather than less, elusive. Though the vision of a literal city had been unrealizable from the first year of the migration, it continued to inform the efforts of Winthrop and other leaders to keep the settlers "knit together" in a single political unit. By the middle of 1634, however, all the leaders could hope for was to keep settlement between the Charles and Merrimack rivers, the boundaries established in the colony's patent. Thus the magistrates' answer to those who felt "straitened" near Boston was to suggest that they select a town site on the lower Merrimack, where the native population had likewise been reduced in 1616-18.[20]

As news of the smallpox epidemic and of the Connecticut Valley's fertility filtered back to the Bay Colony, however, the Merrimack as a potential settlement area was overshadowed. In the summer of 1634, a Newtown party investigated the region and, in the following winter, a group of Watertown men wintered with John Oldham on the Connecticut near the native village of Pyquag, soon to be renamed Wethersfield. During the summer of 1635, a sizable contingent, primarily from Dorchester, established themselves near Plymouth's post and founded Windsor. In the fall a vanguard of thirty-five persons from Newtown (later Cambridge) established Hartford. By mid-1636 the three towns already held about 800 settlers, a figure that made their presence a formidable one next to their post-epidemic neighbors and now-isolated Dutch "Hope."[21]

The problem with these new settlements was that they were

rising faster than Massachusetts Bay could consolidate its authority on the Connecticut. Not only did the area lack an English patent of any kind, the newcomers were ignoring the 1634 treaty with the Pequot and purchasing their land directly from local sachems. The magistrates' strategy of working through the Pequot in order to achieve an orderly expansion was being flouted by upstarts whose actions could instead provoke the Pequot to violence. In an effort to contain and control this new development, the magistrates made use of a dubious patent for the Connecticut Valley that had once been issued by Ferdinando Gorges and had passed through several hands into those of a group of Puritan gentlemen constituted as the Saybrook Company. As Francis Jennings has noted, this company's sudden interest in taking up its lands in 1635 coincided with the beginnings of unauthorized settlement on the Connecticut and the presence in London of John Winthrop, Jr. The company directors, apparently recognizing that in a partnership with Massachusetts Bay lay their only hope of preventing a takeover of the Valley by squatters, named Winthrop, Jr., their governor. Armed with his new title, Winthrop proceeded to Boston and then to the mouth of the Connecticut, arriving as Hartford was being founded upriver in 1635. His first action was to oversee the construction of Fort Saybrook, from where he hoped to govern his subjects, most of whom lived more than thirty miles to the north.[22]

Though an agreement was improvised during the following winter whereby the settlers placed themselves under the nominal jurisdiction of Fort Saybrook, Winthrop's authority over them remained largely fictitious. But among Indians he was in a position to further the policy of undermining and isolating the Pequot. Indeed the site of Fort Saybrook had already been obtained as a gift from the Western Niantic, tributaries of the Pequot. In July 1636 Winthrop, Jr., sought to assert direct authority over the Pequot by calling them to the fort and demanding the murderers of Stone and submission in the form of tribute far in excess of that already being given as "presents." Upon being rebuffed, Winthrop made a separate treaty with the Western Niantic. The irony of this agreement was that though Stone's killers were in fact among the Western Niantic, now tributaries of Saybrook, the Pequot would continue to be held responsible. But it was not legal responsibility that Winthrop was after; it was results. And the result of the treaty was that the Pequot lost their last ally.[23]

Having isolated the Pequot, Massachusetts Bay and Saybrook employed overtly military means to bring about their submission. It was shortly after Winthrop's meeting with the Pequot that John Oldham was murdered, this time by Eastern Niantics, though again the Pequot were held responsible. Then, after the appeal to the Narragansett, came the Massachusetts Bay expedition of September 1636 during which Cutshamekin took a Pequot scalp and in addition the English burned Pequot and Manisean (on Block Island) homes and crops. Saybrook's commanding officer, Lion Gardener, later noted that Cutshamekin's action was, from the Pequot's perspective, the cause and the beginning of hostilities. Until then they had carefully refrained from violence despite repeated English efforts to humiliate and otherwise provoke them. But with the blood of a Pequot shed and no alternative means of obtaining reparation available, they had no choice.[24]

For a time after the assumption of hostilities by the Pequot the tide against them was partially turned, as Fort Saybrook found itself equally isolated. The Pequot began a siege of the fort that coincided with the Antinomian controversy in Boston, which diverted Massachusetts Bay's attention. Despite pleas from Gardener ("Governor" Winthrop, Jr., had returned to Boston) for Massachusetts Bay's support, this desultory siege, along with occasional harassments of English travelers on the Connecticut, continued for nine months. It was relieved only

when events to the north compelled intervention by Massachusetts Bay. In April 1637 the Wethersfield settlers abruptly
broke their purchase agreement with the local natives by driving them from their homes within the town's proclaimed
boundaries. The refugees turned to the only available source
of relief, their former Pequot enemies. Seizing the opportunity
to regain their former dominion in the cause of anti-English resistance, the Pequot employed the strategy they had proposed
to the Narragansett the year before. In a lightning raid they
killed nine settlers working in their fields and took two girls as
prisoners, besides inflicting property damage. Thereupon full-
scale hostilities with the Pequot became official for both Massachusetts Bay and the Connecticut River settlers.[25]

As the war was brewing, Massachusetts Bay had been consumed by its most serious internal quarrel yet. Inspired by
John Cotton but led by Anne Hutchinson, a substantial portion
of the Boston congregation was arguing that virtually all the
New England clergy labored under a heretical "covenant of
works" in presuming to judge and rule on the validity of individual experiences of grace. But the movement was more
than theological, for the Antinomians represented a lay revolt
against clerical authority and, as Emery Battis has shown,
pitted the interests of commercial Boston against those of the
outlying towns. Moreover, in asserting the spiritual equality
of women with men, the movement appeared to its detractors
as a subversion of patriarchal and ministerial authority by
"silly Women laden with diverse lusts."[26]

The Connecticut settlements and the Antinomian conflict
were only the most apparent indicators that Puritan New England's proclaimed collective identity was fading by the mid-
1630s. As David D. Hall argues, the colonists were being overtaken by a spiritual complacency to which the Antinomians
were the boldest response.[27] Though the dimensions of this
complacency have yet to be fully explored by historians, it is

certain that for many colonists the spiritual crisis was, characteristically, a material one as well. As some questioned ministerial restraints on the pursuit of piety, others chafed under the colony's inability to provide the material foundations, in the form of land, for economic independence for themselves and their progeny. In some cases these questions originated with the same person, in others with those in opposition to one another. What the dissenters had in common was a perception that the prevailing vision of the colony placed limitations on the honorable pursuit of individual callings, however those callings were defined.

In the face of this fragmentation and the crises it engendered, the Pequot War served as one means by which Puritan leaders in Massachusetts Bay and in Connecticut, as the breakaway settlements were now being termed, redefined and adjusted New England's proclaimed mission to accord with the realities of settler expansion. The war's ideological significance was established soon after the Wethersfield attack, when John Higginson, chaplain at Fort Saybrook, and Thomas Hooker, a former Boston minister who led the migration to Hartford, wrote Winthrop, Sr., of Connecticut's urgent need of support from Massachusetts Bay. In their letters, the Connecticut leaders cited the need for unity among Puritan saints in doing the Lord's work to argue, in effect, that the older colony had now to accept the fact of Connecticut's independence in order to deal effectively with the Pequot enemy. Higginson asked Winthrop to consider the probability that God had allowed the Pequots to attack the English for three reasons: first, ". . . to make them cleave more close togither, and prize each other, to prevent contentions of Brethren . . ."; second, ". . . to roote out that deeply-rooted securitie and confidence in our owne supposed strength . . ." engendered by the colonists' clear military superiority over the coastal bands; and third, ". . . more seriously to intend this warre then yet they seem to doe." He

went on to remind Winthrop, in a shrewd paraphrase of the latter's *Arbella* address, "that now the eyes of all the Indians in the
countrey are upon the English, to see what they will doe," and
that if decisive action were not forthcoming, "we are like to
have all the Indians in the countrey about our ears. . . ." Winthrop had no difficulty suppressing—at least for the moment—
whatever resentments toward the secessionists he still har-
bored. When, shortly thereafter, Plymouth balked at participating in a war in which it had no stake or grievance, he
reminded Bradford that his colony must "looke at the pe-
quents, and all other Indeans as a common enimie, who though
he may take occasion, of the beginning of his rage, from one
parte of the English, yet if he prevaile, will surly pursue his
advantage, to the rooting out of the whole nation."[28]

The war, as portrayed by the leaders of Massachusetts Bay
and Connecticut, served to remind all English that the differences which divided them were ephemeral compared with the
ties that bound them and promised to clear away the murki-
ness that had lately obscured their sense of divine mission. As
hostilities approached, it became clear to many English that
they and the Pequot stood in for none less than God and Satan
respectively. Rumors circulated of Pequots who were immune
to English swords and rapiers because "there were some Pow-
wowes among them, which work strange things with the help
of Satan." "So insolent were these wicked imps grown," wrote
John Underhill, "that like the devil, their commander, they
run up and down as roaring lions, compassing all corners of
the country for their prey, seeking whom they might devour."[29]

Having located Satan in the Pequot camp, the English forces
could proceed without restraint. The war's outcome was determined in a pre-dawn surprise attack on the Pequot's Mystic
River village while most of the men were away, leaving it in
the hands of between 300 and 700 women, children, and old
men. Despite the sleeping villagers' inability to mount an ef-

fective resistance, Connecticut's Captain John Mason ordered the wigwams burned, while the English and their allies surrounded the village so as to cut down those trying to flee (see fig. 8). In less than an hour, all but seven escapees were dead. The Pequots not present scattered and panicked, and most were captured or killed during the next several months. Many of the men were executed; the rest, along with the women and children, were enslaved and assigned to the colonists, to their Mohegan and Narragansett allies, or to be sold for shipment to the West Indies. Under the terms of the Connecticut-dictated Treaty of Hartford (1638), the Pequot nation was declared dissolved.[30]

For many settlers, the Pequot slaughter was the ideological as well as military turning point in the war and in their conquest of New England. The event inspired rhetorical heights in the most prosaic of Puritan writers who sought to explain its significance. Underhill addressed any John Robinsons among the English who might entertain scruples about the colonists' tactics:

> It may be demanded, Why should you be so furious? (as some have said). Should not Christians have more mercy and compassion? But I would refer you to David's war. When a people is grown to such a height of blood and sin against God and man and all confederates in the action, there he hath no respects to persons, but harrows them and saws them, and puts them to the sword, and the most terriblest death that may be. sometimes the Scripture declareth women and children must perish with their parents. Sometimes the case alters; but we will not dispute it now. We had sufficient light from the Word of God for our proceedings.

Mason, and undoubtedly many others, was able to imagine God's own feeling about the slaughter:

> Thus were they now at their Wits End, who not many Hours before exalted themselves in their great Pride, threatening and

Figure 8. The massacre of the Pequot civilians at their Mystic River village, 1637. The illustration shows Englishmen shooting the Indians as they flee their burning homes. Outside the village is a ring of English troops backed by a second ring, consisting of their Narragansett allies. John Underhill, *Newes from America* (London, 1638). *Courtesy of Chapin Library, Williams College, Williamstown, Mass.*

resolving the utter Ruin and Destruction of all the English,
Exulting and Rejoycing with Songs and Dances; But God was
above them, who laughed his Enemies and the Enemies of his
people to Scorn, making them as a fiery Oven: Thus were the
Stout hearted spoiled, having slept their last Sleep, and none
of their men could find their Hands: Thus did the Lord judge
among the Heathen, filling the Place with Dead Bodies!

And Bradford's earlier reservations vanished in the face of so
powerful a spectacle:

It was a fearful sight to see them thus frying in the fire and the
streams of blood quenching the same, and horrible was the
stink and scent thereof; but the victory seemed a sweet sacri-
fice, and they gave the praise thereof to God, who had wrought
so wonderfully for them, thus to enclose their enemies in their
hands and give them so speedy a victory over so proud and
insulting an enemy.[31]

As these and other characterizations indicated, the Pequot's
most offensive traits were their "pride" and their "insolence."
In emphasizing the sins of individual egotism and defiance of
authority, the Puritan writers seemed to be addressing themselves, albeit obliquely, to the problems that had been beset-
ting their own ranks. The Pequot, even more than the Antinomians, represented a world "turned upside down" with
barbarians triumphing over civilization, Satan over Christ, anarchy over order. Indeed the twin enemies were not entirely
separate in the minds of some Puritans. Thomas Shepard
noted that the internal and external threats "arose and fell together," and a day of thanksgiving was held to commemorate
jointly the military victory and the consolidation of ministerial
ranks following the prosecution of the Antinomians. In the late
stage of the war, male Antinomians refused to muster for combat because their chief opponent, John Wilson, had been appointed chaplain. Despite the fact that one of their number,
John Underhill, had led Massachusetts Bay's troops at Pequot,

the Antinomians were disarmed and their leaders exiled.[32] Like the Pequot, they had, in a legal sense, ceased to exist.

The victory, though primarily a Connecticut accomplishment, was one with which all Puritans could identify. The rhetoric and imagery of the Pequot slaughter were deliberately reminiscent of the Old Testament, particularly of the Israelites "smiting" the Canaanites and driving them from the Promised Land. In 1637 this message was important. The (re)discovery that God had a purpose in mind for the settlers and that that purpose could be happily reconciled with their desire to spread out and expropriate Indian lands marked a significant adjustment of tensions within the New England Puritan movement between individual and communal goals. Freemen could now enjoy material independence without challenging the political-ecclesiastical status quo, while the clergy and magistrates could now count on them to support efforts to define religious and political orthodoxy more rigidly. For with geographic fragmentation a reality, yet a new vision of "New England" was required.

New England IV

As Massachusetts Bay's own population rose from 6500 in 1637 to twice that number in 1643, English settlers streamed into the Connecticut Valley and westward along the coast of Long Island Sound, raising the total in those areas from 800 to about 5500. Slightly more than half of these resided in Connecticut, the rest constituting yet another breakaway colony, New Haven.[33] What is noteworthy about the new settlements is that they were located not on the lands of the conquered Pequot but on those of the small bands who had formerly relied upon the Pequot for protection. These bands were now obliged to accept the protection of the new colonies, the price of which included some of their choicest land as well as payment of tribute and submission to English rule. Like Massachusetts Bay and Plymouth, these colonies played the role of dominant, tribute-collecting powers among depopulated local bands.

In Connecticut, the Mohegans under Uncas served as intermediaries between most subordinate bands and the colony government, much as the Pokanoket under Massasoit did in Plymouth. Uncas rooted his tribute-collecting powers over other Indians not only in the recognition accorded him by the English but in his claim to have succeeded the Pequot. In 1640 he ceded all his territory and that of his tributaries (except what was inhabited and planted) to the colony.[34] The transaction did not open up any new land for settlement; rather it confirmed that which Connecticut had already settled or claimed. Its importance lay in the legal and political benefits it provided both upstart parties. Uncas thereafter received Connecticut's unswerving support as he sought to extend his hegemony to autonomous bands to the north and east. For its part Connecticut was grateful for the deed which certified the transfer. In the absence of a royal patent, it was the next best defense against the incursions and claims of Massachusetts Bay and New Netherland.

Whereas Connecticut replaced the hegemony of the Pequot with that of the Mohegan among the natives within its jurisdiction, New Haven simply inserted itself in the Pequot's role among the coastal bands extending westward from the Quinnipiac River. The best documented instances of this kind of arrangement are the two which formalized the transfer of the Quinnipiac basin itself to the new colony. The first and more critical agreement, signed November 24, 1638, gave New Haven the land around the mouth of the river and its harbor. In it the local sachem Momaquin and his counsellors formally exchanged "the heavy taxes and eminent dangers which they lately felt and feared from the Pequots, Mohawcks, and other Indians" for the comforts afforded by the proximity of English settlers. For these comforts the Quinnipiac Indians gave over all their lands, receiving in exchange a reservation on the east side of the harbor. Even within the reservation, the English had exclusive and unlimited access to the meadow and timber. The natives could, on the other hand, hunt and fish outside the reservation provided that such activities caused no "inconvenience" for the English. The treaty also contained specific stipulations forbidding most social and economic contacts between the two peoples and holding the Indians responsible for the death of any English livestock they killed, even accidentally. (Nothing was said about compensating the Indians for any damage the free-roaming livestock might inflict on their crops.) The natives were also required to obtain the approval of the colony before admitting any outsiders to their community and to inform it of any anti-English plots they heard of from other Indians. Besides their reservation (minus its meadowland and timber) the Quinnipiac received an assortment of coats, tools, and utensils.[35]

Two and a half weeks after the Quinnipiac treaty, New Haven obtained a similar agreement from one Mantowese for the land on both sides of the river from the northerly boundary of the colony's previous acquisition to the river's head. What is curious about the second agreement is that Mantowese was the son of a sachem at Mattabesec (later Middletown) and nephew of the Sequin sachem Sowheag, both located on the Connecticut. It is also noteworthy that, while New Haven's agreement with the Quinnipiac was reached in the presence of all or most of the band on their own territory, Mantowese traveled from his home to New Haven in the company of just one other native. Though the treaty spells out Mantowese's sole right to dispose of the land, these circumstances suggest that because English colonial boundaries happened to cut through his band's territory, Mantowese and his followers had suddenly become a separate band whose loyalties would be directed toward New Haven, while his elders would pay homage to Hartford. Moreover, both treaties stipulated that the Indians subordinate all ties of kinship to the laws and interests of their new colonial rulers.[36]

The underlying explanation, as always, can be found in population figures. Against the New Haven settlers, who numbered 2500 by 1642, the Quinnipiac and the followers of Mantowese could muster but 47 and 10 adult males respectively.[37] Though no figures for other bands within Connecticut and New Haven are known, the consecutive experiences of smallpox and the Pequot War can be assumed to have had similar demographic effects. As a result these bands, too, were easy targets for domination by the newcomers.

Even on Narragansett Bay, where 30,000 natives still outnumbered the settlers by more than ten to one in the early 1640s, the political consequences of English settlement for native communities were beginning to be felt. These consequences first became apparent on the island of Aquidneck (now Rhode Island proper) in 1637 when a party of Antinomians, expelled from Massachusetts Bay, purchased the island in order to establish the settlement of Portsmouth. In accordance with the precedents already established by Roger Williams, the purchasers first approached Wanamataunewit, the Aquidneck sachem, about buying the island. Claiming that such transfers were not within his power, Wanamataunewit referred them to Canonicus and Miantonomi, who not only made the sale but assumed responsibility for evacuating the native inhabitants. Before the year was out, more than eighty English families had settled the island, and by 1643, when Newport had been established at the south end, that figure had risen to somewhere between 120 and 200.[38]

In Narragansett Bay, then, the Narragansett continued the dominant role they had assumed during the fur trade era but, like the Mohegan and Pokanoket, they now served as client and broker for the settlers in their relations with other Indians.

Nevertheless the Narragansett's relationship to Providence, Portsmouth, and Newport only superficially resembled that of the Mohegan to Connecticut and the Pokanoket to Plymouth. The religious dissenters who flocked to Roger Williams's haven of toleration were politically disunited, as well as numerically inferior to both the Narragansett and the other colonies. Moreover, they were ideologically repugnant to the leaders of the other colonies, providing a basis for consensus among those colonies. Thus the Narragansett lacked the substantial English support enjoyed by the Mohegan and Pokanoket. Finally, the Narragansett themselves continued to constitute an object of hostility for their neighbors, especially Connecticut and the Mohegan.

This hostility had erupted even during the Pequot War when the Narragansett openly criticized both the harshness of English warfare and the proposal—heartily endorsed by Uncas—to enslave even those Pequots who voluntarily surrendered and renounced Sassacus's leadership. To the Narragansett, warfare was a contest in which one sought to intimidate and scatter one's enemies through a combination of physical and supernatural weapons. The result might be a favorable shift in the balance of power but certainly not the elimination of any existing communal entities. The Narragansett came out of the war with promises from Massachusetts Bay that they would assume the "hunting" (implying tribute-collecting) privileges formerly enjoyed by the Pequot. They soon found, however, a different English entity—Connecticut—occupying the lands formerly dominated by the Pequot and, in the Treaty of Tartford, were obliged to accept merely a portion of the Pequot survivors as subjects. Moreover, Connecticut had elevated the lowly Uncas to a position of strength and status among Indians and was actively backing his efforts to construct a tributary network among bands within its jurisdiction, many of which had close ties to the Narragansett.[39]

The effective isolation of the Narragansett was completed by

the defection of Massachusetts Bay in 1642. In that year a
group of settlers purchased a tract of land at Shawomet from
the local sachems Pomham and Sacononoco and placed themselves under the "protection and government" of the Bay Colony. In purchasing directly from the local sachems rather than
from the dominant Narragansett, the settlers ran counter to the
precedent recently established in the sale of Aquidneck. On
the other hand, they were in accord with earlier precedents. In
particular the Shawomet purchase followed Roger Williams's
advice to Plymouth a decade earlier that a local sachem, rather
than his or her tribute-collecting superior(s), was the legiti-
mate purveyor of native title. Like Plymouth's purchase on the
Connecticut, moreover, the Shawomet "sale" was in fact a
poorly concealed effort by an outside power to expand into
territory beyond its patent. In this case Massachusetts Bay
sought not only Narragansett land but the arrest of a particularly obstreperous religious radical, Samuel Gorton, and a
small band of his followers who previously settled at Shawomet with Miantonomi's blessing. That the Bay Colony was
prepared to break with its ally had been indicated shortly before when Cutshamekin was briefly jailed in Boston out of a
fear that he was participating in a Narragansett-led conspiracy. The arrest was a signal that the colony no longer needed
the Massachusett sachem in his intermediary role and that it
sought to detach him from the Narragansett altogether. The
move was successful not only in intimidating Cutshamekin into
supporting the colony on whose land he and his people lived
but in helping legitimize the defection of Sacononoco and
Pomham. After his release, the extra-cooperative Cutshamekin
testified that while the latter two sometimes gave presents to
Miantonomi because he was a "great sachem," they were essentially "as free sachems as [Miantonomi] himself."[40] He thus
grounded the colony's argument in native custom as well as
English law.

This assumption by Massachusetts Bay of direct hostility toward the Narragansett and their English friends marked its abandonment of a diplomatic approach to southward expansion and its deferment to the more aggressive approach of Connecticut and the Mohegan.[41] In the face of this consensus of the two leading Puritan powers, the Narragansett made strenuous efforts to escape the fate of the Pequot. As the latter had appealed to them in 1636, they now appealed to others to join in a pan-Indian movement to resist English domination. Though fears of a Narragansett-led conspiracy of all the Indians had regularly been voiced in the colonies since the end of the Pequot War, they more accurately reflected the anxieties aroused in some English minds by even routine trade and diplomatic activities of autonomous Indian bands.[42] After the move into Shawomet, however, English descriptions of Narragansett plotting became more specific than the earlier, more generalized ones.[43] The Saybrook officer, Lion Gardiner, was among the Montauk on eastern Long Island late in 1642 when the Narragansett sought to persuade that band to abandon Connecticut. Gardiner's informant, the leader of a pro-Connecticut faction among the Montauk, noted that whereas Miantonomi formerly received presents during his visits, he now gave them to his listeners. Such was the Narragansett's desperation. And like the Pequot before him, he made an eloquent appeal for pan-Indian unity. As noted at the beginning of the first chapter, he pointed primarily to the threat posed by the English to Indian subsistence. He added that a movement was already in effect that included "all the Sachems from east to west, both Moquakues [?] and Mohauks," who would, on an appointed day, rise "and kill men, women, and children, but no cows, for they will serve to eat till our deer be increased again."[44] No more succinct statement of the impact of English settlement on Indian survival and cultural autonomy can be found in the seventeenth-century sources. Moreover the speech reflects—

like that of the Pequot emissaries to the Narragansett six years earlier—a belated recognition of the need for an *Indian,* as opposed to tribal, identity to counter that of the English. And in its depiction of a pre-English utopia—within the memories of most adults—it anticipated such American Indian prophet movements as those led by Pontiac and Tecumseh, as well as the Ghost Dance.[45] Though an anti-English uprising was part of his plan, Miantonomi's prior record and his friendship with Roger Williams suggest that any movement he led would have been less likely to result in violence than in an effective institutional counterweight to expansion by Connecticut and Massachusetts Bay and in the long-run stabilization of Indian-European relations in and around what was soon to become Rhode Island.

A sudden twist of events in 1643 obliged Miantonomi to carry his message directly to Uncas. In the spring there were charges and countercharges surrounding Miantonomi's alleged hiring of an assassin to kill Uncas, which ended with the would-be assassin himself being murdered and Miantonomi being blamed. But the incident was left unresolved for the moment. In July a Connecticut River sachem, Sequasson, called on the Narragansett for aid against the Mohegan after a battle in which several of his followers had been killed. Miantonomi carefully informed the magistrates of both Connecticut and Massachusetts Bay of his intentions and, receiving no objections, proceeded to Mohegan country. The inaction of the two colonies up to this point indicates quite clearly that they did not yet consider Miantonomi's alleged role in the murder a matter of consequence. Handicapped by a suit of armor lent him by a well-meaning follower of Gorton, he was easily captured by his rival Uncas. It appears to have been at this point that he proposed to Uncas that the two of them ally, cementing their ties through a marriage of Miantonomi to a daughter of Uncas. The Narragansett also hoped to enlist another old antagonist through a marriage of Miantonomi's brother Pessacus to the Pokanoket daughter of Massasoit. Thus Miantonomi turned to the time-honored custom of marriage between members of leading lineages to save his neck as well as to construct an alliance capable of resisting continued English expansion. Though the circumstances under which he made this last appeal for unity made a favorable response highly unlikely, it is significant that Uncas apparently weighed the offer before finally turning his prize captive over to the English.[46]

The unexpected capture of Miantonomi came at a critical moment in New England's political history. Alarmed at Massachusetts Bay's expansion into Shawomet (now Warwick), Roger Williams hastily departed for England to obtain a charter for the colonies around Narragansett Bay. Like the Narragansett, the dissenting settlers here recognized the need for political unity—along with legal protection in the form of a royal patent—to ensure their survival. The self-proclaimed upholders of Puritan orthodoxy in the other four colonies had likewise come to recognize the wisdom of confederation. After five years of wrangling, especially between Connecticut and Massachusetts Bay, they had succeeded in institutionalizing and politicizing their "New England Way" to the extent of forming the United Colonies of New England, an inter-colonial commission consisting of two representatives each from Massachusetts Bay, Connecticut, New Haven, and Plymouth.[47]

While focused on the external threat, the United Colonies represented an effort to redefine Puritan identity in New England. Since the end of the Pequot War, Massachusetts Bay and Connecticut had renewed the mutual recriminations that attended the latter's earlier efforts to establish its independence. Though the idea of an inter-colonial commission had been broached on several occasions, Massachusetts Bay's insistence on dominating any such organization had hitherto been a stumbling block. But with Williams carrying the Rhode Island-Narragansett case to London, they recognized what one Connecticut man had earlier termed their "common Cause." That the foundations of this "Cause" ran deeper than Indians was made apparent by the organization's pointed exclusion of the Narragansett Bay settlements, as well as of New Netherland and the non-Puritan English settlements recently established in what are now New Hampshire and Maine. Whatever their differences, the four member colonies were all governed by men who had passed mutually acceptable tests for sainthood and by principles that carefully defined and enforced orthodoxy in religious, political, and social practice.[48] The Commission was, in short, the closest approximation to a "Citty upon a hill" that could be obtained in a rapidly expanding society of independent farmers.

Yet if Indians were not the actual basis for Puritan unity, they continued to serve as the focus for united action. Despite the Commission's religious foundation, it had no religious functions. Rather its task was to maintain a constant, uniform state of military preparedness, particularly for use against Indians.[49] Once again Indians served as the symbol that enabled the settlers' individualistic, materialistic desires for land to be reconciled with the felt need of many for a religiously based communal identity.

The United Colonies established its leadership in Indian affairs with its first order of business—the case of Miantonomi. The Commissioners certainly recognized that with Williams seeking a charter for Rhode Island from a sympathetic Parliament, the Narragansett would never again be as vulnerable as they were at that moment. Accordingly they tried and convicted Miantonomi for the murder which they had previously ignored and turned him over to Uncas for execution. This deed, which has even repelled many of the perpetrators' otherwise loyal descendants and admirers, was an especially delicate matter for the Commissioners, as reflected in the fact that Uncas was to wait until reaching Mohegan territory before committing the murder. At the same time, several Englishmen would accompany the party to see that the execution was actually carried out. No Indian, not even Uncas, could be trusted alone with the remarkable leader who was urging Indians to bury their present differences in order to recover the autonomy, unity, and abundance of the pre-European past.[50] With his death went the last possibility of an effective native resistance to English Puritan hegemony. For once, the future of "New England" seemed assured.

EPILOGUE

In LESS THAN a generation, the world into which most surviving Indians had been born, and for which they had been
prepared, had vanished. Indeed, Miantonomi's call for united
action to restore it was a revolutionary proposal, in that action
by Indians on such a scale had never before been necessary or
even conceivable. At the same time, many settlers thought of
themselves as migrating to revive a world that had been lost
and, in so doing, spread the revolutionary upheavals in England to North America. As victors, the settlers were able to
preserve an illusion of continuity, while for the Indians, no
such illusions were possible; in reality both peoples had crossed
a critcial historical divide.

A healthy physical environment, the socially and ideologically selective character of the migration, and the willingness
to dominate and, when necessary, wage massive violence
against the Indians permitted the continuation of the rapid
economic and demographic growth that the settlers had known
in England (even as that growth was halting there). And instead of constricting familial landholdings and driving some
young men off the land altogether, as had happened in the old
country, the abundance of available land enhanced family
stability and patriarchal authority by encouraging sons to remain at home to await their inheritance of land.[1] Nevertheless,
the "stable" seventeenth-century New England town, the image
of which has dominated recent social histories of the region,

was only made possible by repeated migrations on the part of many settlers after their arrival and by the continuation of war and "purchase," plus the introduction of reservations by missionaries and others, as means of further reducing the Indians' land base.[2] As a result, New England represented a real alternative both to the increasing hardships being experienced by many marginal smallholders in England and to the indentured servitude that had come to prevail in England's Chesapeake and Caribbean colonies. And whereas indentured servitude supported (before the advent of slavery) the monocultural raising of crops for sale and consumption outside the producing colonies, independent ownership of land plus the presence of merchants in New England's ports provided the resources and habits that nourished an indigenous commercial economy. But there was irony in this nourishing. By the mid-eighteenth century, with most of the region's land in English hands, New England had come full circle to the conditions which had induced the Great Migration from England more than a century earlier—high population combined with a shortage of tillable land; a dependence on the wildly uncertain cycles of a rapidly diversifying economy; growing extremes of wealth and poverty; widespread geographic mobility; the return of destructive epidemics; the breakdown of towns, churches, and families as effective institutions of social control; and the rise of a new religious movement emphasizing individual piety.[3] Despite the intentions and beliefs of many participants, then, the effect of colonization had not been to halt or reverse the processes forming preindustrial England but to carry them across the Atlantic. There the land seized from Indians proved a vital source of both capital and labor for the new economy and society that emerged in the eighteenth century.

For their parts, the natives of New England had passed through a sequence of radical transformations as a consequence of colonization. From the reciprocal networks that had prevailed before the arrival of Europeans, they had entered into specialized trade relationships with both the newcomers and with other Indians. But massive mortality in the face of virgin soil epidemics rendered large tracts of Indian land vulnerable to English settlement. Utilizing their demographic and, when necessary, military advantages, colonists quickly overran the territory around Plymouth and Massachusetts bays, and then the valleys of the lower Connecticut and Housatonic. After the Pequot War, Indians throughout the region were subjected to ever-tightening restrictions on their traditional modes of subsistence. Surviving bands of Massachusett, Pequot, and others who were located near heavy concentrations of English were confined to tiny enclaves, while those groups which retained a larger land base and a greater degree of political integrity and internal autonomy during the middle decades of the seventeenth century did so because they could count on one or the other of the colonies as a protector (in exchange for diplomatic, military, and other services rendered)—the Pokanoket in Plymouth, the Mohegan in Connecticut, and the Narragansett and Eastern Niantic in Rhode Island. But the colonists went on to seize most of the lands of these and other "allies" during and immediately following King Philip's War (1675-76). Thereafter, the Indians continued their descent to the position of a sub-proletariat, often intermarrying with blacks who, like themselves, were confined to the economic and social margins of pre-industrial New England. Although the structural foundations of traditional native society had been all but obliterated, the Indians' very marginality and isolation permitted the survival of strong tribal identities in several enclaves.[4]

In a very real and tangible sense, then, "New England," as we know it in history, was "made" when Indian lands were expropriated for use by English settlers. For it was by that process that the land was removed from a "natural" economy, wherein it was treated as a sacred phenomenon whose powers and gifts were thought to be controlled by supernatural forces, and placed in a nascent capitalist economy where (though hedged in certain respects by the authorities of town, colony, and empire) it became fundamentally a commodity owned by individuals to be bought and sold as they saw fit. Once released from the realm of the sacred, land became a source of wealth whose potential ran far beyond the mere value of its animal, vegetable, and mineral resources. Though most land was employed for subsistence purposes in the seventeenth century, some colonists even then sought to profit from its convertibility to liquid assets.[5]

From a global perspective, then, the expropriation of Indian lands in New England and elsewhere was a variation of the process that drew feudal and peasant lands in Europe into a commercial orbit. For the Indians, however, the task of resisting this expansion was rendered virtually hopeless because of their severe epidemiological and, hence, demographic disadvantages and because of the colonists' readiness and ability to seize on those disadvantages. As a result of these disparities and of the continued gaps between themselves and the dominant group in the realm of culture and values, Indians, unlike peasants, found no firm place in the society that emerged following the loss of their lands. Instead they came to be classified as a separate "race," a status whose legacy of discrimination and inequality persists in our own time.

NOTES

ABBREVIATIONS USED IN THE NOTES

AICRJ	*American Indian Culture and Research Journal*
BASC	*Bulletin of the Archeological Society of Connecticut*
BMAS	*Bulletin of the Massachusetts Archaeological Society*
CCR	J. Hammond Trumbull, ed., *Public Records of the Colony of Connecticut.* 15 vols. 1850-90; reprint ed., New York, 1968.
HNAI	*Handbook of North American Indians.* gen. ed. William C. Sturtevant. 20 vols. Washington, D.C., 1976- .
MCR	Nathaniel B. Shurtleff, ed., *Records of the Governor and Company of the Massachusetts Bay in New England.* 5 vols. Boston, 1853-54.
MHSC	Massachusetts Historical Society, *Collections*
MHSP	Massachusetts Historical Society, *Proceedings*
NEHGR	*New England Historical and Genealogical Register*
NEQ	*New England Quarterly*
NYCD	Edmund Bailey O'Callaghan, ed., *Documents Relative to the Colonial History of the State of New-York.* 15 vols. Albany, 1853-87.
RICR	John R. Bartlett, ed., *Records of the Colony of Rhode Island and Providence Plantations in New England.* 10 vols. 1850-65; reprint ed., New York, 1968.
WMQ	*William and Mary Quarterly*
WP	Allyn B. Forbes, ed., *Winthrop Papers.* 5 vols. Boston, 1929-1947.

INTRODUCTION

1. John Smith, *Travels and Works of Captain John Smith,* ed. Edward Arber (2 vols.; Edinburgh, 1910), 1:259; Thomas Morton, *New English Canaan* (1637), ed. Charles Francis Adams, Jr. (1883; reprint ed., New York, 1967), 121, 133-34;

WP, 2:141; Edward Johnson, *Johnson's Wonder-Working Providence* (1654), ed. J. Franklin Jameson, Original Narratives of Early American History (1910; reprint ed., New York, 1967), 41-42.

2. *Ibid.,* 164-65. For examples of other comments, see the passages quoted herein, pp. 222-24.

3. Cotton Mather, *Magnalia Christi Americana; or, the Ecclesiastical History of New-England* (1702), ed. Thomas Robbins (2 vols.; Hartford, 1855), 2:571-72.

4. Cf. William S. Simmons, "Cultural Bias in the New England Puritans' Perception of Indians," *WMQ* 3d ser., 38 (1981), 56-72, esp. 68 n. 40; Karen Ordahl Kupperman, *Settling with the Indians: The Meeting of English and Indian Cultures in America, 1580-1640* (Totowa, N.J., 1980); Neal Salisbury, "Conquest of the 'Savage': Puritans, Puritan Missionaries, and Indians, 1620-1680" (Ph.D. diss., University of California, Los Angeles, 1972), chaps. 5-7, *passim.* On the providential interpretation of history underlying these accounts, see Keith Thomas, *Religion and the Decline of Magic* (New York, 1971), chap. 4.

5. John Gorham Palfrey, *The History of New England* (5 vols.; Boston, 1858-90), 1 (2d ed., 1876):467; John W. DeForest, *History of the Indians of Connecticut* (1851; reprint ed., Hamden, Conn., 1964), 490. For a striking example of the providential interpretation's continuing influence, compare the full paragraph in Palfrey from which this passage is taken with the one from John Underhill, a participant in the massacre, quoted herein, p. 222. For a larger perspective on the historiographical developments discussed in this paragraph, see Robert M. Berkhofer, Jr., *The White Man's Indian: Images of the American Indian from Columbus to the Present* (New York, 1978), 86-96.

6. Charles M. Andrews, *The Colonial Period of American History* (4 vols.; 1934-38; paper ed., New Haven, 1964); Perry Miller, *The New England Mind: The Seventeenth Century* (New York, 1939); Perry Miller, *The New England Mind: From Colony to Province* (Cambridge, Mass., 1961). The most influential of the social histories are John Demos, *A Little Commonwealth: Family Life in Plymouth Colony* (New York, 1970); Philip J. Greven, Jr., *Four Generations: Population, Land, and Family in Colonial Andover, Massachusetts* (Ithaca and London, 1970); Kenneth A. Lockridge, *A New England Town, the First Hundred Years: Dedham, Massachusetts, 1636-1736* (New York, 1970).

7. Douglas Edward Leach, *Flintlock and Tomahawk: New England in King Philip's War* (New York, 1958), 1; Alden T. Vaughan, *New England Frontier: Puritans and Indians, 1620-1675* (Boston, 1965), 323. Cf. Vaughan's retreat from the remarkable language of this passage in the revised edition of his work. *New England Frontier* (rev. ed., New York, 1979), 323.

8. Vaughan, *New England Frontier* (1965), vii; (1979), xlix.

9. See James Axtell, "The Ethnohistory of Early North America: A Review Essay," *WMQ* 3d ser., 35 (1978), 110-44, for a thorough discussion of the major works dealing with northeastern North America. The one major monograph on New England to reflect the influence of ethnohistory has been Francis Jennings, *The Invasion of America: Indians, Colonialism, and the Cant of Conquest* (Chapel Hill, 1975), a masterpiece of iconoclastic scholarship that, to a significant degree, sets the record straight concerning both the facts of contact between 1630 and 1676 and the ideological quality of most of the evidence bearing on those facts. But Jennings does not provide the specific context needed for understanding what happened between Indians and English in the seventeenth century. Though he offers a good deal of information on native societies in eastern North America in his first part, he does not fully integrate these discussions with the narrative of events in New England that follows. And his account of the colonists bears little relation to the large body of scholarship on the intellectual and social history of Tudor-Stuart England and colonial New England that was produced during the preceding three decades. Cf. Axtell, "Ethnohistory," 133-36; James P. Ronda, "Beyond Thanksgiving: Francis Jennings's *The Invasion of America*," *Journal of Ethnic Studies* 7, no. 2 (1979), 88-94; Richard Drinnon, "Ravished Land," *Indian Historian* 9, no. 4 (1976), 24-26.

10. William H. McNeill, *Plagues and Peoples* (paper ed., Garden City, N.Y., 1976), chaps. 3-5, *passim;* Henry F. Dobyns, "Estimating Aboriginal American Population," with comments and reply, *Current Anthropology* 7 (1966), 395-449; Alfred W. Crosby, "Virgin Soil Epidemics as a Factor in the Aboriginal Depopulation in America," *WMQ* 3d ser., 33 (1976), 289-99; Wilbur R. Jacobs, "The Tip of an Iceberg: Pre-Columbian Indian Demography and Some Implications for Revisions," *ibid.* 31 (1974), 123-32.

11. J. D. Chambers, *Population, Economy, and Society in Pre-Industrial England* (London, 1972), chap. 2.

12. On exploration, see David B. Quinn, *North America from Ear-*

liest Discovery to First Settlements: The Norse Voyages to 1612
(New York, 1977); on the background to European exploitation of North America, see Immanuel Wallerstein, *The Modern
World-System: Capitalist Agriculture and the Origins of the
European World-Economy in the Seventeenth Century* (New
York and London, 1974); on the impact of the fur trade on
native societies, see Harold Hickerson, "Fur Trade Colonialism
and the North American Indians," *Journal of Ethnic Studies*
1, no. 2 (1973), 15-44.

13. On English economic and social development, see Robert
Brenner, "Agrarian Class Structure and Economic Development in Pre-Industrial Europe," *Past and Present* 70 (1976),
30-75; Joan Thirsk, ed., *The Agrarian History of England and
Wales, 1500-1640* (Cambridge, Eng., 1967); Lawrence Stone,
"Social Mobility in England, 1500-1700," *Past and Present* 33
(1966), 16-55. On the sources of Chesapeake migration, see
James Horn, "Servant Emigration to the Chesapeake in the Seventeenth Century," in Thad W. Tate and David L. Ammerman,
eds., *The Chesapeake in the Seventeenth Century: Essays in
Anglo-American Society* (Chapel Hill, 1979), 51-95. On the
social foundations of Puritanism, see Christopher Hill, *Society
and Puritanism in Pre-Revolutionary England* (2d ed., New
York, 1967), chap. 4.

14. See, for example, Sumner Chilton Powell, *Puritan Village: The
Formation of a New England Town* (paper ed., Garden City,
N.Y., 1965); Lockridge, *New England Town;* T. H. Breen,
"Persistent Localism: English Social Change and the Shaping
of New England Institutions," *WMQ* 3d ser., 32 (1975), 3-28;
David Grayson Allen, *In English Ways: The Movement of So-
cieties and the Transferal of English Law and Custom to Mas-
sachusetts Bay in the Seventeenth Century* (Chapel Hill,
1981); James P. Henretta, "Families and Farms: *Mentalité* in
Pre-Industrial America," *WMQ* 3d ser., 35 (1978), 3-32.

15. In my "Conquest of the 'Savage,'" I gave far more weight to
Puritanism as a mediating force between the psychic and the
external, material worlds than now seems warranted. Cf. the
distinguished tradition of critical literary and ideological studies
of Euro-American attitudes and actions toward Indians which
include discussions of New England: Roy Harvey Pearce, *Sav-
agism and Civilization: A Study of the Indian and the American
Mind* (rev. ed., Baltimore, 1967); Richard Slotkin, *Regeneration Through Violence: The Mythology of the American Frontier* (Middletown, Conn., 1973); Richard Drinnon, *Facing
West: The Metaphysics of Indian-Hating and Empire Building*

(paper ed., New York, 1980); Frederick Turner, *Beyond Geography: The Western Spirit Against the Wilderness* (New York, 1980).

16. Nancy Oestereich Lurie, "Indian Cultural Adjustment to European Civilization," in James Morton Smith, ed., *Seventeenth-Century America* (Chapel Hill, 1959), 33-60, esp. 53; Edward H. Spicer, *A Short History of the Indians of the United States* (New York, 1969), chaps. 1-3, *passim;* Mary Young, "Indian Removal and the Attack on Tribal Autonomy: The Cherokee Case," in John K. Mahon, ed., *Indians of the Lower South: Past and Present* (Pensacola, Fla., 1975), 125-42; Jacqueline Peterson, " 'Wild' Chicago: The Formation and Destruction of a Multi-racial Community on the Midwestern Frontier, 1816-1837," in Melvin G. Holli and Peter d'A. Jones, eds., *The Ethnic Frontier: Essays in the History of Group Survival in Chicago and the Midwest* (Grand Rapids, Mich., 1977), 25-71; Richard White, "The Winning of the West: The Expansion of the Western Sioux in the Eighteenth and Nineteenth Centuries," *Journal of American History* 65 (1978), 319-43.

17. Gary B. Nash, *Red, White, and Black: The Peoples of Early America* (Englewood Cliffs, N.J., 1974), 46-97, *passim.*

1: FARMERS AND HUNTERS

1. Lion Gardner, "Leift Lion Gardener his relation of the Pequot Warres," *MHSC* 3d ser., 3 (1833), 154.

2. Douglas S. Byers, "Bull Brook—A Fluted Point Site in Ipswich, Massachusetts," *American Antiquity* 19 (1954), 343-51; Maurice Robbins and George A. Agogino, "The Wapanucket No. 8 Site: A Clovis-Archaic Site in Massachusetts," *ibid.*, 29 (1964), 509-13; George F. MacDonald, "A Review of Research on Paleo-Indian in Eastern North America, 1960-1970," *Arctic Anthropology* 8, no. 2 (1971), 32-41; Robert E. Funk, "Early Man in the Northeast and the Late Glacial Environment," *Man in the Northeast*, no. 4 (1972), 7-39; Don W. Dragoo, "Some Aspects of Eastern North American Prehistory: A Review 1975," *American Antiquity* 41 (1976), 5-10; Robert E. Funk, "Post-Pleistocene Adaptations," in Bruce G. Trigger, ed., *Northeast, HNAI*, 15:16-19. There is a vast ethnographic and theoretical literature on hunting societies. See especially Richard B. Lee and Irven DeVore, eds., *Man the Hunter* (Chicago, 1968); Marshall Sahlins, *Stone Age Economics* (Chicago, 1972); B. J. Williams, *A Model of Band Society*, Memoirs of the Society for

American Archaeology, no. 29, issued as *American Antiquity*
39, no. 4, part 2 (1974). On exogamous marriages, see *ibid.*,
26-29.

3. Dena F. Dincauze, "An Archaic Sequence for Southern New
England," *American Antiquity* 36 (1971), 194-98; Dena F.
Dincauze, "An Introduction to Archaeology in the Greater
Boston Area," *Archaeology of Eastern North America* 2 (1974),
44-47; James A. Tuck, "Early Archaic Horizons in Eastern
North America," *ibid.*, 72-80; Richard I. Ford, "Northeastern
Archeology: Past and Future Directions," *Annual Review of
Anthropology* 3 (1974), 389-92; Dena Ferran Dincauze, *The
Neville Site: 8,000 Years at Amoskeag*, Peabody Museum
Monographs, no. 4 (Cambridge, Mass., 1976); Dena F. Din-
cauze and Mitchell T. Mulholland, "Early and Middle Archaic
Site Distributions and Habitats in Southern New England,"
Annals of the New York Academy of Sciences 288 (1977),
439-56.

4. Joseph R. Caldwell, *Trend and Tradition in the Prehistory of
the Eastern United States*, American Anthropological Association Memoirs, no. 88, Illinois State Museum Scientific Papers,
vol. 10 (Springfield, Ill., 1958), 13-18; William A. Ritchie,
*The Archaeology of Martha's Vineyard, a Framework for the
Prehistory of Southern New England: A Study in Coastal Ecology and Adaptation* (Garden City, N.Y., 1969), 233-34 and *passim*; Dean R. Snow, "Rising Sea Level and Prehistoric Cultural
Ecology in Northern New England," *American Antiquity* 37
(1972), 211-21; David P. Braun, "Explanatory Models for the
Evolution of Coastal Adaptation in Prehistoric New England,"
ibid., 39 (1974), 584-96; James A. Tuck, "Regional Cultural
Development, 3000 to 300 B.C.," in Trigger, ed., *Northeast*,
32-36.

5. Frederick Johnson et al., *The Boylston Street Fishweir*, Papers
of the Robert S. Peabody Foundation for Archaeology, 2 (Andover, Mass., 1942); Dena F. Dincauze, "Prehistoric Occupation of the Charles River Estuary: A Paleogeographic Study,"
BASC, no. 38 (1973), 31; Maurice Robbins, *Wapanucket
no. 6: An Archaic Village in Middleboro, Massachusetts* (Attle-
boro, Mass., 1959), 24-28, 38-73.

6. *Ibid.*, 77-80; William Scranton Simmons, *Cautantowwit's
House: An Indian Burial Ground on the Island of Conanicut in
Narragansett Bay* (Providence, 1970), 14.

7. Don W. Dragoo, "Adena and the Eastern Burial Cult," *Archaeology of Eastern North America* 4 (1976), 1-9; Tuck, "Regional
Cultural Development," 41-43. But cf. Dena F. Dincauze, "The

Late Archaic Period in Southern New England," *Arctic Anthropology* 12, no. 2 (1975), 28-33.

8. Ford, "Northeastern Archeology," 399-400; Dragoo, "Some Aspects of Eastern North American Prehistory," 16-20.

9. On the marginality of Kennebec agriculture, see Dean R. Snow, "Late Prehistory of the East Coast," in Trigger, ed., *Northeast,* 68; Dean R. Snow, "Eastern Abenaki," in *ibid.,* 138. Though now outdated in many particulars, the classic statement on the continuities between Archaic and farming-based cultures remains Caldwell, *Trend and Tradition.* See also James E. Fitting, "Regional Cultural Development, 300 B.C. to A.D. 1000," in Trigger, ed., *Northeast,* 57; Snow, "Late Prehistory," 58-60.

10. Ives Goddard, "Eastern Algonquian Languages," in Trigger, ed., *Northeast,* 70-77; Ives Goddard, "Central Algonquian Languages," in *ibid.,* 586-87; Ives Goddard, "Comparative Algonquian," in Lyle Campbell and Marianne Mithun, eds., *The Languages of Native America: Historical and Comparative Assessment* (Austin and London), 70-132; Frank T. Siebert, Jr., "The Original Home of the Proto-Algonquian People," in *Contributions to Anthropology: Linguistics I (Algonquian)* (Ottawa, 1967), 13-47.

11. Samuel de Champlain, *The Complete Works of Samuel de Champlain,* ed. H. P. Biggar (6 vols.; 1922-36; reprint ed., Toronto and Buffalo, 1971), 1:325-27; Edward Winslow, "Good Newes from New England" (1624), in Alexander Young, ed., *Chronicles of the Pilgrim Fathers* (1841; reprint ed., New York, 1971), 366-67; Roger Williams, *A Key into the Language of America* (1643), ed. John J. Teunissen and Evelyn J. Hinz (Detroit, 1973), 84; Goddard, "Eastern Algonquian Languages," 72.

12. The coinciding of territorial and linguistic boundaries was first pointed out in Dean R. Snow, "A Model for the Reconstruction of Late Eastern Algonquian Prehistory," *Studies in Linguistics* 23 (1973), 77-85.

13. Goddard, "Eastern Algonquian Languages," 70-71; Phillip K. Bock, "Micmac," in Trigger, ed., *Northeast,* 109-10; Vincent O. Erickson, "Maliseet-Passamaquoddy," in *ibid.,* 123-24; Snow, "Eastern Abenaki," 137-38.

14. Goddard, "Eastern Algonquian Languages," 72; Bert Salwen, "Indians of Southern New England and Long Island: Early Period," in Trigger, ed., *Northeast,* 168. Cf. the different linguistic boundaries recorded by John Smith on the Massachusetts-Maine coast in 1614. Smith noticed little difference between the languages of the Eastern Abenaki and Pawtucket

but saw two distinct dialects centered on Massachusetts Bay and on Plymouth Bay and Cape Cod respectively. Smith, *Travels and Works of Captain John Smith*, ed. Edward Arber (2 vols.; Edinburgh, 1910), 1:192.

15. James Mooney, *The Aboriginal Population of America North of Mexico*, Smithsonian Miscellaneous Collections, vol. 8, no. 7 (Washington, D.C., 1928), 3-4. Among the more influential publications to work from Mooney's figures (and in some cases to lower them) were Frank G. Speck, *Territorial Subdivisions and Boundaries of the Wampanoag, Massachuset, and Nauset Indians*, Indian Notes and Monographs 44 (New York, 1928), 12-13; Charles C. Willoughby, *Antiquities of the New England Indians* (1935; reprint ed., New York, 1973), 278-79; A. L. Kroeber, *Cultural and Natural Areas of Native North America*, University of California Publications in American Archaeology and Ethnology 38 (Berkeley and Los Angeles, 1939), 18-33; Alden T. Vaughan, *New England Frontier: Puritans and Indians, 1620-1675* (1965; rev. ed., New York and London, 1979), 28; Lynn Ceci, "The Effect of European Contact and Trade on the Settlement Pattern of Indians in Coastal New York, 1524-1665: The Archaeological and Documentary Evidence" (Ph.D. diss., City University of New York, 1977), 303-7. On the ideological implications of these low estimates, see Francis Jennings, *The Invasion of America: Indians, Colonialism, and the Cant of Conquest* (Chapel Hill, 1975), chap. 2; Woodrow Borah, "The Historical Demography of Aboriginal and Colonial America: An Attempt at Perspective," in William T. Denevan, ed., *The Native Population of the Americas in 1492* (Madison, Wisc., 1976), 19-20.

16. William H. McNeill, *Plagues and Peoples* (paperback ed.; Garden City, N.Y., 1976), chaps. 1-5, *passim;* Alfred W. Crosby, "Virgin Soil Epidemics as a Factor in the Aboriginal Depopulation in America," *WMQ* 3d ser., 23 (1976), 289-99.

17. The assault on the older demographic orthodoxy began with Henry F. Dobyns, "Estimating Aboriginal American Population," with comments and reply, *Current Anthropology* 7 (1966), 395-449. For summaries of the rapidly proliferating literature since then, see Wilbur R. Jacobs, "The Tip of an Iceberg: Pre-Columbian Indian Demography and Some Implications for Revisionism," *WMQ* 3d ser., 31 (1974), 123-32; Henry F. Dobyns, *Native American Historical Demography: A Critical Bibliography*, The Newberry Library Center for the History of the American Indian Bibliographical Series (Bloomington and London, 1976), 10-21; Douglas H. Ubelaker, "Pre-

historic New World Population Size: Historical Review and Current Appraisal of North American Estimates," *American Journal of Physical Anthropology* 45 (1976), 661-66.

18. "The description of the Countrey of Mawooshen," in Samuel Purchas, ed., *Hakluytus Posthumus, or Purchas His Pilgrimes* (20 vols.; 1625; Glasgow, 1906), 19:400-405; Dean R. Snow, *The Archaeology of New England* (New York, 1980), 36-38. Mooney's use of Biard is noted by Douglas H. Ubelaker, "The Sources and Methodology for Mooney's Estimates of North American Indian Populations," in Denevan, ed., *Native Population*, 249, who did not, however, locate the actual citation at *JR*, 3:111.

19. Daniel Gookin, "Historical Collections of the Indians in New England," *MHSC* 1st ser., 1 (1792), 147-49; Mooney, *Aboriginal Population*, 4; Jennings, *Invasion*, 29; Peter Allen Thomas, "In the Maelstrom of Change: The Indian Trade and Cultural Process in the Middle Connecticut Valley, 1635-1665" (unpub. Ph.D. diss., University of Massachusetts, Amherst, 1979), 24-28; Dobyns, "Estimating." Examining Mooney's notes, Ubelaker found that the ethnologist dismissed Gookin's figures as exaggerated but recorded no reason for his judgment. "Sources and Methodology," 249-52, *passim*.

20. S. F. Cook, *The Indian Population of New England in the Seventeenth Century*, University of California Publications in Anthropology 12 (Berkeley, 1976), 13, 23, 27, 30, 35. Estimates originating with Gookin and his informants are also given without citing him in *ibid.*, 47, 51.

21. Cook followed the Polish demographer Ludwik Krzywicki in applying a standard formula derived from accounts from all over North America which provided both kinds of figures. Yet even a cursory understanding of North American cultural diversity should have made clear the futility of employing any such ratio, the more so when no figures from southern New England contributed to the continental "average." Cook also followed Krzywicki in attempting to estimate pre-contact household size. Though he broke the continent into several regions in this case, Cook gained little in accuracy since his "eastern forest and north" alone probably contained as much variation in "household size" as all of North America. On family size, Cook recognized that Gookin's factor of five persons per adult male in 1674 was too low for the demographically more favorable environment of 1600. But his solution was simply to propose instead a range of six to seven as a typical extended or "social" family size among "primitive" peoples everywhere, and

finally to settle on six as a safe bet. *Ibid.*, 4-7; Ludwick Krzy-wicki, *Primitive Society and Its Vital Statistics* (London, 1934), 318-541, *passim*, esp. 318-21.

22. Cook, *Indian Population*, 84.
23. Lawrence C. Wroth, *The Voyages of Giovanni da Verrazzano, 1524-1528* (New Haven and London, 1970), 139-40. On Indian health, see Smith, *Travels and Works*, 1:193; Wood, *New England's Prospect* (1634), ed. Alden T. Vaughan (Amherst, Mass., 1977), 93-94. On warfare, see John Underhill, "Newes from America" (1638), *MHSC* 3d ser., 6 (1837), 26, 27; John Mason, "A Brief History of the Pequot War," *ibid.*, 2d ser., 8 (1826), 149; Williams, *Key*, 237; Jennings, *Invasion*, chap. 9.
24. Williams, *Key*, 118.
25. Sydney V. James, Jr., *Three Visitors to Early Plymouth* ([Plymouth, Mass.], 1963), 79.
26. Cf. Fernand Braudel, *Capitalism and Material Life*, trans. Miriam Kochan (New York, 1967), 7.
27. Gookin, "Historical Collections," 148-49; Salwen, "Indians of Southern New England," 169-70; Champlain, *Works*, 1:336-37; Smith, *Travels and Works*, 1:204-5; J. Franklin Jameson, ed., *Narratives of New Netherland, 1609-1664*, Original Narratives of Early American History (1909; reprint ed., New York, 1967), 39.
28. Champlain, *Works*, 1:398-401; Marc Lescarbot, *The History of New France*, trans. and ed. W. L. Grant (3 vols.; 1907-14; reprint ed., New York, 1968), 2:325-28.
29. Smith, *Travels and Works*, 1:204; Warren K. Moorhead, *The Merrimack Archaeological Survey: A Preliminary Paper* (Salem, Mass., 1931); Cook, *Indian Population*, 13-17, 19-28.
30. Gookin, "Historical Collections," 148; Champlain, *Works*, 1: 335, 340; Smith, *Travels and Works*, 1:192, 204-5; Edward Johnson, *Johnson's Wonder-Working Providence* (1654), ed. J. Franklin Jameson, Original Narratives of Early American History (1910; reprint ed., New York, 1967), 41; James, ed., *Three Visitors*, 29.
31. Gookin, "Historical Collections," 148; Champlain, *Works*, 1: 340. According to Smith, the Indians of the coast as far south as Patuxet, which he called "Accomack," at Plymouth Bay were affiliated with the Massachusett rather than with the Indians of Cape Cod. The discrepancy between him and Gookin as to the Massachusett's southern boundary does not seriously affect the rough population estimates offered here but does suggest that Gookin was reinforcing the rewriting of local Indian history occasioned by Plymouth's treaty with the Pokanoket in 1621. Smith, *Travels and Works*, 1:192; this volume, p. 116.

32. Smith, *Travels and Works*, 1:192; Champlain, *Works*, 1:405, 411, 415; Lescarbot, *History*, 2:332.
33. John Brereton, "A Briefe and True Relation of the Discoverie of the North Part of Virginia" (1602), in Charles Herbert Levermore, ed., *Forerunners and Competitors of the Pilgrims and Puritans* (2 vols.; Brooklyn, 1912), 1:37; Gabriel Archer, "The Relation of Captaine Gosnol's Voyage to the North Part of Virginia" (1625), in *ibid.*, 51; Jameson, ed., *Narratives*, 41. See also the Dutch map in *NYCD*, 1:12-13.
34. Cook, *Indian Population*, 44.
35. Gookin, "Historical Collections," 147-48; Francis Brinley, "Briefe Narrative of the Nanhiganset Countrey," Rhode Island Historical Society, *Publications* 8 (1900), 74.
36. Gookin, "Historical Collections," 147.
37. This calculation is based on Dean Snow's estimate of population density for the Eastern Abenaki plus his figures on the territory of the southern New England Indians. When his "Upper Merrimack" drainage area is included with those to the south, as in Gookin, we get a range of 2.33 to 2.67 per 100 km^2. (But note that Snow's "Lower Connecticut and Central Long Island" includes some territory omitted by Gookin.) Snow's own calculations, as indicated earlier for the Eastern Abenaki, seem to me to underestimate pre-contact family sizes. See Snow, *Archaeology*, 31-42. I am indebted to Professor Snow for sharing this portion of his manuscript with me prior to its publication.
38. Champlain, *Works*, 1:327-28; Martin Pring, "A Voyage . . . for the Discoverie of the North Part of Virginia" (1625), in Levermore, ed., *Forerunners*, 1:65; James, ed., *Three Visitors*, 71; Williams, *Key*, 163, 170; Jameson, ed., *Narratives*, 219; Eva L. Butler, "Algonkian Culture and Use of Maize in Southern New England," *BASC* 22 (1948), 18; Lawrence Kaplan, "Archeology and Domestication in American Phaseolus (Beans)," *Economic Botany* 19 (1965), 359-60; Conrad Heidenreich, *Huronia: A History and Geography of the Huron Indians, 1600-1650* (Toronto, 1971), 184.
39. James, ed., *Three Visitors*, 71; Wood, *New England's Prospect*, 113; Williams, *Key*, 163, 170, 171; Champlain, *Works*, 1:410-11; Dwight B. Heath, ed., *A Journal of the Pilgrims at Plymouth: Mourt's Relation* (New York, 1963), 22; Underhill, "Newes," 7; Butler, "Algonkian Culture," 17-20, 22-24. The well-known story of the Patuxet Squanto showing the Plymouth colonists how to use fish as fertilizer is questioned by Lynn Ceci, who argues that Squanto was demonstrating a technique learned from Europeans rather than an Indian custom. Ceci,

"Fish Fertilizer: A Native North American Practice?," *Science* 188 (4 April 1975), 26-30. Though Ceci is persuasive on the lack of evidence that fish were used this way by New England Indians in general, her argument that Squanto learned the technique from Europeans—probably English colonists in Newfoundland—is at best hypothetical. Thus far no one has considered the possibility that fish fertilizer was a strictly local adaptation by which the Patuxet and, perhaps, a few other coastal groups with high, concentrated populations, small amounts of farmland, and an abundance of fish, had increased their agricultural yields before the depopulation of the late 1610s. On Squanto's youth and early adulthood in pre-epidemic Patuxet, see Neal Salisbury, "Squanto: Last of the Patuxets," in David Sweet and Gary B. Nash, eds., *Struggle and Survival in Colonial America* (Berkeley, 1981), 228-34. Lescarbot reported that the southern New England natives used shells as fertilizer. *History,* 3:195.

40. Butler, "Algonkian Culture," 26-31; M. K. Bennett, "The Food Economy of the New England Indians, 1605-75," *Journal of Political Economy* 63 (1955), 369-87. Cf. the survey of food remains at several archaeological sites in Frederick W. Warner, "The Foods of the Connecticut Indians," *BASC* 37 (1972), 27-47. Lynn Ceci argues that Indians on Long Island and in what is now New York City only began to farm (and then minimally) after European colonization obliged them to adopt year-round sedentary settlement patterns. This argument is of course consistent with her assertion, noted above (n. 15), that the pre-contact population of this area was lower even than Mooney estimated. It is unclear whether subsistence conditions in the area Ceci has studied differed radically from those in southern New England or whether Ceci's failure to consider diseases led her to conclusions at such sharp variance with the evidence offered here. Ceci, "Effect," chap. 2.

41. Jameson, ed., *Narratives,* 105-8, *passim;* Wood, *New England's Prospect,* 106, 107; Thomas Morton, *New English Canaan* (1637), ed. Charles Francis Adams, Jr. (1883; reprint ed., New York, 1967), 138; Edward Winslow, "The Glorious Progress of the Gospel amongst the Indians in New England" (1649), *MHSC* 3d ser., 4 (1834), 81; William Hubbard, *A General History of New England* (1682; 1848 ed. reprinted, New York, 1972), 30-31, Williams, *Key,* 164-66, 168-69, 224.

42. *JR,* 3:77-83; Calvin Martin, *Keepers of the Game: Indian-Animal Relationships and the Fur Trade* (Berkeley, 1978), 42; Butler, "Algonkian Culture," 9-11; Peter A. Thomas, "Contrastive Subsistence Strategies and Land Use as Factors for Under-

standing Indian-White Relations in New England," *Ethnohistory* 23 (1976), 5-11; Thomas, "Maelstrom," 96-117.

43. Kent V. Flannery, "Archeological Systems Theory and Early Mesoamerica," in Betty Meggers, ed., *Anthropological Archeology in the Americas* (Washington, D.C., 1968), 67-78; Caldwell, *Trend and Tradition*, 11-14; Snow, "Late Prehistory," 58-60, 64-69. Cf. Melvin L. Fowler, "Agriculture and Village Settlement in the North American East: The Central Mississippi Valley Area, A Case History," in Stuart Struever, ed., *Prehistoric Agriculture* (Garden City, N.Y., 1971), 391-403.

44. Harold C. Conklin, "The Study of Shifting Cultivation," *Current Anthropology* 2 (1961), 27-61.

45. See especially Hu Maxwell, "The Use and Abuse of Forests by the Virginia Indians," *WMQ* 1st ser., 19 (1910), 73-103.

46. Clifford Geertz, *Agricultural Involution: The Process of Ecological Change in Indonesia* (Berkeley and Los Angeles, 1963), 16-24; Edward C. Higbee, "The Three Earths of New England," *Geographical Review* 42 (1952), 425-38.

47. Wood, *New England's Prospect*, 38; Williams, *Key*, 191; William Morell, "Morell's Poem on New-England" (*ca.* 1625), *MHSC* 1st ser., 1 (1792), 132; Morton, *New English Canaan*, 172; Higbee, "Three Earths," 426-27; Gordon M. Day, "The Indian as an Ecological Factor in the Northeastern Forest," *Ecology* 34 (1953), 329-46; S. K. Bromley, "An Indian Relict Area," *Scientific Monthly* 60 (1945), 153-54; Calvin Martin, "Fire and Forest Structure in the Aboriginal Eastern Forest," *Indian Historian* 6, no. 4 (1973), 38-42, 54; Geertz, *Agricultural Involution*, 16.

48. Williams, *Key*, 160-61, 164, 189, 190, 191-92; Wood, *New England's Prospect*, 100; Butler, "Algonkian Culture," 20-21, 24-26; John Witthoft, *Green Corn Ceremonialism in the Eastern Woodlands*, Occasional Contributions from the Museum of Anthropology of the University of Michigan 13 (Ann Arbor, 1949), 5-11.

49. John Josselyn, *An Account of Two Voyages to New-England* (1675; Boston, 1865), 106-7; Martin, *Keepers of the Game, passim*.

50. Champlain, *Works*, 1:410-11; Heath, ed., *Journal*, 22; Butler, "Algonkian Culture," 23-24. During his visit in the late spring of 1524, Verrazzano found the Indians of Narragansett Bay still eating corn, some of which they presented to him and his crew. Wroth, *Verrazzano*, 138, 139, 140.

51. *JR*, 3:79; Gordon M. Day, "An Agawam Fragment," *International Journal of Linguistics* 33 (1967), 244-47.

52. Kenneth M. Morrison, "Towards a History of Intimate En-

counters: Algonkian Folklore, Jesuit Missionaries, and Ki-wakwe, the Cannibal Giant," *AICRJ* 3, no. 4 (1979), 55.

53. Williams, *Key*, 194; Simmons, *Cautantowwit's House*, chap. 4, *passim*.

54. Frank G. Speck, "Penobscot Tales and Religious Beliefs," *Journal of American Folk-lore* 48 (1935), 75-79.

55. Wendell S. Hadlock, "Three Contact Burials from Eastern Massachusetts," *BMAS* 10 (1948-49), 65; Simmons, *Cautantowwit's House*, 59-62, 67-68.

56. Werner Müller, "North America," in Walter Krickberg et al., *Pre-Columbian American Religions*, trans. Stanley Davis (London, 1968), 161-70, esp. 168; Kenneth M. Morrison, "The People of the Dawn: The Abnaki and Their Relations with New England and New France; 1600-1727" (Ph.D. diss., University of Maine, 1975), 18-25; Martin, *Keepers of the Game*, 35.

57. Williams, *Key*, 190, 191.

58. William Jones, "The Algonkin Manitou," *Journal of American Folk-lore* 18 (1905), 183-90; Müller, "North America," 154; Simmons, *Cautantowwit's House*, 51; Martin, *Keepers of the Game*, 34. For a discussion that includes equivalents of manitou in the Siouan and Iroquoian language families, see the editor's introduction in Elisabeth Tooker, ed., *Native North American Spirituality of the Eastern Woodlands* (New York, 1979), 11-30.

59. Williams, *Key*, 173.

60. *JR*, 2:77-79; 3:101-3; Wood, *New England's Prospect*, 112-14; Williams, *Key*, 103, 117, 121, 122, 170, 207. See also the sexual distinctions in burial goods in Simmons, *Cautantowwit's House*, 44-46.

61. James, ed., *Three Visitors*, 79; Winslow, "Good Newes," 363; Josselyn, *Account*, 50. For the equivalent rites for young women, see Winslow, "Good Newes," 364; Morton, *New English Canaan*, 145.

62. *JR*, 3:103-5; Winslow, "Good Newes," 364; Williams, *Key*, 86, 115, 117, 185.

63. Wroth, *Verrazzano*, 138-39; Brereton, "Relation," 40; Archer, "Relation," 48-49; Pring, "Voyage," 64.

64. Judith K. Brown, "A Note on the Division of Labor by Sex," *American Anthropologist* 72 (1970), 1073-78; Judith K. Brown, "Economic Organization and the Position of Women among the Iroquois," *Ethnohistory* 17 (1970), 151-67; Anthony F. C. Wallace, *The Death and Rebirth of the Seneca* (New York, 1970), 28-30.

65. Patrilocal residence is implied in the numerous references to divorce in which women are reported to have left their husbands, voluntarily or involuntarily, rather than the reverse. See, for example, Winslow, "Good Newes," 364; Wood, *New England's Prospect*, 99-100; Gookin, "Historical Collections," 149. For an argument that the Narragansett may have reckoned kinship matrilineally, see William S. Simmons, and George Aubin, "Narragansett Kinship," *Man in the Northeast* 9 (1975), 21-31. An essay that appeared after this manuscript was complete argues briefly but cogently that the sexual division of labor among coastal Algonquian horticulturalists was far less pronounced than has traditionally been assumed, both before and during the colonial period. See Robert Steven Grumet, "Sunksquaws, Shamans, and Tradeswomen: Middle Atlantic Coastal Algonkian Women During the 17th and 18th Centuries," in Mona Etienne and Eleanor Leacock, eds., *Women and Colonization: Anthropological Perspectives* (New York, 1980), 43-62.

66. James, ed., *Three Visitors*, 72; Williams, *Key*, 115; Gookin, "Historical Collections," 149; Thomas, "Maelstrom," 32-36; Lorraine E. Williams, "Ft. Shantok and Ft. Corchaug: A Comparative Study of Seventeenth Century Culture Contact in the Long Island Sound Area" (Ph.D. diss., New York University, 1972), 30.

67. Winslow, "Good Newes," 361-62; Williams, *Key*, 170, 206.

68. *JR*, 2:73. See also *ibid.*, 1:73-75, 3:87-91; Bock, "Micmac," 115-16; Erikson, "Maliseet-Passamaquoddy," 131; Snow, "Eastern Abenaki," 140; Morrison, "People of the Dawn," 38-43.

69. Williams, *Key*, 202; Wood, *New England's Prospect*, 97.

70. Winslow, "Good Newes," 361-62; Williams, *Key*, 201, 203, 227, 235. For a discussion of band leadership from the perspective of political anthropology, see Thomas, "Maelstrom," 38-44. Thomas emphasizes the impact of European contact on traditional patterns of sachem selection.

71. *JR*, 1:73-77; 3:91; Morton, *New English Canaan*, 150-51; Wood, *New England's Prospect*, 100-101.

72. Winslow, "Good Newes," 357-60; Wood, *New England's Prospect*, 100-101; William S. Simmons, "Southern New England Shamanism: An Ethnographic Reconstruction," in William Cowan, ed., *Papers of the Seventh Algonquian Conference, 1975* (Ottawa, 1976), 217-56, *passim*.

73. Williams, *Key*, 193, 231, 120, 124, 203; Winslow, "Good Newes," 359; Jameson, ed., *Narratives*, 87; Wood, *New England's Prospect*, 98; Benjamin Basset, "Fabulous Traditions

and Customs of the Indians of Martha's Vineyard," *MHSC* 1st ser., 1 (1792), 140.

74. Claude Lévi-Strauss, *The Savage Mind* (Chicago, 1966), 30-33; Wood, *New England's Prospect*, 103-4.

75. *Ibid.*, 104; Lévi-Strauss, *Savage Mind*, 30-31.

76. Wood, *New England's Prospect*, 85.

77. Josselyn, *Account*, 105; John Josselyn, *New-England's Rarities* (1672), ed. Edward Tuckerman (Boston, 1865), 38. On conversational etiquette, cf. Wallace, *Death and Rebirth*, 76. On the possibility that such rituals represented nativistic responses to Europeans, see William Turnbaugh, "Elements of Nativistic Pipe Ceremonialism in the Post-Contact Northeast," *Pennsylvania Archeologist* 47 (1977), 1-7.

78. Thomas Shepard, "The Clear Sun-shine of the Gospel Breaking forth upon the Indians in New-England" (1648), *MHSC* 3d ser., 4 (1834), 60; Williams, *Key*, 152, 207; Wood, *New England's Prospect*, 92; Morton, *New English Canaan*, 145-46; Winslow, "Good Newes," 358; Josselyn, *Account*, 99-100; A. Irving Hallowell, "Some Psychological Characteristics of the Northeastern Indians" (1946), in his *Culture and Experience* (Philadelphia, 1955), chap. 6; Harold Hickerson, "Some Implications of the Theory of the Particularity, or 'Atomism,' of Northern Algonkians," with comments, *Current Anthropology* 8 (1967), 313-43, esp. 323.

79. Morton, *New English Canaan*, 138; Winslow, "Glorious Progress," 81; Williams, *Key*, 193; *JR*, 3:89-91; Howard M. Chapin, *Sachems of the Narragansetts* (Providence, 1931), appendices.

80. Williams, *Key*, 202; Winslow, "Good Newes," 360-61; Wood, *New England's Prospect*, 98. For more recent examples, see Speck, *Territorial Subdivisions*, 32-33; Anthony F. C. Wallace, "Political Organization and Land Tenure among the Northeastern Indians, 1600-1830," *Southwestern Journal of Anthropology* 13 (1957), 306-7; Vaughan, *New England Frontier*, 32-33; Jennings, *Invasion*, 110-16.

81. Cf. Thomas, "Maelstrom," 32-38; T. J. C. Brasser, "The Coastal Algonkians: People of the First Frontiers," in Eleanor Burke Leacock and Nancy Oestereich Lurie, eds., *North American Indians in Historical Perspective* (New York, 1971), 65-66; Salwen, "Indians of Southern New England," 168. On the distinguishing characteristics of "bands," "tribes," and "chiefdoms," the classic statement is Elman R. Service, *Primitive Social Organization: An Evolutionary Perspective* (2d ed.; New York, 1971).

82. Marcel Mauss, *The Gift: Forms and Functions of Exchange in Archaic Societies*, trans. Ian Cunnison (London, 1954), 3.

83. Thus early European visitors found wampum shells from Long Island Sound near the Bay of Fundy, and European copper, obtained from Indians in the latter region, in southern New England. On copper in the south, see Wroth, *Verrazzano*, 138; Brereton, "Relation," 34-35, 38-39; Archer, "Relation," 46. Lescarbot noted late in the first decade of the seventeenth century that, unable to procure wampum from southern New England, the Micmac were obtaining what they considered a poor substitute from the French. *History*, 3:158. Also on wampum, see herein, p. 49.

2: HUNTERS AND TRADERS

1. Charles Hudson, *The Southeastern Indians* (Knoxville, Tenn., 1976), 97.
2. T. J. C. Brasser, "The Coastal Algonkians: People of the First Frontiers," in Eleanor Burke Leacock and Nancy Oestereich Lurie, eds., *North American Indians in Historical Perspective* (New York, 1971), 66-71.
3. See David Beers Quinn, *England and the Discovery of America, 1481-1620* (New York, 1974), chap. 1, for a comprehensive discussion of his own and other arguments.
4. David B. Quinn, *North America from Earliest Discovery to First Settlements: The Norse Voyages to 1612* (New York, 1977), chap. 5, *passim* and pp. 513-17.
5. Bernard G. Hoffman, *Cabot to Cartier: Sources for a Historical Ethnography of Northeastern North America, 1497-1550* (Toronto, 1961), 11; Quinn, *North America*, 119, 123, 126, 131-32.
6. Lawrence C. Wroth, *The Voyages of Giovanni da Verrazzano, 1524-1528* (New Haven and London, 1970), 134-40.
7. *Ibid.*, 140-41.
8. Richard I. Ford, "Northeastern Archeology: Past and Future Directions," *Annual Review of Anthropology* 3 (1974), 394; John Witthoft, "Archaeology as a Key to the Colonial Fur Trade," *Minnesota History* 40 (1966), 205. Lynn Ceci assumes that the copper Verrazzano saw was acquired directly from earlier European visitors, which is possible but less likely than the explanation offered here. Lynn Ceci, "The Effect of European Contact and Trade on the Settlement Pattern of Indians in Coastal New York, 1524-1665: The Archeological and Documentary Evidence" (Ph.D. diss., City University of New York, 1977), 143-44. Cf. Malcolm C. Webb, "Exchange Networks: Prehistory," *Annual Review of Anthropology* 3 (1974), 346-47; Wilcomb E. Washburn, "Symbol, Utility, and Aesthetics in the Indian Fur Trade," *Minnesota History* 40 (1966), 198-202.

9. Dean R. Snow, "Abenaki Fur Trade in the Sixteenth Century," *Western Canadian Journal of Anthropology* 6 (1976), 3-11; Hoffman, *Cabot to Cartier*, 125-30; Quinn, *North America*, 160-162, 352.

10. H. P. Biggar, ed., *The Voyages of Jacques Cartier*, Publications of the Public Archives of Canada 11 (Ottawa, 1924), 49-57; Bruce G. Trigger, *The Children of Aataentsic: A History of the Huron People to 1660* (2 vols.; Montreal and London, 1976), 1:177-78.

11. Biggar, ed., *Voyages of Cartier*, 60-67, 80-81; Trigger, *Children*, 1:178-83.

12. A short-lived Portuguese colony on Cape Breton Island in the 1520s found the Micmac there to be "submissive." H. P. Biggar, ed., *The Precursors of Jacques Cartier, 1497-1534* (Ottawa, 1911), 197.

13. Biggar, ed., *Voyages of Cartier*, 177-78; Bernard G. Hoffman, "The Historical Ethnography of the Micmac of the Sixteenth and Seventeenth Centuries" (Ph.D. diss., University of California, Berkeley, 1955), 29-30. On the Micmac advantage, cf. Trigger, *Children*, 1:216.

14. H. P. Biggar, *The Early Trading Companies of New France* (Toronto, 1901), 25; Quinn, *North America*, 524; Hoffman, *Cabot to Cartier*, 32, 201.

15. Biggar, ed., *Voyages of Cartier*, 53. Cartier does not say explicitly that the Micmac had a surplus but this can be reasonably concluded from the context, especially by contrasting his remarks to those he made about the Stadaconans. Cf. Trigger, *Children*, 1:178.

16. Quinn, *North America*, 524-32, 535; Biggar, *Early Trading Companies*, 28-29, 32-33; Hoffman, "Historical Ethnography," 31-32; Marcel Trudel, *The Beginnings of New France, 1524-1663*, trans. Patricia Claxton (Toronto, 1973), 57-58; Harold A. Innis, *The Fur Trade in Canada* (rev. ed.; New Haven, 1962), 15-16. For the locations of some of the more prominent fishing stations after the turn of the century, see Lescarbot, *History*, 2:284. Additional scattered figures on fur trade volume can be found in D. B. Quinn, "The Voyage of Etienne Bellenger to the Maritimes in 1583: A New Document," *Canadian Historical Review* 43 (1962), 341-42; Biggar, *Early Trading Companies*, 63; Wilson D. Wallis and Ruth Sawtell Wallis, *The Micmac Indians of Eastern Canada* (Minneapolis, 1955), 10. On the difficulties of achieving an overall quantitative picture, see Quinn, *North America*, 513.

17. Alfred Goldsworthy Bailey, "The Ordeal of the Eastern Algon-

quians," in his *Culture and Nationality* (Toronto and Montreal, 1972), 30; Quinn, *North America,* 348. Scholars are not in unanimous agreement as to the ethnic identities and dialects of several eastern Canadian and northern New England Algonquian groups described in early colonial documents, and to the continuity between those groups and contemporary Indian communities. I follow here the usages accepted by most ethnohistorians and linguists, including the authors of the relevant essays in Bruce G. Trigger, ed., *Northeast, HNAI* 15 (Washington, D.C., 1978. The one group which has not been positively identified is that on the Saco River at Chouacoet. Cf. the maps in *ibid.,* 138, 161.

18. Alfred Goldsworthy Bailey, *The Conflict of European and Algonkian Cultures, 1504-1700: A Study in Canadian Civilization* (2d ed.; Toronto, 1969), 47; Hoffman, "Historical Ethnography," 31; Calvin Martin, "The Four Lives of a Micmac Copper Pot," *Ethnohistory* 22 (1975), 113-16. The long scholarly debate on the effects of the European fur trade on the traditional values and institutions of the northern Algonquians is succinctly reviewed in *ibid.,* 117-20.

19. Marc Lescarbot, *The History of New France,* trans. and ed. W. L. Grant (3 vols.; 1907-14; reprint ed., New York, 1968), 2:281-82, 3:168; *JR,* 3:69, 105-7; Bailey, *Conflict,* 47; Hoffman, "Historical Ethnography," 231-36.

20. *JR,* 1:75; Bernard G. Hoffman, "Souriquois, Etechemin, and Kwĕdĕch: A Lost Chapter in American Ethnography," *Ethnohistory* 2 (1955), 66; Trigger, *Children,* 1:213, 216; Bailey, *Conflict,* 12-13, 50-53.

21. *JR,* 1:77, 177; 3:81, 105-9, 111; Alfred W. Crosby, "Virgin Soil Epidemics as a Factor in the Aboriginal Depopulation in America," *WMQ* 3d ser., 33 (1976), 289-99; Dean R. Snow, *The Archaeology of New England* (New York, 1980), 35-36. With Snow, I see Virginia Miller's pre-contact figure for the Micmac of 35,000 as unjustifiably high. Miller, "Aboriginal Micmac Population: A Review of the Evidence," *Ethnohistory* 23 (1976), 117-27. Lescarbot estimated less than 2000 for the Micmac in the early 1610s—an even lower figure than Biard's. *JR,* 2:73.

22. Calvin Martin, "The European Impact on the Culture of a Northeastern Algonquian Tribe: An Ecological Interpretation," *WMQ* 3d ser., 31 (1974), 17-24; Calvin Martin, *Keepers of the Game: Indian-Animal Relationships and the Fur Trade* (Berkeley, 1978), 53.

23. Lescarbot, *History,* 2:355; *JR,* 3:81, 1:173-75.

24. Cf. Martin, *Keepers of the Game,* which argues that Indians engaged in the relentless pursuit of wildlife as revenge upon the animals for having caused the diseases.

25. For an account of contemporary Micmac that argues for continuity with the pre-contact and colonial periods, see Jeanne Guillemin, *Urban Renegades: The Cultural Strategy of American Indians* (New York and London, 1975).

26. Innis, *Fur Trade,* 16-19.

27. Trudel, *Beginnings of New France,* chap. 4; Lescarbot, *History,* 2:211-16; W. J. Eccles, *France in America* (New York, 1972), 14.

28. Samuel de Champlain, *The Works of Samuel de Champlain,* ed. H. P. Biggar (6 vols.; 1922-36; reprint ed., Toronto and Buffalo, 1971), 1:295, 296.

29. *Ibid.,* 367-68; Lescarbot, *History,* 2:280-81. Lescarbot places the village just 500 paces from the French fort but Champlain's map does not show it, suggesting that the Indians moved there after the fort was established. Cf. *ibid.,* 3:274-75 and Champlain, *Works,* 1:259.

30. Lescarbot, *History,* 2:354-55; *JR,* 1:75-77.

31. Trudel, *Beginnings of New France,* chap. 11.

32. Champlain, *Works,* 1:314-16, 363-65; Lescarbot, *History,* 2: 322.

33. Champlain, *Works,* 1:326, 414.

34. *Ibid.,* 349-55.

35. *Ibid.,* 397-401; Lescarbot, *History,* 2:325-28.

36. Champlain, *Works,* 1:407-31; Lescarbot, *History,* 2:330-37.

37. Douglas R. McManis, *European Impressions of the New England Coast, 1497-1620* (Chicago, 1972), 83-85, summarizes these arguments.

38. Champlain, *Works,* 1: maps facing 346, 358, 401, 421.

39. *Ibid.,* 326.

40. *Ibid.,* 394.

41. *Ibid.,* 299, 364; Lescarbot, *History,* 2:323.

42. Champlain, *Works,* 1:321, 329-30.

43. Lescarbot, *History,* 2:323-24. Alvin Morrison has stressed the insulting nature—by the standards of Indian protocol—of Messamouet's conduct, in "Membertou's Raid on the Chouacoet 'Almouchiquois'—The Micmac Sack of Saco in 1607," in William Cowan, ed., *Papers of the Sixth Algonquian Conference, 1974* (Ottawa, 1975), 150-51.

44. Lescarbot, *History,* 2:324-25, 327; Champlain, *Works,* 1: 395-96.

45. Champlain, *Works,* 1:435-36, 442-43, 457; Lescarbot, *History,*

3:273; Marc Lescarbot, "The Defeat of the Armouchiquois Savages by Chief Membertou and His Savage Allies," trans. Thomas Goetz, in William Cowan, ed., *Papers of the Sixth Algonquian Conference, 1974* (Ottawa, 1975), 160.

46. Champlain, *Works*, 1:445.
47. Lescarbot, "Defeat," 162-63. Sasinou's conflict with other Abenaki bands was noted by James Davies, a member of the English colony at Sagadahoc (to be discussed in the next chapter), and by Champlain but not by Lescarbot. Davies also noted Sasinou's earlier enmity with the Micmac. Davies, "The Relation of a Voyage, unto New England," in Charles Herbert Levermore, ed., *Forerunners and Competitors of the Pilgrims and Puritans* (2 vols.; Brooklyn, 1912), 1:363, 372; Champlain, *Works*, 1:457. Alvin Morrison has difficulty ascertaining Sasinou's motives because he assumes the existence of an "Abenaki confederacy" led by "superchief Bashaba," of which Sasinou and his band were a part. "Membertou's Raid," 152-53.
48. Lescarbot, "Defeat," 170, 168, 169, 172, 174.
49. Lescarbot, *History*, 3:264; Lescarbot, "Defeat," 168, 176-77.
50. Lescarbot, *History*, 2:368-69n.; JR, 1:67.
51. *Ibid.*, 69-71; Lescarbot, *History*, 2:233; Trudel, *Beginnings of New France*, 84, 88.
52. JR, 1:77, 108-13, 121; 2:135-61, 89.
53. *Ibid.*, 2:89, 1:163.
54. *Ibid.*, 2:121, 1:213.
55. *Ibid.*, 1:25-51, 2:81-87, 211-17; Trudel, *Beginnings of New France*, 108-11.
56. JR, 3:56, 245-47.
57. *Ibid.*, 2:9-23, 93-99.
58. *Ibid.*, 1:163, 2:15-19, 51-53.
59. Cf. Morrison, "People of the Dawn," 70-73; Robert Conkling, "Legitimacy and Conversion in Social Change: The Case of French Missionaries and the Northeastern Algonkian," *Ethnohistory* 21 (1974), 1-24, esp. 12-13.
60. James P. Ronda, "The Missionary as Cultural Revolutionary: Two Seventeenth-Century Examples" (unpub. paper presented to the meeting of the American Studies Association, San Antonio, November 1975).
61. JR, 2:75-77; James P. Ronda, "The European Indian: Jesuit Civilization Planning in New France," *Church History* 41 (1972), 385-95.
62. JR, 2:19-23, 95-99.
63. *Ibid.*, 33-45, 49-53.
64. *Ibid.*, 247-49, 3:239-43, 261-73; Lucien Campeau, "La Pre-

mière Mission des Jésuites en Nouvelle-France (1611-1613)," in *Cahiers d'Histoire des Jésuites* 1 (Montreal, 1972), 27-41.

65. *JR*, 2:249-75, 3:4-19, 275-83, 4:8-79; Campeau, "La Première Mission," 41-47.

66. John Smith, *Travels and Works of Captain John Smith*, ed. Edward Arber (2 vols.; Edinburgh, 1910), 1:188, 200, 205; 2:937. Smith's own haul was "neer 1100 Bever skinnes, 100 Martins, and neer as many Otters." *Ibid.*, 1:188.

67. *Ibid.*, 1:192; Snow, "Abenaki Fur Trade," 7-8.

68. Smith, *Travels and Works*, 1:203, 218.

69. *Ibid.*, 206.

70. Gookin, "Historical Collections of the Indians in New England," *MHSC* 1st ser., 1 (1792), 148-49. On the discrepancy between Smith's and Gookin's identifications of the Patuxet, see above, chap. 1, n. 31.

71. Bert Salwen, "Indians of Southern New England and Long Island: Early Period," in Trigger, ed., *Northeast*, 168; Brasser, "Coastal Algonquians," 65.

72. Trigger, *Children*, 1:209, 214-28. Based on both archaeological and documentary evidence, Trigger's account is the most thorough and reasoned explanation of the long-debated "disappearance of the St. Lawrence Iroquoians."

73. *Ibid.*, 228-36, 247-61.

74. J. Franklin Jameson, ed., *Narratives of New Netherland, 1609-1664*, Original Narratives of Early American History (1909; reprint ed., New York, 1967), 7, 18-23; Allen W. Trelease, *Indian Affairs in Colonial New York: The Seventeenth Century* (1960; reprint ed., Port Washington, N.Y., 1970), 26-27.

75. Thomas J. Condon, *New York Beginnings: The Commercial Origins of New Netherland* (New York and London, 1968), 18-25; Van Cleaf Bachman, *Peltries or Plantations: The Economic Policies of the Dutch West India Company in New Netherland, 1623-1639* (Baltimore, 1969), 7-10; Simon Hart, *The Prehistory of the New Netherland Company* (Amsterdam, 1959), 26-34.

76. Trelease, *Indian Affairs*, 31-32.

77. Trigger, *Children*, 1:229; Bruce G. Trigger, "The Mohawk-Mahican War (1624-28): The Establishment of a Pattern," *Canadian Historical Review* 52 (1971), 276-86.

78. Jameson, ed., *Narratives*, 39-44, 309.

79. *Ibid.*, 41, 42. The Dutch also noted the Narragansett's unique dual sachemship, for which see also Wroth, *Verrazzano*, 138; Roger Williams, *A Key into the Language of America* (1643), ed. John J. Teunissen and Evelyn J. Hinz (Detroit, 1973),

201; Howard M. Chapin, *Sachems of the Narragansetts* (Providence, 1931), 6-7. In the Dutch map based on accounts of Block's expedition, the "Wapanoos" are placed on both sides of Narragansett Bay and the "Nahicans" on the east end of Long Island because of a cartographer's copying error. See I. N. Phelps Stokes, *The Iconography of Manhattan Island, 1498-1909* (6 vols.; 1915-28; reprinted, New York, 1967), 2:70. The map is reproduced in *ibid.*, plate 23, and *NYCD*, 1: between pp. 12 and 13.

80. Jameson, ed., *Narratives*, 42-43. Jameson identifies these rivers as the Thames and the Four Mile respectively, but a careful reading of the written account, by Johan de Laet, indicates that these identifications are erroneous. De Laet does not say, as Jameson says he does, that the Pequot's river is a different one from the "Sagamore" (actually, the Mystic) mentioned earlier in the same paragraph (42-43). Moreover, he misidentifies de Laet's "Fisher's Hook" as Montauk Point instead of Fisher's Island (42). Correction of these two errors, plus a recognition that the "small island . . . southwest by south" from the Mystic must be Mason's Island (43), points more definitely to the Thames as the Mohegan's "Frisian River." Though the Thames is hardly "small," as de Laet describes it, it should be noted that he was not impressed by the size of the Connecticut either and that only the Hudson impressed him as "great" (42-45, *passim*). See also the locations of the "Pequats" and "Morhicans" on the Dutch map cited in the preceding note, and the discussion of subsequent events in this region in the chapters that follow.

81. Jameson, ed., *Narratives*, 43.

82. *Ibid.* Cf. Sidney S. Rider, *The Lands of Rhode Island as they Were Known to Caunonicus and Miantunnomu when Roger Williams Came in 1636* (Providence, 1904), figs. on pp. 293-95. That the Pequot and Mohegan had long lived where Block found them is corroborated by the recent findings of both archaeologists and linguists. See Bert Salwen, 'A Tentative 'In Situ' Solution to the Mohegan-Pequot Problem," in William R. Young, ed., *An Introduction to the Archaeology and History of the Connecticut Valley Indian* (Springfield, Mass., 1969), 81-88; Ives Goddard, "Eastern Algonquian Languages," in Trigger, ed., *Northeast*, 72. But most historians and anthropologists continue to perpetuate parts or all of the myth, which originated with the English settlers, that the Pequots were "outsiders" who "invaded" New England from the west and that the Mohegan "seceded" from them in the mid-1630s. Re-

cent variations on this theme include Carroll Alton Means, 'Mohegan-Pequot Relationships, as Indicated by the Events Leading to the Pequot Massacre of 1637 and Subsequent Claims in the Mohegan Land Controversy," *BASC* 21 (1947), 33; Alden T. Vaughan, *New England Frontier: Puritans, and Indians, 1620-1675* (1965; rev. ed., New York, 1979), 55-56; P. Richard Metcalf, "Who Should Rule at Home? Native American Politics and Indian-White Relations," *Journal of American History* 61 (1973-74), 654-56; William Burton and Richard Lowenthal, "The First of the Mohegans," *American Ethnologist* 1 (1974), 589-99; Francis Jennings, *The Invasion of America: Indians, Colonialism, and the Cant of Conquest* (Chapel Hill, 1975), 199.

3: HOSTS AND VISITORS

1. On the differing effects of furs and land on European relations with Indians, see Gary B. Nash, *Red, White, and Black: The Peoples of Early America* (Englewood Cliffs, N.J., 1974), chap. 5, *passim*, esp. 119-20. On the English preference for fish to that of the French for furs, see Douglas R. McManis, *European Impressions of the New England Coast, 1497-1620* (Chicago, 1972), 90. On sassafras, see Charles Manning and Merrill Moore, "Sassafras and Syphilis," *NEQ* 9 (1936), 473-75.

2. David B. Quinn, *North America from Earliest Discovery to First Settlements: The Norse Voyages to 1612* (New York, 1977), 129, 130, 385-86.

3. David Beers Quinn, ed., *The Voyages and Colonising Enterprises of Sir Humphrey Gilbert* (2 vols.; London, 1940), 1:49-100; 2:*passim;* McManis, *European Impressions*, chap. 2. On Norumbega, see also Sigmund Diamond, "Norumbega: New England Xanadu," *American Neptune* 11 (1951), 96-107.

4. David Beers Quinn, *England and the Discovery of America, 1481-1620* (New York, 1974), 239-40.

5. John Brereton, "A Briefe and True Relation of the Discoverie of the North Part of Virginia" (1602), in Charles Herbert Levermore, ed., *Forerunners and Competitors of the Pilgrims and Puritans* (2 vols.; Brooklyn, 1912), 1:31-32; Gabriel Archer, "The Relation of Captaine Gosnol's Voyage to the North Part of Virginia" (1625), in *ibid.*, 43-45.

6. Brereton, "Relation," 32-41; Archer, "Relation," 45-53.

7. *Ibid.*, 49-50, 53-54; Manning and Moore, "Sassafras and Syphilis."

8. Brereton, "Relation," 40-41.

9. Martin Pring, "A Voyage . . . for the Discoverie of the North Part of Virginia" (1625), in Levermore, ed., *Forerunners*, 1: 62-64, 66-67. On the site of Pring's fortress, see David B. Quinn, "Martin Pring at Provincetown in 1630?," *NEQ* 40 (1967), 78-91.

10. See Quinn, *England and the Discovery of America*, 388-91, for background.

11. James Rosier, "A True Relation of the Most Prosperous Voyage Made this Present Yeere 1605, by Captaine George Waymouth" (1605), in Levermore, ed., *Forerunners*, 1:323-38, 342.

12. Quinn, *North America*, 131-32.

13. Samuel de Champlain, *The Works of Samuel de Champlain*, ed. H. P. Biggar (6 vols.; 1922-36; reprint ed., Toronto and Buffalo, 1971), 1:364-65.

14. See Richard Arthur Preston, *Gorges of Plymouth Fort* (Toronto, 1953), for a thorough biography.

15. James Phinney Baxter, ed., *Sir Ferdinand Gorges and His Province of Maine* (3 vols.; Boston, 1890), 1:204; 2:10-11; 3:146, 147, 168-70; John Stoneman, "The Voyage of M. Henry Challons . . . ," in Samuel Purchas, ed., *Hakluytus Posthumus, or Purchas His Pilgrimes* (1625; 20 vols.; Glasgow, 1906), 19: 284-97. Baxter's assertion that Sassacomit and Manedo were one and the same person seems unlikely. Cf. Baxter, *Gorges*, 1:204n., with Rosier, "True Relation," 351, and Charles Deane, "Indians Kidnapped from Maine," *MHSP* 2d ser., 2 (1885-86), 35-38. Gorges caused untold confusion for generations of scholars when he included the Patuxet Indian Squanto ("Tasquantum") among Waymouth's captives in his *Brief Relation* (1658), in Baxter, ed., *Gorges*, 2:8. The fact that Squanto was not included in Gorges's *Brief Relation* (1622) or, even more critically, in the list made by Rosier at the time, suggests that Gorges's memory was failing him in old age. See Deane, "Indians Kidnapped," esp. 36-37. Gorges's own text in the earlier *Brief Relation* indicates that he first heard of Squanto through Captain Thomas Dermer in 1618 when the latter two were in Newfoundland, four years after Squanto had been kidnapped by another English crew. Baxter, ed., *Gorges*, 1:212; this volume, p. 107. Nor was this the only instance when Gorges confused the names of former Indian acquaintances in his old age. See Preston, *Gorges*, 396-97 n.3; 400 n.29; 402 n.55. Squanto's presence among Waymouth's captives has seemed to some to be supported by John Smith's mention of an Indian named "Tantum" whom he "set on shore at Cape Cod" in 1614 but the link is tenuous: Smith visited Squanto's home village

of Patuxet *before* reaching Cape Cod on that voyage, and Smith did not mention "Tantum" in accounts of New England he published in 1616, 1620, and 1622, only inserting him in a 1624 edition. John Smith, *Travels and Works of Captain John Smith*, ed. Edward Arber (2 vols.; Edinburgh, 1910), 2:732; Philip L. Barbour, *The Three Worlds of Captain John Smith* (Boston, 1964), 317. However, it is highly possible that Sassacomit was the same as Samoset, the Abenaki from Pemaquid who, along with Squanto, greeted the Plymouth colonists in 1621 (see p. 114), and that herein was the source of confusion in the aging Gorges's mind.

16. Baxter, ed., *Gorges*, 2:14; James Davies, "The Relation of a Voyage, unto New England" (1607), in Levermore, ed., *Forerunners*, 1:368-69, 374; William Strachey, *The Historie of Travell into Virginia Britania* (1612), ed. Louis B. Wright and Virginia Freund, Hakluyt Society Publications 2d ser., 103 (London, 1953), 164-65.

17. Davies, "Relation," 374, 375; Strachey, *Historie*, 169, 172.

18. Baxter, ed., *Gorges*, 1:206-7; 2:15-17; Strachey, *Historie*, 173. See, for example, Henry S. Burrage, *The Beginnings of Colonial Maine, 1602-1658* (Portland, Me., 1914), 96; Preston, *Gorges*, 145-48; Dean R. Snow, "Abenaki Fur Trade in the Sixteenth Century," *Western Canadian Journal of Anthropology* 6 (1976), 7.

19. Strachey, *Historie*, 170-71; Baxter, ed., *Gorges*, 3:161; *JR*, 2:45-47; 3:223; Alden T. Vaughan, *New England Frontier: Puritans and Indians, 1620-1675* (rev. ed.; New York and London, 1979), 14; Kenneth M. Morrison, "The People of the Dawn: The Abnaki and Their Relations with New England and New France, 1600-1727" (Ph.D. diss., University of Maine, 1975), 68-70.

20. Robert Juet, "The Third Voyage of Master Henry Hudson" (1625), in Levermore, ed., *Forerunners*, 2:392-94; J. Franklin Jameson, ed., *Narratives of New Netherland, 1609-1664*, Original Narratives of Early American History (1909; reprint ed., New York, 1967), 7.

21. Smith, *Travels and Works*, 2:696-97; Baxter, ed., *Gorges*, 1:210; 2:20-21. Again, Gorges's account of 1658 confuses the facts as presented in all earlier ones, including his own. *Ibid.*, 2:19-20, 23-25.

22. *Ibid.*, 1:207-8.

23. Smith, *Travels and Works*, 1:205, 206. See also *ibid.*, 188, 204.

24. *Ibid.*, 187-88, 240; 2:700, 936; Barbour, *Three Worlds*, 305-6.

25. Smith, *Travels and Works*, 1:189-91, 193-94; 2:699, 891-92, 937.

26. *Ibid.*, 1:193, 218; Barbour, *Three Worlds*, 315-17. Barbour's assertion (*ibid.*, 316) that Tahanedo "had last been seen or heard of [when Sagadahoc was abandoned] in 1607," and its implication that Smith was taking a big gamble, overlooks Sir Francis Popham's annual visits as well as the virtual certainty that Smith had met Tahanedo the year before.

27. Smith, *Travels and Works*, 1:191, 205, 218-19, 262-64; 2:925, 955-56; Edmund S. Morgan, *American Slavery, American Freedom: The Ordeal of Colonial Virginia*, 77.

28. Smith, *Travels and Works*, 1:198-99.

29. Alden T. Vaughan, *American Genesis: Captain John Smith and the Founding of Virginia* (Boston and Toronto, 1975), 34-37, 43-51; J. Frederick Fausz, "The Powhatan Uprising of 1622: A Historical Study of Ethnocentrism and Cultural Conflict" (Ph.D. diss., College of William and Mary, 1977), 219-51.

30. Barbour, *Three Worlds*, 317-24.

31. Smith, *Travels and Works*, 1:219; 2:698-99; Baxter, ed., *Gorges*, 1:209-11; William Bradford, *Of Plymouth Plantation*, ed. Samuel Eliot Morison (New York, 1967), 83-84; Dwight B. Heath, ed., *A Journal of the Pilgrims at Plymouth: Mourt's Relation* (New York, 1963), 52, 70.

32. Baxter, ed., *Gorges*, 2:196-97; Alvin H. Morrison, "Membertou's Raid on the Chouacoet 'Almouchiquois'—The Micmac Sack of Saco in 1607," in William Cowan, ed., *Papers of the Sixth Algonquian Conference, 1974* (Ottawa, 1975), 153.

33. Smith, *Travels and Works*, 2:933, wrote that "they had three plagues in three yeares successively," while others assumed that it was a single epidemic. The beginning in 1616 is established in Baxter, ed., *Gorges*, 2:19, and Dermer noted in 1619 that many were still suffering. See Purchas, *Hakluytus Posthumus*, 19:129-30. The most authoritative assessments are Herbert U. Williams, "The Epidemic of the Indians of New England, 1616-1620, with Remarks on Native American Infections," *Bulletin of the Johns Hopkins Hospital* 20 (1909), 340-49; Sherburne F. Cook, "The Significance of Disease in the Extinction of the New England Indians," *Human Biology* 45 (1973), 485-508; Alfred W. Crosby, "God . . . Would Destroy Them, and Give Their Country to Another People . . . ," *American Heritage* 29, no. 6 (1978), 38-43. For diagnoses other than plague, see P. M. Ashburn, *The Ranks of Death: A Medical History of the Conquest of America*, ed. Frank D. Ashburn (New York, 1947), 88-90; John Duffy, *Epidemics in Colonial America* (Baton Rouge, 1953), 43, 140-41; E. Wagner Stearn and Allen E. Stearn, *The Effect of Smallpox on the Destiny of the Amerindian* (Boston, 1945), 21-22; Robert

Austin Warner, "The Southern New England Indians to 1725:
A Study in Culture Contact" (Ph.D. diss., Yale University,
1935), 284-85; Daniel Gookin, "Historical Collections of the
Indians in New England," *MHSC* 1st ser., 1 (1972), 148.

34. Baxter, ed., *Gorges*, 2:19; Smith, *Travels and Works*, 1:258,
259; 2:933; Purchas, *Hakluytus Posthumus*, 19:130; Thomas
Morton, *New English Canaan* (1637), ed. Charles Francis
Adams, Jr. (1883; reprint ed., Boston, 1967), 130-32; Phineas
Pratt, "A Declaration of the Affairs of the English People that
First Inhabited New England" (1662), *MHSC* 4th ser., 4
(1858), 479-80; Bradford, *Plymouth*, 83-84; Nathaniel Morton, *New Englands Memoriall*, ed. Howard J. Hall (New York,
1937), 27-28; Alfred W. Crosby, "Virgin Soil Epidemics as a
Factor in the Aboriginal Depopulation in America," *WMQ* 3d
ser., 23 (1976), 289-99.

35. Baxter, ed., *Gorges*, 2:19, 77; Purchas, *Hakluytus Posthumus*,
19:129; Smith, *Travels and Works*, 1:259; 2:933; Everett
Emerson, ed., *Letters from New England, 1629-1638* (Amherst, Mass., 1976), 68. Edward Johnson, who did not arrive
in New England until 1636, included the Pequot among the
Indians struck. Johnson, *Johnson's Wonder-Working Providence*, ed. J. Franklin Jameson, Original Narratives of Early
American History (1910; reprint ed., New York, 1967), 41.
The claim is not supported by any other writer and is doubtful
in view of the Pequot's strength during the 1620s and early
1630s.

36. Cf. Cook, "Significance of Disease," 487. This conclusion departs from that in my "Red Puritans: The 'Praying Indians' of
Massachusetts Bay and John Eliot," *WMQ* 3d ser., 31
(1974), 35.

37. Smith, *Travels and Works*, 1:204; William Wood, *New England's Prospects* (1634), ed. Alden T. Vaughan (Amherst,
Mass., 1977), 38; Morton, *New English Canaan*, 132-33.

38. Purchas, *Hakluytus Posthumus*, 19:130, Heath, ed., *Journal*,
52, 55, 63, 64. I assume this inclusion because Nemasket lay
directly between Plymouth and the "Massasoits" whom the
narrator of the account refers to as "our next bordering neighbors." *Ibid.*, 52.

39. *Ibid.*, 52. Again, the narrator has clearly lumped the three villages into a single "Nauset" unit.

40. Dermer in Bradford, *Plymouth*, 82; Emerson, ed., *Letters*, 37,
68; Smith, *Travels and Works*, 1:259. See also the English maps
from the 1630s in fig. 7 herein; and Samuel Abbot Green, *Ten
Fac-simile Reproductions relating to New England* (Boston,
1902), between pp. 24 and 25.

41. Emerson, ed., *Letters*, 68-69; Smith, *Travels and Works*, 1:259.
42. Johnson, *Wonder-Working Providence*, 41; Crosby, "Virgin Soil Epidemics," 293-94; Cook, "Significance of Disease," 477-79; Crosby, "God . . . Would Destroy Them," 40.
43. Heath, ed., *Journal*, 78; Sydney V. James, ed., *Three Visitors to Early Plymouth* [Plymouth, Mass.], 1963), 31-32; Bradford, *Plymouth*, 89; Thomas Lechford, *Plain Dealing: or, Newes from New-England* (1642), ed. J. Hammond Trumbull (1836; reprint ed., New York and London, 1970), 121-22. On the death of Nanapeshamet, see also below, p. 272, n. 18.
44. Roger Williams, *The Complete Writings of Roger Williams* (7 vols.; New York, 1963), 6:316-17; *CCR*, 3:275-76.
45. Emerson, ed., *Letters*, 68, 69; Heath, ed., *Journal*, 55.
46. Edward Winslow, "Good Newes from New England" (1624), in Alexander Young, ed., *Chronicles of the Pilgrim Fathers* (1841; reprint ed., New York, 1971), 358-59; Warner, "Southern New England Indians," 284; Crosby, "God . . . Would Destroy Them," 40; Dena F. Dincauze, "An Introduction to Archaeology in the Greater Boston Area," *Archaeology of Eastern North America* 2 (1974), 57; Morton, *New English Canaan*, 132-33; Bradford, *Plymouth*, 87. See also Johnson, *Wonder-Working Providence*, 41.
47. Morton, *New English Canaan*, 130-32 and n.; Smith, *Travels and Works*, 2:933. Squanto later convinced some Indians that Plymouth could inflict the plague on its enemies at will. See Bradford, *Plymouth*, 99; Morton, *New English Canaan*, 245.
48. Baxter, ed., *Gorges*, 1:209-10, 212, 215; Smith, *Travels and Works*, 1:219; Heath, ed., *Journal*, 55; Bradford, *Plymouth*, 81; *Hakluytus Posthumus*, 19:129. This and the following two paragraphs are adapted from my "Squanto: Last of the Patuxets," in David Sweet and Gary B. Nash, eds., *Survival and Struggle in Colonial America* (Berkeley, 1981), chap. 12.
49. Purchas, *Hakluytus Posthumus*, 19:129-30, 131-33; Bradford, *Plymouth*, 83; Heath, ed., *Journal*, 52.
50. Bradford, *Plymouth*, 82, 83; Baxter, ed., *Gorges*, 2:29; Smith, *Travels and Works*, 1:258-59; James, ed., *Three Visitors*, 27. Squanto's status was mentioned only by the Plymouth colony's detractor, Thomas Morton, in *New English Canaan*, 243-45. Though Morton failed to distinguish Squanto and Samoset, the former's behavior, both with Dermer and at the first meeting with the settlers, leaves little doubt that it was he who was the captive.
51. On Vines, see Baxter, ed., *Gorges*, 2:18-19; Preston, *Gorges*, 161, 400. On Dermer, see Purchas, *Hakluytus Posthumus*, 19:129-34; Bradford, *Plymouth*, 81-83; Baxter, ed., *Gorges*, 1:215-

17, 219-22; 2:28-30; Preston, *Gorges*, 163-64. As Gorges and Preston indicate, a voyage by one Edward Rowcraft in 1618, like Dermer's an ill-fated one (but not because of Indians), contributed additional intelligence.

52. Baxter, ed., *Gorges*, 1:218-19; 2:30-31; Preston, *Gorges*, 164-77.

53. Bradford, *Plymouth*, 82. Bradford, the Plymouth colony leader and historian, later wrote that, even after landing at Cape Cod, the expedition hoped to sail southward and was deterred only by heavy winds and rough waters. Yet it was also Bradford who printed the portion of Dermer's letter recommending Plymouth, stating that he had received it from a mutual friend. Cf. Bradford, *Plymouth*, 59-60 and 81-82. Moreover, Charles M. Andrews has shown that New England was the first choice of the leaders of the expedition at the time of its departure from England and that the delay in sealing Gorges's charter was the principal reason for taking the "Pierce patent" granting permission to settle in Virginia. Andrews concluded from this that they in fact planned to go to Virginia, but his own evidence and that in Bradford suggest, alternatively, that taking the Pierce patent was merely a precautionary move, it having already been granted them when they *were* considering Virginia, and that the intent to sail southward from Cape Cod was not a serious one. Charles M. Andrews, *The Colonial Period of American History* (4 vols.; 1934-38; paper ed., New Haven and London, 1964), 1:262-64. Cf. Ruth A. McIntyre, *Debts Hopeful and Desperate: Financing the Plymouth Colony* ([Plymouth, Mass.], 1963), 21. In any event, Gorges granted the new settlement an official patent as soon as he heard of its establishment. Preston, *Gorges*, 198-99; Andrews, *Colonial Period*, 1:279-81.

4: SURVIVORS AND PILGRIMS

1. Charles M. Andrews, *The Colonial Period of American History* (4 vols.; 1934-38; paper ed., New Haven and London, 1964), 1:248-78, is a thorough account of the voyage's background but see also Ruth A. McIntyre, *Debts Hopeful and Desperate: Financing the Plymouth Colony* ([Plymouth, Mass.], 1963), 11-20. Thomas W. Perry, "New Plymouth and Old England: A Suggestion," *WMQ* 3d ser., 18 (1961), 251-54, offers a useful perspective. George D. Langdon, Jr., *Pilgrim Colony: A History of New Plymouth, 1620-1691* (New Haven and London, 1966), 2-11, is superficial for what purports to be a comprehensive history of Plymouth.

2. William Bradford, *Of Plymouth Plantation*, ed. Samuel Eliot Morison (New York, 1967), 75-76. See also Dwight B. Heath, ed., *A Journal of the Pilgrims at Plymouth: Mourt's Relation* (New York, 1963), 17-18; Andrews, *Colonial Period*, 1:290-92.

3. Heath, ed., *Journal*, 26, 37, and 19-37, *passim;* David B. Quinn, "Martin Pring at Provincetown in 1603?," *NEQ* 40 (1967), 88.

4. Bradford, *Plymouth*, 77-79.

5. *Ibid.*, 84. Cf. William S. Simmons, "Cultural Bias in the New England Puritans' Perception of Indians," *WMQ* 3d ser., 38 (1981), 65-66.

6. Heath, ed., *Journal*, 56-57; Bradford, *Plymouth*, 80-81; Nathaniel Morton, *New Englands Memoriall* (1669), ed. Howard J. Hall (New York, 1937), 24.

7. John Smith, *Travels and Works of Captain John Smith*, ed. Edward Arber (2 vols.; Edinburgh, 1910), 1:292.

8. Thomas Morton, *New English Canaan* (1637), ed. Charles Francis Adams, Jr. (1883; reprint ed., New York, 1967), 244-45. On Squanto and fish fertilizer, cf. Bradford, *Plymouth Plantation*, 85; Erhard Rostlund, "The Evidence for the Use of Fish as Fertilizer in Aboriginal North America," *Journal of Geography* 56 (1957), 222-28; Lynn Ceci, "Fish Fertilizer: A Native North American Practice?," *Science* 188 (4 April 1975), 26-30; Howard S. Russell, *Indian New England Before the Mayflower* (Hanover, N.H., and London, 1980), 166-67.

9. Heath, ed., *Journal*, 61-62, 66. Bradford gave a less hopeful account of this mission in *Plymouth*, 87.

10. Heath, ed., *Journal*, 60-61.

11. *Ibid.*, 62-65, 67.

12. *Ibid.*, 66, 92.

13. *Ibid.*, 73-76; Bradford, *Plymouth*, 88-89. Though Pokanoket by birth, Hobbamock had, according to the friendly Phineas Pratt, "fleed for his live from his Sacham to Plimouth," suggesting that, like Squanto, he was an outcast without a band connection. Pratt, "A Declaration of the Affairs of the English People that First Inhabited New England" (1662), *MHSC* 4th ser., 4 (1858), 485.

14. Immediately prior to the Nemasket incident, Plymouth had made friendly contact with bands at Cummaquid and Nauset on Cape Cod. Heath, ed., *Journal*, 69-71.

15. Morton, *New Englands Memoriall*, 29; Heath, ed., *Journal*, 58; Sydney V. James, Jr., ed., *Three Visitors to Early Plymouth* ([Plymouth, Mass.], 1963), 11-12; Bradford, *Plymouth*, 89.

16. Bradford, *Plymouth*, 89; Heath, ed., *Journal*, 78. Frank G.

272   NOTES TO PAGES 121-22

Speck equates Obbatinewat with Obtakiest, presumably on the
basis of orthographic similarity, but the latter is phonologically
closer to Phineas Pratt's "Aberdikees" and "Abordikees." Cf.
Speck, *Territorial Subdivisions and Boundaries of the Wampanoag, Massachusett, and Nauset Indians,* Indian Notes and
Monographs 44 (New York, 1928), 98; and Pratt, "Declaration," 484-86, *passim.* This choice is even more plausible because the Indian leader in a skirmish described in almost
identical terms by two different authors is called "Abordikees"
by Pratt, who knew him by that name in 1622, and "Chickataubut" by Thomas Morton (no relation to Nathaniel), who
maintained friendly contact with him through the rest of the
decade. Though the reasons for the sachem's name change are
not specified in any document, such a practice was common
among southern New England Algonquians for a variety of
reasons. Cf. Roger Williams, *A Key into the Language of
America* (1643), ed. John T. Teunissen and Evelyn J. Hinz
(Detroit, 1973), 96; Edward Winslow, "Good Newes from
New England" (1624), in Alexander Young, ed., *Chronicles
of the Pilgrim Fathers* (1841; reprint ed., New York, 1971),
363-64; John Josselyn, *An Account of Two Voyages to New-
England* (1675; Boston, 1865), 100.
17. Though Winslow wrote that the Massachusett had grown some
corn for the colony in 1622, he explicitly stated that they had
done so "upon our motion," implying that it was not as part of
a previous treaty agreement. Winslow, "Good Newes," 302. On
the "loss" of treaties and other documents and their subsequent
distortion in accounts by colonial leaders, cf. Francis Jennings,
*The Invasion of America: Indians, Colonialism, and the Cant
of Conquest* (Chapel Hill, 1975), 182; Andrews, *Colonial
Period,* 1:357-58.
18. Heath, ed., *Journal,* 78, notes that Nanapeshamet had recently
died but gives no date. The date 1619 has been assigned by
several secondary authors, most notably Alonzo Lewis and
James R. Newhall, *History of Lynn, Essex County, Massachusetts* (2 vols.; Lynn, Mass., 1890), 1:35; Bert Salwen, "Indians
of Southern New England and Long Island: Early Period," in
Bruce G. Trigger, ed., *Northeast, HNAI* 15:170.
19. Heath, ed., *Journal,* 78-79. See also Bradford, *Plymouth,* 89.
20. Winslow, "Good Newes," 284, is the most complete account
but see also Bradford, *Plymouth,* 96-97; James, ed., *Three
Visitors,* 12. On the incident's meaning, see Howard M. Chapin,
Sachems of the Narragansetts (Providence, 1931), 11, but cf.
Alfred W. Crosby, "God . . . Would Destroy Them, and Give

Their Country to Another People . . . ," *American Heritage* 29, no. 6 (1978), 41-42.

21. Winslow, "Good Newes," 285-92; Bradford, *Plymouth*, 98-99. I have explored these events and Squanto's motives at greater length in "Squanto: Last of the Patuxets," in David Sweet and Gary B. Nash, eds., *Survival and Struggle in Colonial America* (Berkeley, 1981), 241-43. For a somewhat different interpretation of Squanto, see Frank Shuffleton, "Indian Devils and Pilgrim Fathers: Squanto, Hobomock, and the English Conception of Indian Religion," *NEQ* 49 (1976), 114-15.

22. Winslow, "Good Newes," 284-85, 295; Bradford, *Plymouth*, 97, 110, 111. For a description of the fort, see James, ed., *Three Visitors*, 11.

23. Winslow, "Good Newes," 304-5, 308-9.

24. Samuel Eliot Morison in Bradford, *Plymouth*, 64n. See also Stephen Saunders Webb, "Army and Empire: English Garrison Government in Britain and America, 1569 to 1763," *WMQ* 3d ser., 34 (1977), 6.

25. Winslow, "Good Newes," 325.

26. Andrews, *Colonial Period*, 1:261-67, *passim;* McIntyre, *Debts*, 14-17, 24-26; Bradford, *Plymouth*, 100 and 100-111, *passim.*

27. Bradford, *Plymouth*, 108, 109.

28. Winslow, "Good Newes," 276-77, 296-300, 302, 309-12, 323-24, 327-45; Bradford, *Plymouth*, 113-20; Morton, *New Englands Memoriall*, 40-44; Pratt, "Declaration"; Morton, *New English Canaan*, 179, 245-62. For briefer references, see R. G. Marsden, ed., "A Letter of William Bradford and Isaac Allerton, 1623," *American Historical Review* 8 (1902-3), 298-99; James, ed., *Three Visitors*, 30-31. Accounts by historians sympathetic to Plymouth include Charles Francis Adams, Jr., *Three Episodes in Massachusetts History* (2 vols.; Boston, 1896), 1: 59-104; David Bushnell, "The Treatment of the Indians in Plymouth Colony," *NEQ* 26 (1953), 194; Alden T. Vaughan, *New England Frontier: Puritans and Indians, 1620-1675* (rev. ed., New York, 1979), 82-88. More critical are George F. Willison, *Saints and Strangers* (New York, 1945), 214-30; Jennings, *Invasion*, 186-87; Karen Ordahl Kupperman, "Thomas Morton, Historian," *NEQ* 50 (1977), 660-62.

29. Winslow, "Good Newes," 297-98; Bradford, *Plymouth*, 113.

30. Winslow, "Good Newes," 302.

31. *Ibid.*, 327-30; Bradford, *Plymouth*, 115.

32. Winslow, "Good Newes," 327-28, 330, 332-33; Morton, *New English Canaan*, 252-53; Bradford, *Plymouth*, 116.

33. Pratt, "Declaration," 482; Morton, *New English Canaan*, 249-

52. Bradford and Winslow claimed that more than one Wessagusset man was stealing corn, while Morton and Pratt asserted that there was only one. Winslow, "Good Newes," 327; Bradford, *Plymouth*, 115; Pratt, "Declaration," 482; Morton, *New English Canaan*, 249.

34. Bradford, *Plymouth*, 115; Winslow, "Good Newes," 309-11, 323-24.

35. *Ibid.*, 330-34; Bradford, *Plymouth*, 117-18; Pratt, "Declaration," 483-84.

36. Winslow, "Good Newes," 336.

37. *Ibid.*, 336-39, 341, 342, 343; Morton, *New English Canaan*, 248-49, 253; Pratt, "Declaration," 485-86; Bradford, *Plymouth*, 118.

38. Winslow, "Good Newes," 344; Morton, *New English Canaan*, 253-54. "But if the Plimmouth Planters had really intended good to Master Weston, or those men," Morton shrewdly asked, "why had they not kept the Salvages alive in Custody, untill they had secured the other English?" *Ibid.*, 254.

39. Some Plymouth men had apparently taken some bearskins from the grave of Obtakiest's mother, a severe religious offense, in the previous November. Morton's inclusion of this incident among the causes of Massachusett hostility was dismissed by his editor, Charles Francis Adams, Jr., who did not recognize that Winslow's Obtakiest and Morton's Chickataubut were one and the same person. *New English Canaan*, 170, 247.

40. Pratt, "Declaration," 480.

41. Bradford, *Plymouth*, 116, 118; Winslow, "Good Newes," 341-42; Morton, *New English Canaan*, 254; Marsden, ed., "Letter," 299.

42. Morton, *New English Canaan*, 254-55; Everett Emerson, ed., *Letters from New England, 1629-1638* (Amherst, Mass., 1976), 68.

43. Winslow, "Good Newes," 345.

44. Bradford, *Plymouth*, 374-75.

45. *Ibid.*, 372-73.

46. Winslow, "Good Newes," 331.

47. *Ibid.*, 325-26; Heath, ed., *Journal*, 68. An Anglican minister, William Morell, encountered a similar objection to monogamy among Massachusett men at around the same time. "Morell's Poem on New-England" (*ca.* 1625), *MHSC* 1st ser., 1 (1792), 138. On Morell's presence at Massachusetts Bay, see herein, p. 153.

48. Winslow, "Good Newes," 355; Heath, ed., *Journal*, 83.

49. Winslow, "Good Newes," 325-26, 355-56.

50. *Ibid.*, 356; Williams, *Key*, 194-97. Cf. Thomas Morton's con-

struing of Kiehtan's dissatisfaction in such a way that it closely resembled God's in the story of Noah and the ark. *New English Canaan*, 167-68.

51. Winslow, "Good Newes," 356, 359. Cf. Shuffleton, "Indian Devils," 110-14; Simmons, "Cultural Bias," esp. 60-63. As Shuffleton points out, Winslow studiously avoided noting that one of Plymouth's loyal Indian friends was a pniese who had taken his name from this deity. *Ibid.*, 112.

52. Neal Salisbury, "Red Puritans: The 'Praying Indians' of Massachusetts Bay and John Eliot," *WMQ* 3d ser., 31 (1974), 39. Cf. William S. Simmons, "Conversion from Puritan to Indian," *NEQ* 52 (1979), 197-218, *passim;* Simmons, "Cultural Bias," *passim.* The latter is an excellent introduction to the larger belief systems underlying English attitudes toward Indians.

53. Marsden, ed., "Letter," 297; Andrews, *Colonial Period*, 1:334-38; Richard Arthur Preston, *Gorges of Plymouth Fort* (Toronto, 1953), 225-29; Henry S. Burrage, *The Beginnings of Colonial Maine* (Portland, Me., 1914), 160-75; Christopher Levett, "A Voyage into New England" (1628), in Maine Historical Society, *Collections* 1st ser., 2 (1847), 73-109.

54. Emmanuel Altham, commissioned by the Adventurers to establish Plymouth's fishing industry and fur trade, estimated that he saw about 400 English vessels between Monhegan Island and Cape Ann during the 1623 season. James, ed., *Three Visitors*, 25. During the same year, Sir Ferdinando Gorges accused the fishermen of corrupting, cheating, and arming the Indians while he was trying to secure a fish licensing monopoly in New England waters from Parliament. Baxter, ed., *Gorges*, 2:41-42; Preston, *Gorges*, 186-96, 233-42. For other complaints about the trading of guns to Indians, see James, ed., *Three Visitors*, 16, 32; Marsden, "Letter," 295. Winslow saw the thriving trade as evidence that Plymouth could profit from it too. "Good Newes," 371.

5: CLIENTS AND TRADERS

1. William Bradford, *Of Plymouth Plantation*, ed. Samuel Eliot Morison (New York, 1967), 120-21.

2. *Ibid.*, 120-21, 144-45; Darret B. Rutman, *Husbandmen of Plymouth: Farms and Villages in the Old Colony, 1620-1692* (Boston, 1967), 11-13.

3. Charles M. Andrews, *The Colonial Period of American History* (4 vols.; 1934-38; paper ed., New Haven, 1964), 1:281, 283-84.

4. Sydney V. James, Jr., ed., *Three Visitors to Early Plymouth*

([Plymouth, Mass.], 1963), 42-52, *passim;* Bradford, *Plymouth,* 140, 163, 175-77; R. G. Marsden, ed., "A Letter from William Bradford and Isaac Allerton, 1623," *American Historical Review* 8 (1902-3), 296; Andrews, *Colonial Period,* 1: 284, 300; Ruth A. McIntyre, *Debts Hopeful and Desperate: Financing the Plymouth Colony* ([Plymouth, Mass.], 1963), 28-29.

5. Bradford, *Plymouth,* 139, 178.

6. *Ibid.,* 139; James, ed., *Three Visitors,* 36.

7. *Ibid.,* 17. The letter in which Pory makes his comment also includes a brief description of Gorges's fortified fishing station at Damariscove Island, off the Maine coast, suggesting that this was his source on Abenaki trading habits. *Ibid.,* 15-16.

8. Bradford, *Plymouth,* 178.

9. *Ibid.,* 170-75, 181-83, 192-93, 194-200; James, ed., *Three Visitors,* 77-78; Andrews, *Colonial Period,* 1:284-87. On the coincidence of the Kennebec success and the formation of the Undertakers, cf. Henry S. Burrage, *The Beginnings of Colonial Maine, 1602-1658* (Portland, Me., 1914), 185-86.

10. Bradford, *Plymouth,* 191.

11. Francis Jennings, *The Invasion of America: Indians, Colonialism, and the Cant of Conquest* (Chapel Hill, 1975), 155-56; Peter Allen Thomas, "In the Maelstrom of Change: The Indian Trade and Cultural Process in the Middle Connecticut Valley, 1635-1665" (Ph.D. diss., University of Massachusetts, Amherst, 1979), 49-51.

12. Cf. Daniel Gookin, "Historical Collections of the Indians in New England," *MHSC* 1st ser., 1 (1792), 147-48; William S. Simmons, "Narragansett," in Bruce G. Trigger, ed., *Northeast, HNAI* 15:190-91.

13. Bert Salwen, "Indians of Southern New England and Long Island: Early Period," in *ibid.,* 161 (fig. 1), 172; Howard M. Chapin, *Sachems of the Narragansetts* (Providence, 1931), 109. William Wood and Edward Johnson both noted that the Pequot derided the Narragansett as "women-like men" (Wood) during the heat of their rivalry in the early 1630s. William Wood, *New England's Prospect* (1634), ed. Alden T. Vaughan (Amherst, Mass., 1977), 81; Edward Johnson, *Johnson's Wonder-Working Providence,* ed. J. Franklin Jameson, Original Narratives of Early American History (1910; reprint ed., New York, 1967), 163. For the possibility that a Pequot-as-men, Narragansett-as-women dichotomy may once have expressed a more harmonious relationship, cf. the similar one between the Iroquois and the Delaware in the eighteenth century as discussed

by Jay Miller, "The Delaware as Women: A Symbolic Solution," *American Ethnologist* 1 (1974), 507-14.

14. J. Franklin Jameson, ed., *Narratives of New Netherland, 1609-1664*, Original Narratives of Early American History (1909); reprint ed., New York, 1967), 86, 87. The Dutch account of this incident, by Nicholas Wassenaer, identifies the victim as "chief" of, variously, the "Sickenanes," "Sickenames," and "Sickenamers," an identification which editor Jameson took to mean the Sequin of the Connecticut River. Evidence that the Dutch used these terms to refer to the Pequot rather than the Sequin is most obvious in documents referring to both groups. In 1614, Adriaen Block identified both the "Pequatoos" of the "river of the Siccanamos" and the "Sequins" of the "Fresh [Connecticut] River." *Ibid.*, 42-43. Cf. *NYCD*, 1: map between pp. 12 and 13. In 1633, New Netherland concluded a treaty with the 'Sickenames," who were, it is clear from the context, the Pequots. The treaty was also assented to by the "Sequeen." *Ibid.*, 2:139-40. On the background to the treaty, see herein, p. 207.

15. T. J. Brasser, *Indians of Long Island, 1600-1964* (Colorado Springs, 1966), 15; Mary W. Herman, "Wampum as a Money in Northeastern North America," *Ethnohistory* 3 (1956), 21-33; Bradford, *Plymouth*, 203. By far the most thorough and provocative study of wampum and its impact on Indian-European relations is Lynn Ceci, "The Effect of European Contact and Trade on the Settlement Pattern of Indians in Coastal New York, 1524-1665: The Archeological and Documentary Evidence" (Ph.D. diss., City University of New York, 1977). However, much of Ceci's argument is not supported by her evidence, especially her contention that, on one hand, wampum was unknown to the Indians before the beginnings of the European trade and, on the other, that such a trade had begun on a regular basis by 1600. See *ibid.*, 15-19, 168-70. The only instance she actually cites of wampum passing into European hands before 1622 suggests the kind of exchange that was, from an Indian perspective, traditional rather than the rationalized one that evolved later. Nor is there evidence that the recipient (Henry Hudson in 1609) understood the gift in the later terms. *Ibid.*, citing Jameson, ed., *Narratives*, 22-24. Her inference that Block encountered a thriving wampum trade during his 1614 expedition is hypothetical in the extreme. Ceci, "Effect," 180-84. Finally, her assertion that wampum shells could not have been drilled with stone and, thus, had to await the arrival of European metal drills is directly contra-

dicted by Roger Williams's informants. Cf. *ibid.*, 15-16; Williams, *A Key into the Language of America* (1643), ed. John J. Teunissen and Evelyn J. Hinz (Detroit, 1973), 213. It is apparent that metal drills helped transform wampum to a mass-produced commodity but not to create it as an item of religious and cultural significance for the natives.

16. Jameson, ed., *Narratives*, 86; Van Cleaf Bachman, *Peltries or Plantations: The Economic Policies of the Dutch West India Company in New Netherland, 1623-1639* (Baltimore, 1969), 21-22, 93; Allen W. Trelease, *Indian Affairs in Colonial New York: The Seventeenth Century* (1960; reprint ed., Port Washington, N.Y., 1970), 48; James, ed., *Three Visitors*, 69-70.

17. Bradford, *Plymouth*, 203; Ceci, "Effect," 208-10; Jameson, ed., *Narratives*, 87; "Pedigree of Uncas," *NEHGR*, 10 (1856), 228; *CCR*, 3:479; Salwen, "Indians of Southern New England," 172-73.

18. On Dutch activity, see the comment by Isaack de Rasieres, secretary to the governor of New Netherland, that Dutch traders "by occasion came so far northward with their shallop, and met with sundry of the Indians, who told them that they were within half a day's journey of your Plantation," and Bradford's demand of March 19 that the Dutch "forbear to trade with the natives in this bay, and river of Narragansett and Sowams." Bradford, *Plymouth*, 379; William Bradford, "Governor Bradford's Letter Book," *MHSC* 1st ser., 3 (1794), 52. That the Manomet post had been constructed and used before receipt of Rasieres's letter is clear from the sequence in Bradford's history. See *Plymouth*, 192-93, 194. In his edition of this work, Samuel Eliot Morison carelessly lumped these events under the heading, "Trading with the Dutch at Buzzards Bay," when in fact Bradford describes, first, trade in and from the bay (with Indians, not the Dutch) and then, after discussing a separate matter, the beginning of Dutch-Plymouth correspondence (not trade).

19. *Ibid.*, 195. May is the latest date because that is when Isaac Allerton took the document to England. See *ibid.*, 193n., 194. The document and its date are significant because of Bradford's own assertion, farther on in his history, that Plymouth had no knowledge of wampum's existence, much less its value, until Rasieres brought it to them in person later that year. *Ibid.*, 203. His implication that Plymouth was utterly ignorant of the trade to the west until this time is the reason for the detailed chronology in this paragraph.

20. See the quote in n. 18 above from Bradford, "Letter Book," 52.

The version of this letter included in Morison's edition of *Plymouth Plantation* omits this aggressive portion. Cf. Bradford, *Plymouth*, 380.

21. Bradford, "Letter Book," 53-54; Bradford, *Plymouth*, 203-4; James, ed., *Three Visitors*, 74. Bradford placed this event in his annal for 1628, apparently so that his discussions of the Dutch and wampum would lead directly into the trade of guns to Indians and then to Thomas Morton's post at Ma-re Mount (discussed below), which began that year. However, all other evidence, including Bradford's own letters, points precisely to the date given here.

22. Ceci, "Efect," 46-47, 198; Bradford, *Plymouth*, 203-4.

23. Cf. Andrews, *Colonial Period*, 1:342, who estimates fifty settlers between Massachusetts Bay and the mouth of the Piscataqua. I have accounted for these plus the thirty at Mt. Woolaston (to be discussed below), whom Andrews did not think had arrived yet, and the fishing station at Monhegan Island.

24. Charles Knowles Bolton, *The Real Founders of New England: Stories of Their Life along the Coast, 1602-1628* (Boston, 1929), chaps. 2-7, *passim;* Andrews, *Colonial Period*, 1:336-42.

25. William Morell, "Morell's Poem on New-England" (*ca.* 1625), *MHSC* 1st ser., 1 (1792), 130-39, esp. 139; Samuel Maverick, "A Briefe Discription of New England and the Severall Towns Therein" (1660), *NEHGR*, 39 (1885), 38.

26. Compare the estimate of English settlers above, n. 23, with those given for the natives in 1631 by Thomas Dudley in Everett Emerson, ed., *Letters from New England, 1629-1638* (Amherst, Mass., 1976), 69.

27. John White, "The Planters Plea" (1630), in Peter Force, ed., *Tracts and Other Papers . . .* (4 vols.; Washington, D.C., 1837), 2, no. 3:38-42; Frances Rose-Troup, *John White: The Patriarch of Dorchester and the Founder of Massachusetts, 1575-1648* (New York, 1930), 49-106, *passim;* Frances Rose-Troup, *The Massachusetts Bay Company and Its Predecessors* (New York, 1930), 10-15; Clifford K. Shipton, *Roger Conant: A Founder of Massachusetts* (Cambridge, Mass., 1945), 28-67; Andrews, *Colonial Period*, 1:344-52; Richard P. Gildrie, *Salem, Massachusetts, 1626-1683: A Covenant Community* (Charlottesville, Va., 1975), 1-5.

28. Bradford, *Plymouth*, 204.

29. *Ibid.*, 182, 193, 200-202; Burrage, *Beginnings of Colonial Maine*, 186-88.

30. Bradford, "Letter Book," 56-57.

31. James, ed., *Three Visitors*, 16, 31-32; Bradford, *Plymouth*, 89; Marsden, ed., "Letter," 295; Christopher Levett, "A Voyage into New England" (1628), in Maine Historical Society, *Collections* 1st ser., 2 (1847), 93; Bradford, "Letter Book," 57.

32. Bradford, *Plymouth*, 204-6; Thomas Morton, *New English Canaan* (1637), ed. Charles Francis Adams, Jr. (1883; reprint ed., New York, 1967), 276; Phineas Pratt, "A Declaration of the Affairs of the English People that First Inhabited New England" (1662), in *MHSC* 4th ser., 4 (1858), 478; Christopher Hill, *Society and Puritanism in Pre-Revolutionary England* (2d ed.; New York, 1967), 183-94, esp. 185. On the name "Ma-re Mount," cf. Karen Ordahl Kupperman, "Thomas Morton, Historian," *NEQ* 50 (1977), 662; Richard Slotkin, *Regeneration Through Violence: The Mythology of the American Frontier* (Middletown, Conn., 1973), 61.

33. Bradford, "Letter Book," 61-64; Bradford, *Plymouth*, 207-10; Morton, *New English Canaan*, 276-89. Samuel Eliot Morison's comments in *Plymouth Plantation* overlook Bradford's remark that the list in his letter book is incomplete. Cf. *Plymouth*, 208-9n. and "Letter Book," 63.

34. *MCR*, 1:392; Bradford, "Letter Book," 63; Emerson, ed., *Letters*, 37; Wood, *New England's Prospect*, 94. Higginson and Wood both arrived in 1629, just one year after Morton's arrest and Bradford's accusatory letter.

35. Bradford, *Plymouth*, 205-6.

36. For a discussion of Morton's treatment in history and, particularly, literature, that favors his detractors, see John P. McWilliams, Jr., "Fictions of Merry Mount," *American Quarterly* 29 (1977), 3-30. For an argument that Morton has been wrongly overlooked by historians, see Kupperman, "Thomas Morton." Two recent studies in the tradition described here are parts of longer, incisive treatments of literary and ideological manifestations of American racism: Slotkin, *Regeneration Through Violence*, 58-65; and Richard Drinnon, *Facing West: The Metaphysics of Indian-Hating and Empire-Building* (paper ed., New York, 1980), 1-61, esp. 3-20, 24-26, 57-60. Even the best and most recent effort to reconstruct the events at Ma-re Mount focuses on the maypole as symbol of cultural conflict instead of examining that conflict from the perspectives of all parties. See Michael Zuckerman, "Pilgrims in the Wilderness: Community, Modernity, and the Maypole at Merry Mount," *NEQ* 50 (1977), 255-77.

37. Morton, *New English Canaan*, 123, 144-45, 256-57, 276-82, 289; Bradford, *Plymouth*, 205-6.

38. Morton, *New English Canaan*, 137, 148-50, 175-78, 179-242, *passim*, 268-70.
39. *Ibid.*, 134, 139-41, 150-53, 167-69.
40. *Ibid.*, 162-65.
41. Cf. Morton's own conclusion, *ibid.*, 287.
42. Bradford, *Plymouth*, 215-22, 386-87. Plymouth eventually succeeded in having Ashley arrested for selling guns to the Indians. Again, as with Morton, Bradford reinforced the charge with a statement about the suspect's "uncleanness with Indian women." In 1635, however, Plymouth lost the post when it was seized by the French. *Ibid.*, 226-34, 237-46, 275-79; William A. Roberts, "The Fur Trade in New England in the Seventeenth Century" (Ph.D. diss., University of Pennsylvania, 1958), 44-46.
43. White, "Planters Plea," 42-43; Rose-Troup, *Massachusetts Bay Company*, 16-94, *passim;* Rose-Troup, *John White*, 107-231, *passim;* Shipton, *Roger Conant*, 68-87; Andrews, *Colonial Period*, 1:352-74; Bradford, *Plymouth*, 206, 216; Gildrie, *Salem*, 5-19; Darret B. Rutman, *Winthrop's Boston: Portrait of a Puritan Town, 1630-1649* (Chapel Hill, 1965), 178.
44. Morton, *New English Canaan*, 304-13, 336-38, 342-45; Bradford, *Plymouth*, 216-17; *MCR*, 1:74, 75; Emerson, ed., *Letters*, 74; John Winthrop, *The History of New England from 1630 to 1649*, ed. James Savage (2 vols.; rev. ed., Boston, 1853), 1:41-43; *WP*, 2:267. Morton joined forces with Sir Ferdinando Gorges during the 1630s in order to regain a foothold in New England but did not return until 1643. After residing in Plymouth, Rhode Island, and Maine, he was arrested by Massachusetts Bay authorities for slandering them in *New English Canaan*. After about a year in the Boston jail, he was released and returned to Maine, where he died in 1647. Charles Francis Adams, Jr., introduction to *New English Canaan*, 49-92.

6: SURVIVORS AND SAINTS

1. Charles Edward Banks, *The Planters of the Commonwealth* (Boston, 1930), 14-15; Norman C. P. Tyack, "Migration from East Anglia to New England before 1660" (Ph.D. diss., University of London, 1951), 33-41. Cf. T. H. Breen and Stephen Foster, "Moving to the New World: The Character of Early Massachusetts Immigration," *WMQ* 3d ser., 30 (1973), 191-92.
2. Mildred Campbell, *The English Yeoman under Elizabeth and the Early Stuarts* (New Haven, 1942), chap. 3; Joan Thirsk, "Industries in the Countryside," in F. J. Fisher, ed., *Essays in*

the Economic and Social History of Tudor and Stuart England
(Cambridge, Eng., 1961), 70-88; Joan Thirsk, "The Farming
Regions of England," in Thirsk, ed., *The Agrarian History of
England and Wales* 4: *1500-1640* (Cambridge, Eng., 1967),
40-80, *passim;* C. W. Chalkin, *Seventeenth-Century Kent: A
Social and Economic History* (London, 1965), 10-13, 17, 27,
54-57, 60-64, 69-72; Tyack, "Migration," 90-124; Alan Everitt,
Change in the Provinces: The Seventeenth Century (Leicester,
Eng., 1972), 22.

3. Chalkin, *Seventeenth-Century Kent,* 123-24; Peter Clark, "The
Migrant in Kentish Towns, 1580-1640," in Peter Clark and
Paul Slack, eds., *Crisis and Order in English Towns, 1500-
1700: Essays in Urban History* (London, 1972), 117-63, esp.
134-38. Clark terms these men "betterment migrants," as opposed to the far more numerous and impoverished "subsistence
migrants." On the "industrious sort," see Christopher Hill, *Society and Puritanism in Pre-Revolutionary England* (2d ed.,
New York, 1967), chap. 4, esp. p. 133.

4. Tyack, "Migration," 101-6, 124-53, 168-76; Peter Clark, *En-
glish Provincial Society from the Reformation to the Revolution:
Religion, Politics, and Society in Kent, 1500-1640* (Rutherford,
N.J., 1970), 317-22, 353-56; Chalkin, *Seventeenth-Century
Kent,* 35; Breen and Foster, "Moving to the New World," 206.

5. Charles Edward Banks, *Topographical Dictionary of 2885
Emigrants to New England, 1620-1650* (1937; reprint ed.,
Baltimore, 1969), xii-xiii. On the distribution within East
Anglia, see Tyack, "Migration," 3-7, 33-45. See also G. E.
Fussell, "Social and Agrarian Background of the Pilgrim Fa-
thers," *Agricultural History* 7 (1933), 183-202; Breen and
Foster, "Moving to the New World," 194, 195, 197. On patriar-
chalism and familial continuity, see Philip J. Greven, Jr., *Four
Generations: Population, Land, and Family in Colonial An-
dover, Massachusetts* (Ithaca and London, 1970), esp. 265-69;
John J. Waters, "The Traditional World of the New England
Peasants: A View from Seventeenth-Century Barnstable,"
NEHGR, 130 (1976), 3-21; John J. Waters, "American Colo-
nial Stem Families: Persisting European Patterns in the New
World" (unpub. paper, 1978); Thomas R. Cole, "Family,
Settlement, and Migration in Southeastern Massachusetts,
1650-1805," *NEHGR,* 132 (1978), 171-85; Hill, *Society and
Puritanism,* chap. 13.

6. Norman O. Brown, *Life Against Death: The Psychoanalytic
Meaning of History* (paper ed., New York, 1959), chap. 14;
Michael Walzer, *Revolution of the Saints: A Study in the*

Origins of Radical Politics (Cambridge, Mass., 1965), esp. 312-13; Hill, *Society and Puritanism*, esp. chap. 4; Christopher Hill, "Protestantism and the Rise of Capitalism," in Fisher, ed., *Essays in Economic and Social History*, 26.

7. Max Weber, *The Protestant Ethic and the Rise of Capitalism*, trans. Talcott Parsons (New York, 1930), 98-128; Hill, *Society and Puritanism*, chaps. 13-14.

8. *Ibid.*, chaps. 4-6; Weber, *Protestant Ethic*, chap. 5; Walzer, *Revolution of the Saints*, chap. 6.

9. Cf. Walzer, *Revolution of the Saints;* Edmund S. Morgan, *Visible Saints: The History of a Puritan Idea* (New York, 1963), chaps. 1-3; Edmund S. Morgan, *Roger Williams: The Church and the State* (New York, 1967); Hill, *Society and Puritanism*, chap. 4.

10. See esp. John Horton, "Two Bishops and the Holy Brood: A Fresh Look at a Familiar Fact," *NEQ* 40 (1967), 339-46; Tyack, "Migration," chaps. 8-11.

11. Everett Emerson, ed., *Letters from New England, 1629-1638* (Amherst, Mass., 1976), 36-37; Dwight B. Heath, ed., *A Journal of the Pilgrims at Plymouth: Mourt's Relation* (New York, 1963), 84, 94; John White, "The Planters Plea" (1630), in Peter Force, ed., *Tracts and Other Papers . . .* (4 vols.; Washington, D.C., 1837), 2, no. 3: 3.

12. *WP*, 2: 91-92; Heath, ed., *Journal*, 94-95; White, "Planters Plea," 3.

13. Emerson, ed., *Letters*, 75; Edward Winslow, "Good Newes from New England" (1624), in Alexander Young, ed., *Chronicles of the Pilgrim Fathers* (1841; reprint ed., New York, 1967), 372. See also Ebenezer Hazard, ed., *Historical Collections, Consisting of State Papers and Other Authentic Documents* (2 vols.; Philadelphia, 1792-94), 1:148.

14. John Smith, *Travels and Works of Captain John Smith* (2 vols.; Edinburgh, 1910), 1:208-9.

15. Heath, ed., *Journal*, 51; Emerson, ed., *Letters*, 106; Winslow, "Good Newes," 272; Roger Clap, "Memoirs of Captain Roger Clap," in Alexander Young, ed., *Chronicles of the First Planters of Massachusetts Bay* (1846; reprint ed., New York, 1970), 350.

16. Genesis 1:28; Psalms 115:16; White, "Planters Plea," 1-2; *WP*, 2:118, 120; Emerson, ed., *Letters*, 37; Heath, ed., *Journal*, 91-92; Chester E. Eisinger, "The Puritans' Justification for Taking the Land," *Essex Institute Historical Collections* 84 (1948), 131-43; Wilcomb E. Washburn, "The Moral and Legal Justification for Dispossessing the Indians," in James Morton Smith,

ed., *Seventeenth-Century America* (Chapel Hill, 1959), 25; Hill, *Society and Puritanism*, 142.

17. *MCR*, 1:17; White, "Planters Plea," 15. See also *ibid.*, 29.

18. *MCR*, 1:384; Winslow, "Good Newes," 274.

19. Charles M. Andrews, *The Colonial Period of American History* (4 vols.; 1934-38; paper ed., New Haven, 1964), 1: chap. 19; *MCR*, 1:385, 394, 400. For a thorough account of the Virginia uprising and the reaction in England, see J. Frederick Fausz, "The Powhatan Uprising of 1622: A Historical Study of Ethnocentrism and Cultural Conflict" (Ph.D. diss., College of William and Mary, 1977), 353-443.

20. *WP*, 2:295.

21. The English estimates are from Darret B. Rutman, *Winthrop's Boston: Portrait of a Puritan Town, 1630-1649* (Chapel Hill, 1965), 178. For the Indian figures, see herein, pp. 103-5.

22. *WP*, 2:136-37; Emerson, ed., *Letters*, 37, 106; William Wood, *New England's Prospect* (1634), ed. Alden T. Vaughan (Amherst, Mass., 1977), 75-76, 102.

23. Emerson, ed., *Letters*, 68-69; John Winthrop, *The History of New England from 1630 to 1649*, ed. James Savage (2 vols.; 2d ed.; Boston, 1853), 1:31, 58.

24. *Ibid.*, 71-72; Wood, *New England's Prospect*, 79. Subsequent Puritan mythmakers portrayed the incident as a "Tarrentine" attack upon the English rather than upon local Indians. See Edward Johnson, *Johnson's Wonder-Working Providence*, ed. J. Franklin Jameson, Original Narratives of Early American History (1910; reprint ed., New York, 1967), 78-79; Thomas Cobbet, "A Narrative of New England's Deliverances" (1677), in *NEHGR*, 7 (1853), 210-11.

25. E.g., "The Charlestown Records," in Young, ed., *Chronicles of Massachusetts Bay*, 374; Smith, *Travels and Works*, 2:934; Alonzo Lewis and James R. Newhall, *History of Lynn, Essex County, Massachusetts* (2 vols.; Lynn, Mass., 1890), 1:40, 130-32; Sidney Perley, *Indian Land Titles of Essex County, Massachusetts* (Salem, Mass., 1912), 49-50; Wood, *New England's Prospect*, 62. Cf. the argument in Francis Jennings, "Virgin Land and Savage People," *American Quarterly* 23 (1971), 526-28, which assumes that the absence of any Indian-to-English deeds before 1634 means that the English simply occupied land during this period without regard for Indian reactions or for the Massachusetts Bay Company's instructions. But Jennings misses the essential point regarding purchase in these instructions, viz., that title need be purchased only if an Indian insisted; I am suggesting here that no Indians had (yet) insisted though, as we shall see, they soon did.

26. Emerson, ed., *Letters*, 31, 37, 73, 74; Thomas Morton, *New English Canaan* (1637), ed. Charles Francis Adams, Jr. (1883; reprint ed., New York, 1967), 144, 174; *MCR*, 1:83, 102, 106, 132, 406; *WP*, 3:82; Clap, "Memoirs," 353.

27. *MCR*, 1:73, 84, 89, 91, 92, 96, 100-101, 102; Winthrop, *History*, 1:59, 74, 103-4; Emerson, ed., *Letters*, 81-82. The question of English-Indian intermarriage was raised but then deferred by the General Court in 1635, perhaps because a rumored match failed to materialize. See *MCR*, 1:140. For an argument that the colony's legal protection of Indians in the early years stemmed from a feeling of military insecurity, see Lyle Koehler, "Red-White Power Relations and Justice in the Courts of Seventeenth-Century New England," *AICRJ* 3, no. 4 (1979), 2-5.

28. *MCR*, 1:67, 87, 88, 99, 102, 121, 133, 143; Winthrop, *History*, 1:67.

29. In addition to the references in the preceding note, see *ibid.*, 103-4; Emerson, ed., *Letters*, 111-12.

30. Wood, *New England's Prospect*, 75-95, *passim;* 96-97, 101-2. Wood reassured skeptics that English guns would easily diffuse any instance of Indian resistance. See *ibid.*, 94-95, 102-3.

31. Emerson, ed., *Letters*, 64; Winthrop, *History*, 1:74-75. For typical portrayals of Winthrop, see, for example, Edmund S. Morgan, *The Puritan Dilemma: The Story of John Winthrop* (Boston and Toronto, 1958); Richard S. Dunn, *Puritans and Yankees: The Winthrop Dynasty of New England, 1630-1717* (1962; paper ed., New York, 1971), 1-56, esp. 3-4. Thomas Morton was satirizing the image that prevailed even then when he depicted Winthrop as "Joshua Temperwell" in *New English Canaan*, 310 et seq. On the identity and significance of the structure Winthrop occupied, see Roger Williams's translation of the term "Wetuomémese": "*A little house;* which their women and maids live apart in, foure, five, or six dayes, in the time of their monethly sicknesse, which custome in all parts of the Countrey they strictly observe, and no *Male* may come into that house." *A Key into the Language of America*, ed. John J. Teunissen and Evelyn J. Hinz (Detroit, 1973), 117.

32. *MCR*, 1:101, 388; Emerson, ed., *Letters*, 81-82; Winthrop, *History*, 1:43, 45, 65.

33. "Charlestown Records," 377-78; *MCR*, 1:85, 90, 385, 392; Winthrop, *History*, 1:59, 105, 106-7; Emerson, ed., *Letters*, 82-83.

34. Johnson, *Wonder-Working Providence*, 86-87. Cf. Wood, *New England's Prospect*, 102.

35. "Charlestown Records," 386-87; Winthrop, *History*, 1:137-38,

142-43, 146-47; John Duffy, "Smallpox and the Indians in the American Colonies," *Bulletin of the History of Medicine* 25 (1951), 327-29; Sherburne F. Cook, "The Significance of Disease in the Extinction of the New England Indians," *Human Biology* 45 (1973), 491-93, 499-500; Alfred W. Crosby, "Virgin Soil Epidemics as a Factor in the Aboriginal Depopulation in America," *WMQ* 3d ser., 33 (1976), 289-99, esp. 290. William Bradford reported on the epidemic's striking the Indians of the Connecticut River in his annal for 1634; the epidemic he reported for 1633 is a different one, as is clear from the dates and symptoms he gives. Cf. Bradford, *Plymouth Plantation,* ed. Samuel Eliot Morison (New York, 1967), 260-61 and 270-71.

36. Winthrop, *History* 1:137-38, 142, 143, 147-48; "New Englands First Fruits" (1643), in Samuel Eliot Morison, *The Founding of Harvard College* (Cambridge, Mass., 1935), 422-23; Johnson, *Wonder-Working Providence,* 79-80; WP, 3:149. For earlier signs of John's interest in Christianity, see Emerson, ed., *Letters,* 68; WP, 3:74.

37. "Charlestown Records," 387; Johnson, *Wonder-Working Providence,* 79; WP, 3:172. Johnson, not an eyewitness, misdates the epidemic in 1631 but his references to the death of Sagamore John and other events make clear that he was referring to the one under discussion here. Johnson also states that the colonists bought land earlier but this assertion corresponds to his contemporaries' efforts to legitimize their holdings and not to any recorded transaction before or during 1633.

38. Lewis and Newhall, *History of Lynn,* 1:40, 130-32; Perley, *Indian Land Titles,* 49-50; Wood, *New England's Prospect,* 62; *MCR,* 1:112, 151-52; John Noble and John F. Cronin, eds., *Records of the Court of Assistants of the Massachusetts Bay, 1630-1692* (3 vols.; Boston, 1901-28), 2:49, 50, 51-52, 54-55. Wood and Dexter were among the Lynn settlers who founded Sandwich on Cape Cod in 1637. See Lewis and Newhall, *History of Lynn,* 1:113, 119.

39. Winthrop, *History,* 1:63; Samuel Hugh Brockunier, *The Irrepressible Democrat: Roger Williams* (New York, 1940), 41-42; Perry Miller, *Roger Williams: His Contribution to the American Tradition* (paper ed., New York, 1962), 28-29; Richard P. Gildrie, *Salem, Massachusetts, 1626-1683: A Covenant Community* (Charlottesville, Va., 1975), 24-25.

40. Winthrop, *History,* 1:109; WP 3:86; Roger Williams, *The Complete Writings of Roger Williams* (7 vols.; New York, 1963), 6:2; Edmund J. Carpenter, *Roger Williams: A Study of the Life, Times and Character of a Political Pioneer* (New

York, 1909), 224; Gildrie, *Salem*, 24-25; Wood, *New England's Prospect*, 110. Wood's editor, Alden T. Vaughan, identifies the unnamed missionary as "presumably" John Eliot, despite the absence of any evidence suggesting that Eliot began his missionary work before another decade had passed and the fact that at least two notable Williams scholars have identified their subject with the passage. See J. Hammond Trumbull in Williams, *Complete Writings*, 1:63-64; Brockunier, *Irrepressible Democrat*, 47.

41. Bradford, *Plymouth*, 257; Williams, *Complete Writings*, 2:46; 4:461; Brockunier, *Irrepressible Democrat*, 46-48, Washburn, "Moral and Legal Justification," 25; Gildrie, *Salem*, 31.

42. *MCR*, 1:394; Bradford, *Plymouth*, 257; *WP*, 4:454. On the purchases being rooted in competing desires to establish sovereignty in the Connecticut Valley, see Francis Jennings, *The Invasion of America: Indians, Colonialism, and the Cant of Conquest* (Chapel Hill, 1975), 133-34.

43. *WP*, 3:147. For a discussion that places Williams's dismissal in the contexts of both Salem and Massachusetts Bay politics, see Gildrie, *Salem*, 31-36.

44. Williams, *Complete Writings*, 2:46, 47. Cf. Ruth Barnes Moynihan, "The Patent and the Indians: The Problem of Jurisdiction in Seventeenth-Century New England," *AICRJ* 2, no. 1 (1977), 8-18.

45. Winthrop, *History*, 1:145-46; *MCR*, 1:112; Williams, *Complete Writings*, 6:333, 336-37, 406-8; *WP*, 4:38; *RICR*, 1:18, 22-26; Carpenter, *Roger Williams*, 225-26; Roger Williams, *An Answer to a Scandalous Paper . . .* (Providence, 1945); Sydney V. James, "The Worlds of Roger Williams," *Rhode Island History* 37 (1978), 104-5. James's essay is one of the few discussions of Williams to attempt to reconcile his many activities into a coherent whole. See *ibid.*, 98-109.

46. Winthrop, *History*, 1:209-10; Williams, *Complete Writings*, 4:461-62.

47. Perley, *Indian Land Titles*, 26. See also Suffolk County, Mass., *Suffolk Deeds* (11 vols.; Boston, 1880-1900), 1:34, 43; D. Hamilton Hurd, comp., *History of Middlesex County, Massachusetts* (3 vols.; Philadelphia, 1890), 1:8, 3:812; "Boston Town Records," in City of Boston, *Second Report of the Record Commissioners* (Boston, 1877), 6, 11-12; *MCR*, 1:196, 201, 254, 292, 317.

48. *MCR*, 1:394 (my emphasis); Alden T. Vaughan, *New England Frontier: Puritans and Indians, 1620-1675* (rev. ed., New York, 1979), esp. 104-15; Wilcomb E. Washburn, *The Indian*

in America (New York, 1975), 82-83. Vaughan's thesis is further weakened by the fact that most such transfers were not formalized until the 1680s when the towns, belatedly heeding Williams's argument, sought title independent of a Crown endeavoring to establish a "Dominion of New England" over the colonies. See Jennings, "Virgin Land and Savage People," 526.

49. Hurd, comp., *History of Middlesex County*, 3:812.
50. Bernard Bailyn, *The New England Merchants in the Seventeenth Century* (Cambridge, Mass., 1955), 26-30; Winthrop, *History*, 1:135; *MCR*, 1:108, 157; Francis X. Moloney, *The Fur Trade in New England* (Cambridge, Mass., 1931), 68-69.

7: LOSERS AND WINNERS

1. "The Charlestown Records," in Alexander Young, ed., *Chronicles of the First Planters of the Colony of Massachusets Bay* (1846; reprint ed., New York, 1970), 377-78; William Wood, *New England's Prospect* (1634), ed. Alden T. Vaughan (Amherst, Mass., 1977), 81.
2. John Winthrop, *The History of New England from 1630 to 1649*, ed. James Savage (2 vols.; 2d ed., Boston, 1853), 1:62, 69-70; William Bradford, *Of Plymouth Plantation*, ed. Samuel Eliot Morison (New York, 1967), 258.
3. Winthrop, *History*, 1:87; Roger Williams, *The Complete Writings of Roger Williams* (7 vols.; New York, 1963), 6:225, 317, 407; Edmund J. Carpenter, *Roger Williams: A Study of the Life, Times and Character of a Political Pioneer* (New York, 1909), 224. The post apparently stood at the location marked "Old Plymouth" on William Wood's map (fig. 7).
4. *CCR*, 3:479-80.
5. *NYCD*, 1:287; 2:139-40. The notice of the first purchase also appears in J. Franklin Jameson, ed., *Narratives of New Netherland, 1609-1664*, Original Narratives of Early American History (1909; reprint ed., New York, 1967), 309. The deed for this purchase is lost and no Dutch documents identify the Indian seller(s), but the mouth of the Connecticut was occupied by the Western Niantic who later gave a tract there to an English party. See herein, p. 217.
6. Influential accounts incorporating all or portions of this interpretation include John W. DeForest, *History of the Indians of Connecticut* (1853; reprint ed., Hamden, Conn., 1964), 58-156, *passim;* Carroll Alton Means, "Mohegan-Pequot Relationships, as Indicated by the Events Leading to the Pequot Massacre of 1637 and Subsequent Claims in the Mohegan

Land Controversy," *BASC* 21 (1947), 26-34; Alden T. Vaughan, *New England Frontier: Puritans and Indians, 1620-1675* (rev. ed., New York and London, 1979), 55-56, 115-16, 122-54, *passim;* P. Richard Metcalf, "Who Should Rule at Home? Native American Politics and Indian-White Relations," *Journal of American History* 61 (1973-74), 654-56; William Burton and Richard Lowenthal, "The First of the Mohegans," *American Ethnologist* 1 (1974), 589-99; Francis Jennings, *The Invasion of America: Indians, Colonialism, and the Cant of Conquest* (Chapel Hill, 1975), 186-227, *passim.*

7. Winthrop, *History,* 1:225; Bradford, *Plymouth,* 258-59; *WP,* 4:454.

8. Winthrop, *History,* 1:87, 103, 106-7; 132, 133-34, 146.

9. *Ibid.,* 146-147; Bradford, *Plymouth,* 270-71.

10. On Pequot strength, see Williams's map in *WP,* 3:414. On Wequash, see especially *ibid.;* Increase Mather, *Early History of New England* (1677), ed. Samuel G. Drake (Boston, 1864), 169-70. On Soso, see Elisha R. Potter, *The Early History of Narragansett,* published as Rhode Island Historical Society, *Collections* 3(1835), see pp. 245-48, 263-67; *WP,* 3:445; Williams, *Complete Writings,* 6:340; Williams, *Key,* 131-32. In a letter to Winthrop in July 1637, Williams wrote that Wequash "slue" Soso but stated in the next paragraph that he had "allmost slaine him." Soso's mark on a deed dated 1660 indicates that the latter is correct. Cf. *WP,* 3:445; Potter, *Early History,* 243.

11. *CCR,* 3:479. Historians and anthropologists, such as those cited above in n. 6, have misinterpreted Uncas's actions during these years because they have assumed that the Pequot and the Mohegan constituted a single "tribe" under a single sachem who was chosen according to rigid rules of succession. These misimpressions derive primarily from the "Pedigree of Uncas," *NEHGR,* 10 (1856), 227-28, prepared with English legal assistance in 1679, long after his rivals were dead, as part of the Mohegans' claim to Pequot lands. As noted in Chapter 1, sachems belonged to prominent lineages but the choices of actual leaders were made by band members.

12. Winthrop, *History,* 1:176-77; Jennings, *Invasion,* 189-96, 227.

13. As in the case of Stone, Jennings demonstrates that the Pequot were not the perpetrators. But whereas he argues that the culprit, one Ausdah, was a Narragansett who was merely sheltered by the Niantics, a letter from Williams to Winthrop in 1640 identifies Ausdah as a member of the latter. Cf. Jennings, *Invasion,* 206-9; *WP,* 4:269-70.

14. The truce of 1634 between the two groups had been mediated

by Massachusetts Bay without a face-to-face meeting of Pequots and Narragansetts precisely because of the humiliation
that such a meeting would have entailed for the former. See
Winthrop, *History*, 1:177-78.

15. Bradford, *Plymouth*, 294-95; Winthrop, *History*, 1:234.
16. *RICR*, 1:22-25; *WP*, 3:502; Winthrop, *History*, 1:209; Williams,
    Complete Writings, 6:316, 335.
17. Edward Johnson, *Johnson's Wonder-Working Providence*, ed.
    J. Franklin Jameson, Original Narratives of Early American
    History (1910; reprint ed., New York, 1967), 161-64.
18. Winthrop, *History*, 1:233, 234, 236-38. For Williams' memory
    of his role, see his *Complete Writings*, 6:231-32, 269, 338-39.
19. *CCR*, 3:479; *WP*, 3:270.
20. Darret B. Rutman, *Winthrop's Boston: Portrait of a Puritan
    Town, 1630-1649* (Chapel Hill, 1965), 178-79; *MCR*, 1:119,
    128, 146, 148, 358-60; Winthrop, *History*, 1:157, 159, 167-69,
    191, 206-7.
21. Winthrop, *History*, 1:162, 223; Charles M. Andrews, *The Co-
    lonial Period of American History* (4 vols.; 1934-38; paper ed.,
    New Haven, 1964), 2:70-73, 74-75, 80-81; Evarts B. Greene
    and Virginia Harrington, *American Population before the Fed-
    eral Census of 1790* (New York, 1932), 47.
22. *CCR*, 1:5; DeForest, *History*, 83-84; Andrews, *Colonial Period*,
    1:403-4; 2:73-74, 75-76; Jennings, *Invasion*, 197-98.
23. *Ibid.*, 204-6.
24. Above, n. 13; Lion Gardener, "Leift Lion Gardener his relation
    of the Pequot Warres," *MHSC* 3d ser., 3 (1833), 141-42, 151.
    A very different explanation of the causes of the war is pre-
    sented by Lynn Ceci, who argues that it was fundamentally a
    contest for control of New England's wampum mint. Ceci
    cogently demonstrates that the English sought control of the
    wampum industry and trade in order to establish a regulated
    currency, based on wampum, for themselves. There can be little
    doubt of wampum's importance but, as the argument offered
    here should indicate, English numbers and land-hunger (both
    of which Ceci overlooks) were the critical factors shaping
    English policy. See Ceci, "The Effect of European Contact and
    Trade on the Settlement Pattern of Indians in Coastal New
    York, 1524-1665: The Archeological and Documentary Evi-
    dence" (Ph.D. diss., City University of New York, 1977),
    210-14.
25. Gardener, "Relation," 142-48; *CCR*, 1:19-20; Winthrop, *His-
    tory*, 1:312-31; DeForest, *History*, 105-15.
26. Emery Battis, *Saints and Sectaries: Anne Hutchinson and the*

Antinomian Crisis in the Massachusetts Bay Colony (Chapel Hill, 1962), esp. chap. 17; Rutman, *Winthrop's Boston,* chap. 5; David D. Hall, ed., *The Antinomian Controversy, 1636-1638: A Documentary History* (Middletown, Conn., 1968), 3-20; Johnson, *Wonder-Working Providence,* 28, 127-29, *passim,* 132-33. On the movement's anti-patriarchalism, cf. Ben Barker-Benfield, "Anne Hutchinson and the Puritan Attitude toward Women," *Feminist Studies* 1, no. 2 (1972), 65-96; Michael J. Colocurcio, "Footsteps of Anne Hutchinson: The Context of *The Scarlet Letter,*" *ELH* 39 (1972), 459-94. Lyle Koehler, "The Case of the American Jezebels: Anne Hutchinson and Female Agitation During the Years of Antinomian Turmoil, 1636-1640," *WMQ* 3d ser., 31 (1974), 55-78; Mary Maples Dunn, "Saints and Sisters: Congregational and Quaker Women in the Early Colonial Period," *American Quarterly* 30 (1978), 585-88.

27. David D. Hall, *The Faithful Shepherd: The New England Ministry in the Seventeenth Century* (Chapel Hill, 1972), 156-66.

28. *WP,* 3:404-8, 417; Winthrop, *History,* 1:260-61.

29. Johnson, *Wonder-Working Providence,* 168; John Underhill, "Newes from America" (1638), in *MHSC* 3d ser., 6 (1837), 15. See also John Hull, "The Diaries of John Hull," in American Antiquarian Society, *Transactions and Collections* 3 (1857), 171-72; Johnson, *Wonder-Working Providence,* 164; Nathaniel Morton, *New Englands Memoriall* (1669), ed. Howard J. Hall (New York, 1937), 99; Mather, *Early History,* 184. Cf. William S. Simmons, "Cultural Bias in the New England Puritans' Perception of Indians," *WMQ* 3d ser., 38 (1981), 67-68.

30. Underhill, "Newes from America," 23-25; John Mason, "A Brief History of the Pequot War" (1736), in *MHSC* 2d ser., 8 (1826), 138-41; Gardener, "Relation," 149-50; Jennings, *Invasion,* 220-22. On enslavement, see Almon Wheeler Lauber, *Indian Slavery in Colonial Times within the Present Limits of the United States* (New York, 1913), 124-25; Winthrop, *History,* 1:277-80, *passim.* Cf. *WP,* 3:434, 450, 459; William Hubbard, *The History of the Indian Wars in New England* (1677), ed. Samuel G. Drake (1865; reprint ed., 2 vols. in 1, New York, 1970), 1:38-39. The Treaty of Hartford can be conveniently consulted in Vaughan, *New England Frontier,* 341-42.

31. Underhill, "Newes," 25; Mason, "Brief History," 140-41; Bradford, *Plymouth,* 296.

32. Hall, ed., *Antinomian Controversy,* 253; Thomas Shepard, *God's Plot: The Paradoxes of Puritan Piety,* ed. Michael McGiffert (Amherst, Mass., 1972), 66, 68; *MCR,* 1:204, 211-12;

Winthrop, *History*, 1:290-91; Battis, *Saints and Sectaries*, 211-12.

33. Rutman, *Winthrop's Boston*, 179; Greene and Harrington, *American Population*, 47.

34. The deed is reprinted in DeForest, *History*, 495. See also De-Forest's discussion in *ibid.*, 183-84.

35. Charles J. Hoadley, ed., *Records of the Colony and Plantation of New Haven, from 1638 to 1649* (Hartford, 1857), 1-5.

36. *Ibid.*, 5-7.

37. For subsequent deed/treaties in New Haven, see DeForest, *History*, 167-68.

38. Francis Brinley, "Briefe Narrative of the Nanhiganset Countrey," in Rhode Island Historical Society, *Publications*, 8 (1900), 74; Carl Bridenbaugh, *Fat Mutton and Liberty of Conscience: Society in Rhode Island, 1636-1690* (Providence, 1974), 8 and n.; Sydney V. James, *Colonial Rhode Island: A History* (New York, 1975), 20, 25-28; *RICR*, 1:45-51.

39. Underhill, "Newes," 27; *WP*, 3:434, 4:120; Jennings, *Invasion*, 223-26; Vaughan, *New England Frontier*, 341.

40. Samuel Gorton, "Simplicities Defense against Seven-headed Policy" (1646), in Peter Force, ed., *Tracts and Other Papers* . . . (4 vols.; Washington, D.C., 1837), 4, no. 6; 21; *MCR*, 2:26-27, 38, 40-41; Winthrop, *History*, 2:95-96, 144-48. Cf. the different view of native precedent in Jennings, *Invasion*, 261-65. Gorton presents his side of his long-standing dispute with Massachusetts Bay in "Simplicities Defense," 24-44, *passim*, while the colony's case appears in Edward Winslow, *Hypocrisie Unmasked* (1646; reprint ed., New York, 1968). On Gorton's thought and its contexts, see Philip F. Gura, "The Radical Thought and Ideology of Samuel Gorton: New Light on the Relation of English to American Puritanism," *WMQ* 3d ser., 36 (1979), 78-100.

41. Cf. Jennings' contrast between Connecticut's "crashing conquest methods" and Massachusetts Bay's "nibbling technique," in *Invasion*, 261.

42. See, for example, the fear of a Narragansett-Mohawk conspiracy in *WP*, 4:258-59; Winthrop, *History*, 2:9. On the long-standing Mohawk-Narragansett friendship, see *RICR*, 1:295.

43. Cf. John A. Sainsbury, "Miantonomo's Death and New England Politics, 1630-1645," *Rhode Island History* 30 (1971), 116-17, 120.

44. Gardener, "Relation," 154-55. See also "Relation of the Plott—Indian," in *MHSC* 3d ser., 3 (1833), 161-64; *MCR*, 2:23-24; Winthrop, *History*, 2:95.

45. James Mooney, *The Ghost-Dance Religion and the Sioux Out-*

break of 1890, Bureau of American Ethnology, 14th Annual
Report, 1892-93 (Washington, D.C., 1896), is the classic study
of such movements.

46. David Pulsifer, ed., *Acts of the Commissioners of the United
Colonies of New England* (2 vols., in Nathaniel B. Shurtleff
and David Pulsifer, eds., *Records of the Colony of New Plymouth* 9-10, Boston, 1859), 1:10-11; Winthrop, *History,* 2:155,
157; Sainsbury, "Miantonomo's Death," 117; Winslow, *Hypocrisie Unmasked,* 72-73, 86; William Harris, *A Rhode Islander
Reports on King Philip's War: The Second William Harris
Letter of August, 1676,* ed. Douglas Edward Leach (Providence, 1963), 55-57; Winthrop, *History,* 2:97.

47. Samuel Hugh Brockunier, *The Irrepressible Democrat: Roger
Williams* (New York, 1940), 135; Pulsifer, ed., *Acts,* 1:3-8.

48. Jennings, *Invasion,* 258-59; *WP,* 4:36; Pulsifer, ed., *Acts,* 1:3-4;
Johnson, *Wonder-Working Providence,* 219; Winthrop, *History,*
2:121; Neal Emerson Salisbury, "Conquest of the 'Savage':
Puritans, Puritan Missionaries, and Indians, 1620-1680" (Ph.D.
diss., University of California, Los Angeles, 1972), 120-21.

49. Pulsifer, ed., *Acts,* 1:4-8, 12; Salisbury, "Conquest of the
'Savage'," 122.

50. Pulsifer, ed., *Acts,* 1:10-12, 15; Winthrop, *History,* 2:162.

EPILOGUE

1. Philip J. Greven, Jr., *Four Generations: Population, Land, and
Family in Colonial Andover, Massachusetts* (Ithaca, N.Y.,
1970).

2. T. H. Breen and Stephen Foster, "Moving to the New World:
The Character of Early Massachusetts Immigration," *WMQ*
3d ser., 30 (1973), 209-11; Linda Auwers Bissell, "From One
Generation to Another: Mobility in Seventeenth-Century Windsor, Connecticut," *ibid.* 31 (1974), 79-110; Ralph J. Crandall,
"New England's Second Great Migration: The First Three
Generations of Settlement, 1630-1700," *NEHGR,* 129 (1975),
347-60; Francis Jennings, *The Invasion of America: Indians,
Colonialism, and the Cant of Conquest* (Chapel Hill, 1975),
part II; Neal Salisbury, "Red Puritans: The 'Praying Indians'
of Massachusetts Bay and John Eliot," *WMQ* 3d ser., 31
(1974), 27-54.

3. The economic and demographic aspects of this argument are
presented in Kenneth A. Lockridge, "Land, Population, and
the Evolution of New England Society, 1630-1790," *Past and
Present* 39 (1968), 62-80.

4. Cf. Edward H. Spicer, *Cycles of Conquest: The Impact of*

Spain, Mexico, and the United States on the Indians of the Southwest, 1533-1960 (Tuscon, 1962), chap. 20. These developments in New England are elaborated somewhat in Neal Salisbury, *The Indians of New England: A Critical Bibliography* (Bloomington and London, 1981), and those through King Philip's War will be the subject of a succeeding volume to this one.

5. On this last point, see, for example, Bernard Bailyn, *The New England Merchants in the Seventeenth Century* (Cambridge, Mass., 1955), 102-3, 118-19; Richard S. Dunn, "John Winthrop, Jr., and the Narragansett Country," *WMQ* 3d ser., 13 (1956), 68-86; Jennings, *Invasion*, 278-80; Theodore B. Lewis, "Land Speculation and the Dudley Council of 1686," *WMQ* 3d ser., 31 (1974), 255-72; Richard L. Bushman, *From Puritan to Yankee: Character and the Social Order in Connecticut* (Cambridge, Mass., 1967), chap. 6.

INDEX

INDEX

Abbaamacho. *See* Hobbamock (Indian deity)

Abenaki, Eastern, Indians: and Biard, 74, 75; and Chouacoet, 66, 69–70; and English explorers and traders, 90–95, 110; and epidemics, 102–3; and French, 60–61, 62, 67, 69, 70, 75, 77, 99; kidnappings of, 53, 90–91, 95; and Micmac, 61, 67, 69–70, 71, 99, 101, 156; and Montagnais, 61; and Plymouth, 144–46, 151–52, 163, 208; precontact, 20, 24, 30, 36, 37, 42, 62, 251n.37; and southern New England Indians, 76–78; and Verrazzano, 52–53

Abenaki, Eastern, language, 20, 247n.14

Abenaki, Western, Indians, 27

Abenaki, Western, language, 20

Abenaki Indians. *See* Abenaki, Eastern, Indians

Adams, Charles Francis, Jr., 247n.39

Adventurers, Plymouth: back colony, 111, 139; question support for colony, 134–35, 140, 143–44, 145; sell out to Undertakers, 146

Agawam (Pawtucket village), 27, 129, 183, 184. *See also* Ipswich, Massachusetts Bay; Pawtucket Indians

Agriculture: in England, 166–67, 168; French offer, to Abenaki, 61; Indian adoption of, 18, 19, 33; and Indian beliefs, 11, 34–39 passim; and Indian diet, 31–32; as Indian subsistence, 9, 30–34, 39; Indian women and, 30–31, 39, 40–41, 42; of Indians, and English rule, 177, 200; of Kennebec Abenaki, 19, 67; in Plymouth, 142–43, 189; social-economic effects of on Indians, 22, 42, 44. *See also* Farmers, English

Alcohol, and Indians, 56, 81, 185

Altham, Emmanuel, 156, 275n.54

Algonquian, Eastern, languages, 19–21

Algonquin Indians, 79

Algonquian language family, 20

Allerton, Isaac, 112, 139, 163, 164, 278n.19

Andrews, Charles M., 5, 270n.53, 279n.23

Androscoggin River, 20

297